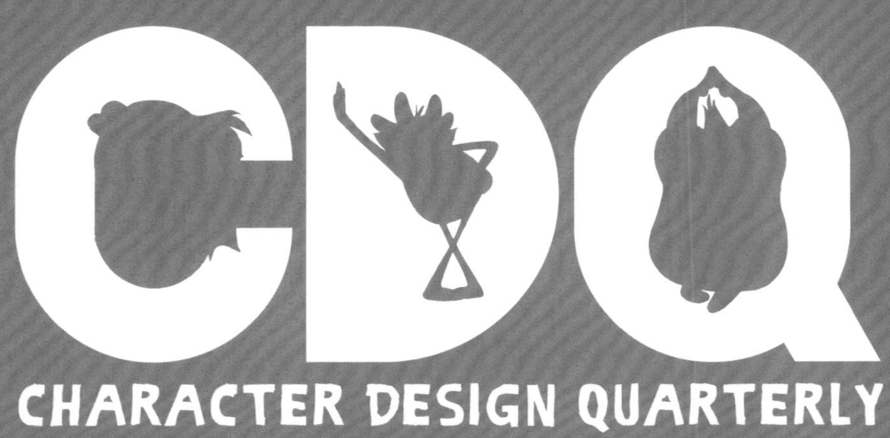

CDQ
CHARACTER DESIGN QUARTERLY

CONTENTS

WELCOME TO *CHARACTER DESIGN QUARTERLY 19*

This issue we are positively bursting with personality, with big emotions, big expressions, and big ideas popping from every page.

Taraneh Karimi is our cover artist, returning to *CDQ* to share more of her magical artwork. As well as sitting down with us for a wide-ranging interview, Taraneh also provides an in-depth look at how the stunning cover was put together.

An animal stampede rushes through the rest of the pages, with jaguars, wolves, guinea pigs, and even a princely frog all crammed between the covers. We've got tutorials from Melany Altuna, Justin Runfola, and Felipe Rodriguez showing us how to bring all sorts of cute and creepy creatures to life!

Elsewhere, interviews with Chris Ables and Federico Etchegaray give us insights into working with some of the biggest names in animation, and Gray Young gives us a fascinating look at how to create effective storyboards. With even more tutorials, features, and wonderful gallery artwork to explore, *CDQ 19* is the last word in character design...well, until next issue!

SAM DRAPER
EDITOR

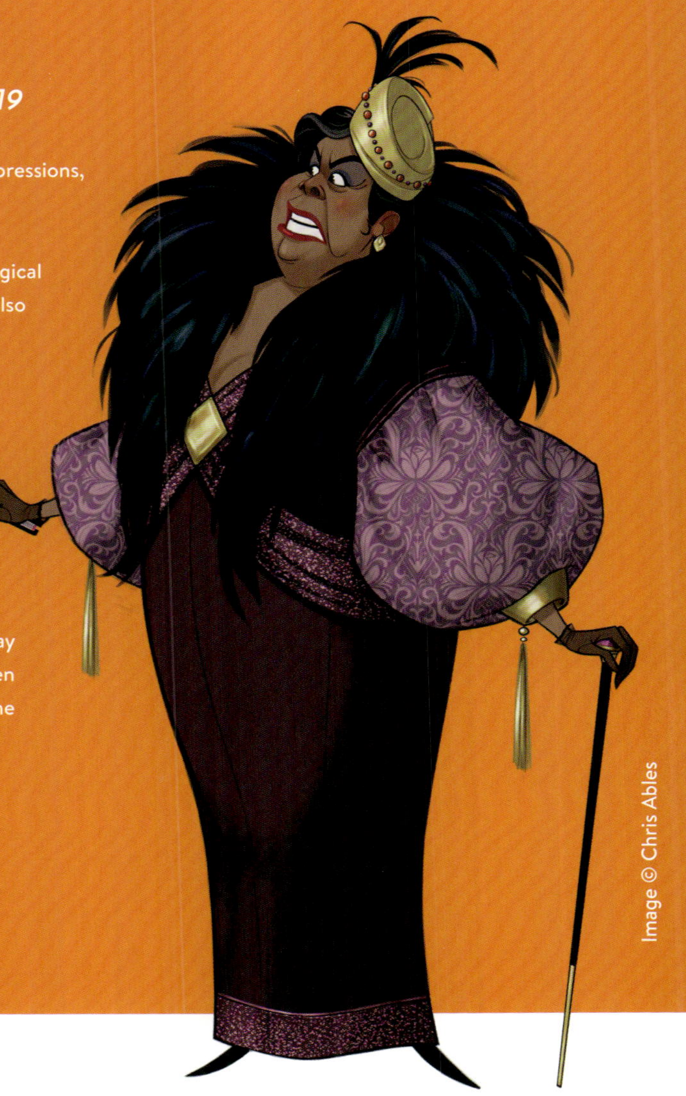

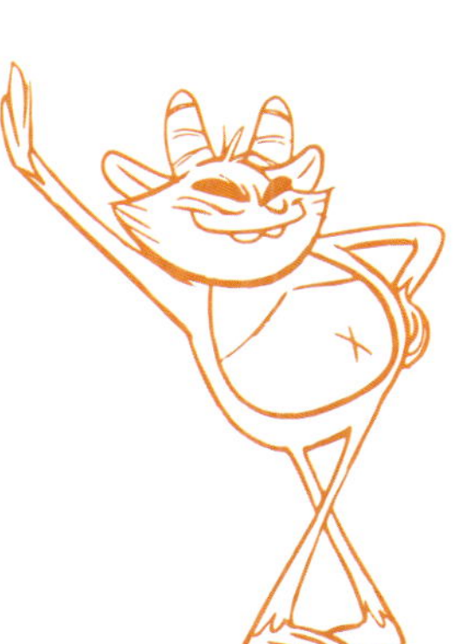

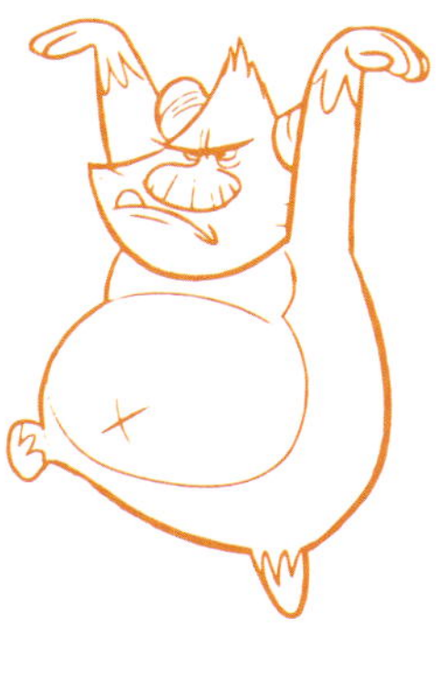

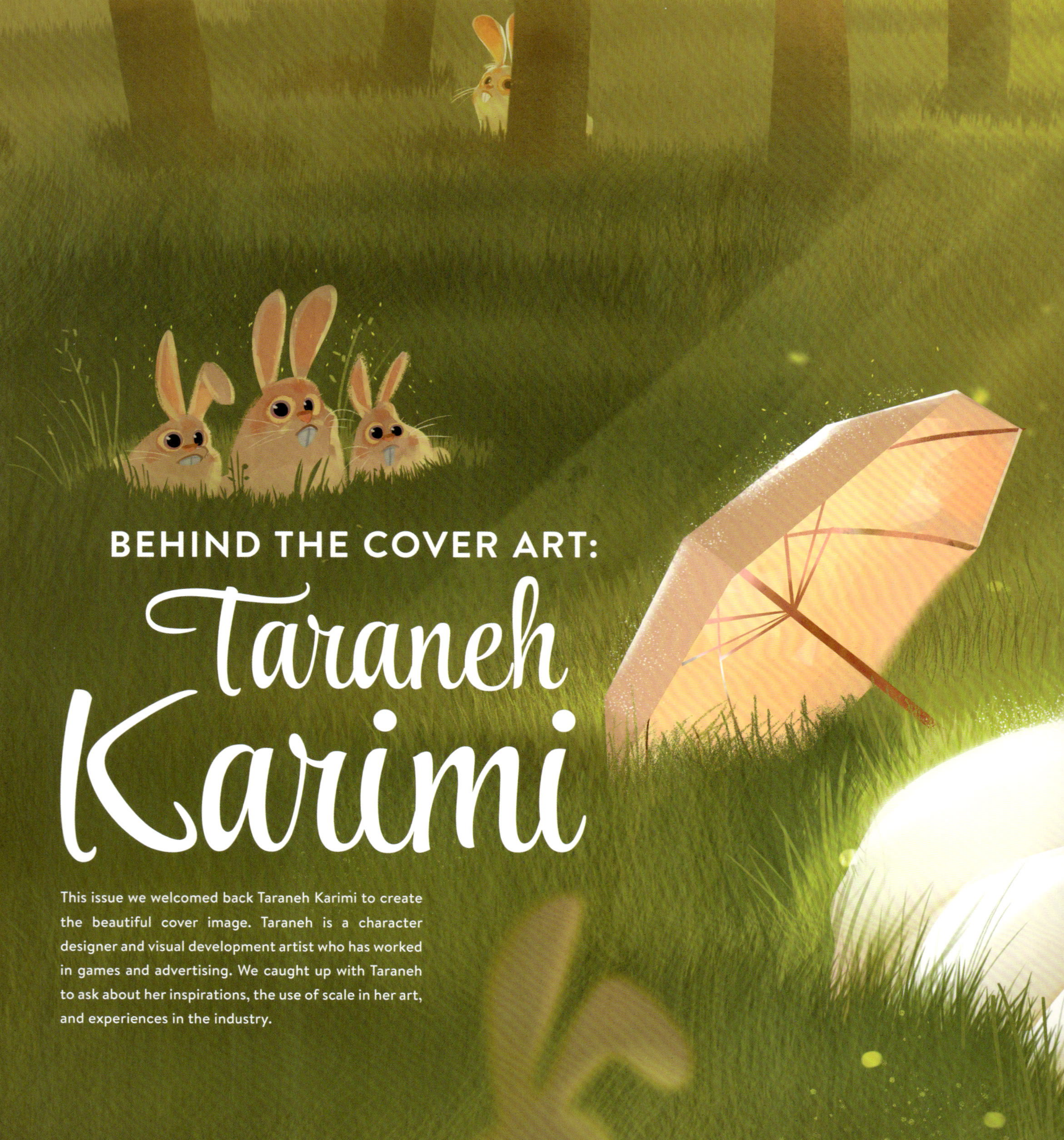

BEHIND THE COVER ART:
Taraneh Karimi

This issue we welcomed back Taraneh Karimi to create the beautiful cover image. Taraneh is a character designer and visual development artist who has worked in games and advertising. We caught up with Taraneh to ask about her inspirations, the use of scale in her art, and experiences in the industry.

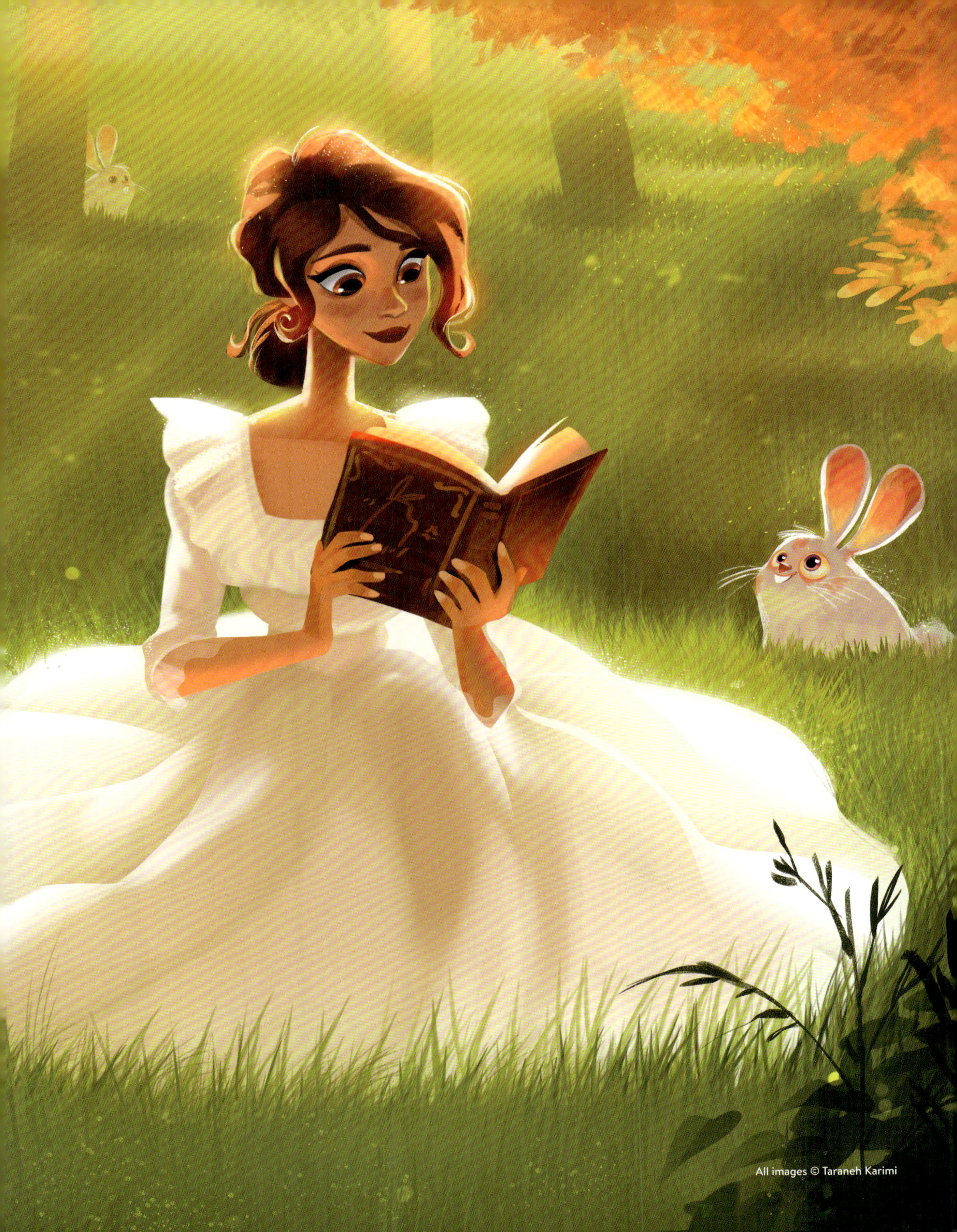
All images © Taraneh Karimi

Hi Taraneh! You're fast becoming one of our favorite artists here at *CDQ*, could you tell the readers a little bit about yourself, and how you started in character design?

I am honored and thrilled to hear that! *CDQ* is one of my favorite magazines and it feels so rewarding to be able to share my story in a magazine that has inspired me so much over the past couple of years.

I started working on characters as a hobby around seven years ago. At the time, I was working as an illustrator in motion graphics. I was mostly drawing myself, or people around me, in my everyday life. That's how my curiosity for anatomy and expressions grew and I decided to dedicate more time to studying it.

One of the most striking elements of your work is your impressive use of scale to create a sense of fantasy and wonder – where did this idea come from?

I've always been fascinated by nature – a leaf dancing in the wind can give me the same joy and wonder as a magical forest. As a kid, I always tried to imagine the world that was hidden behind everything, and I think I've brought that secret part of life into my work too. Contrasting real and fantasy worlds by showing them alongside one another can emphasize the differences, and helps create beautiful stories.

This spread: *Human Rights* – An attempt to capture the inequality in the world, with humor

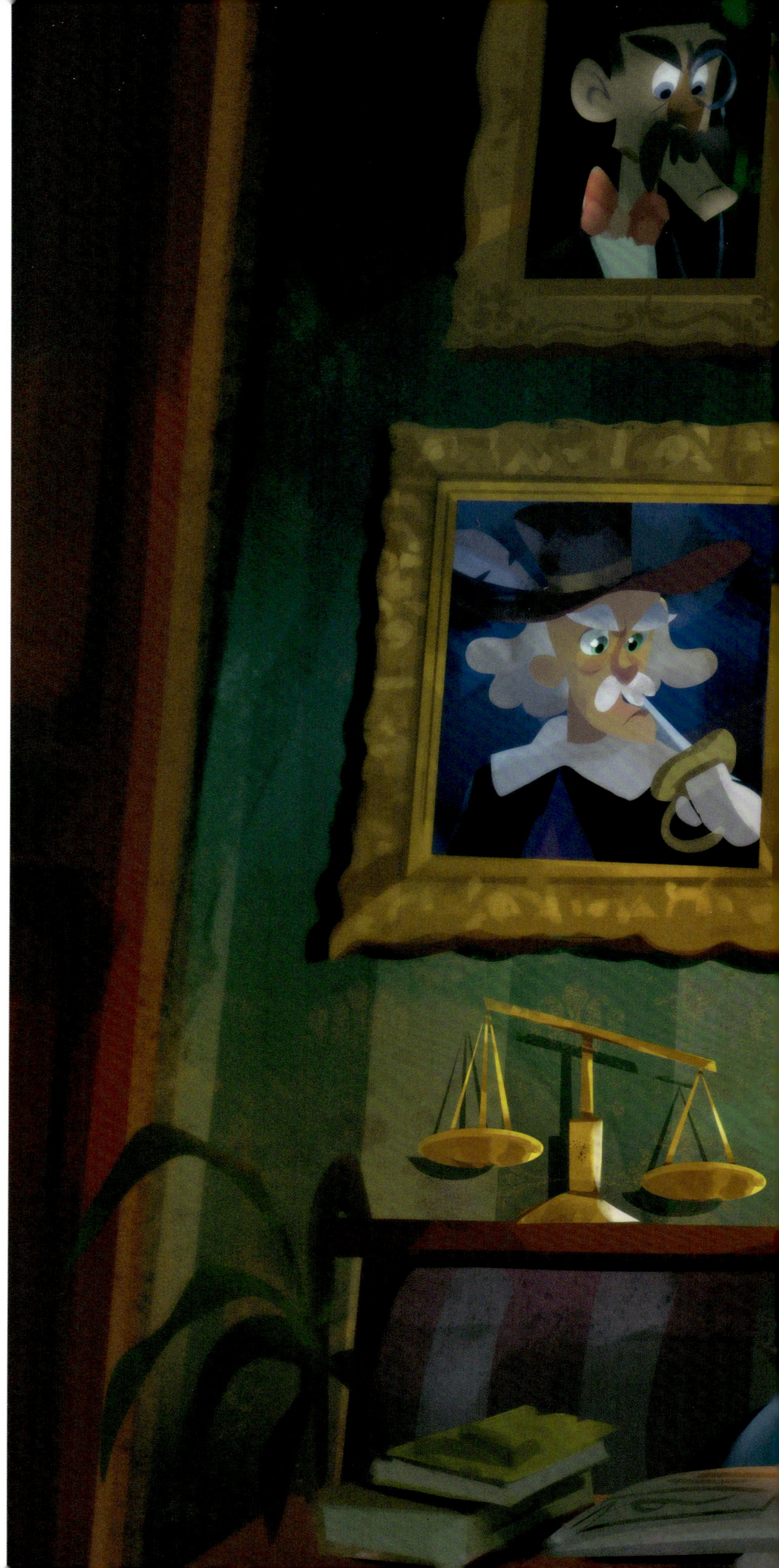

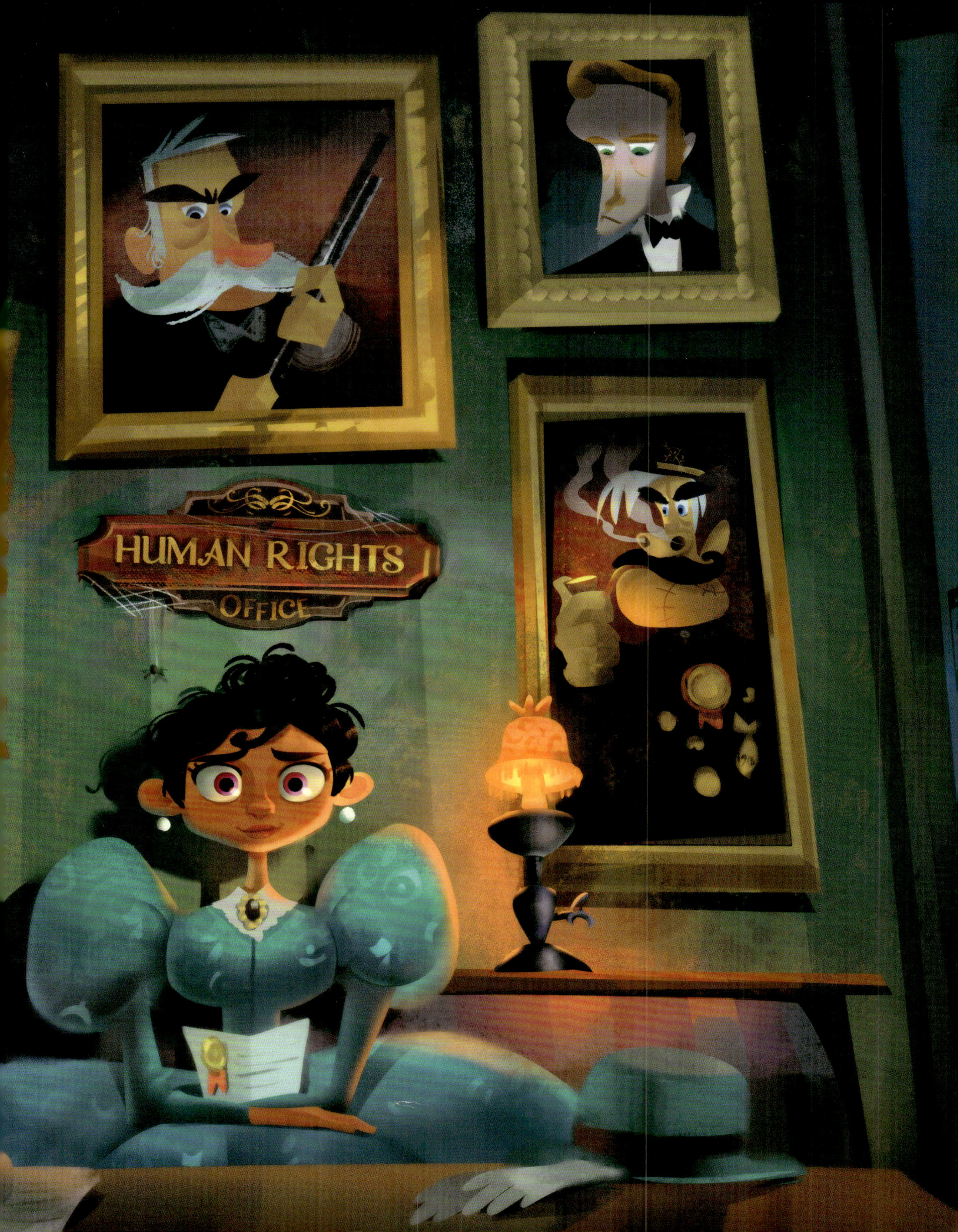

HUMAN RIGHTS
OFFICE

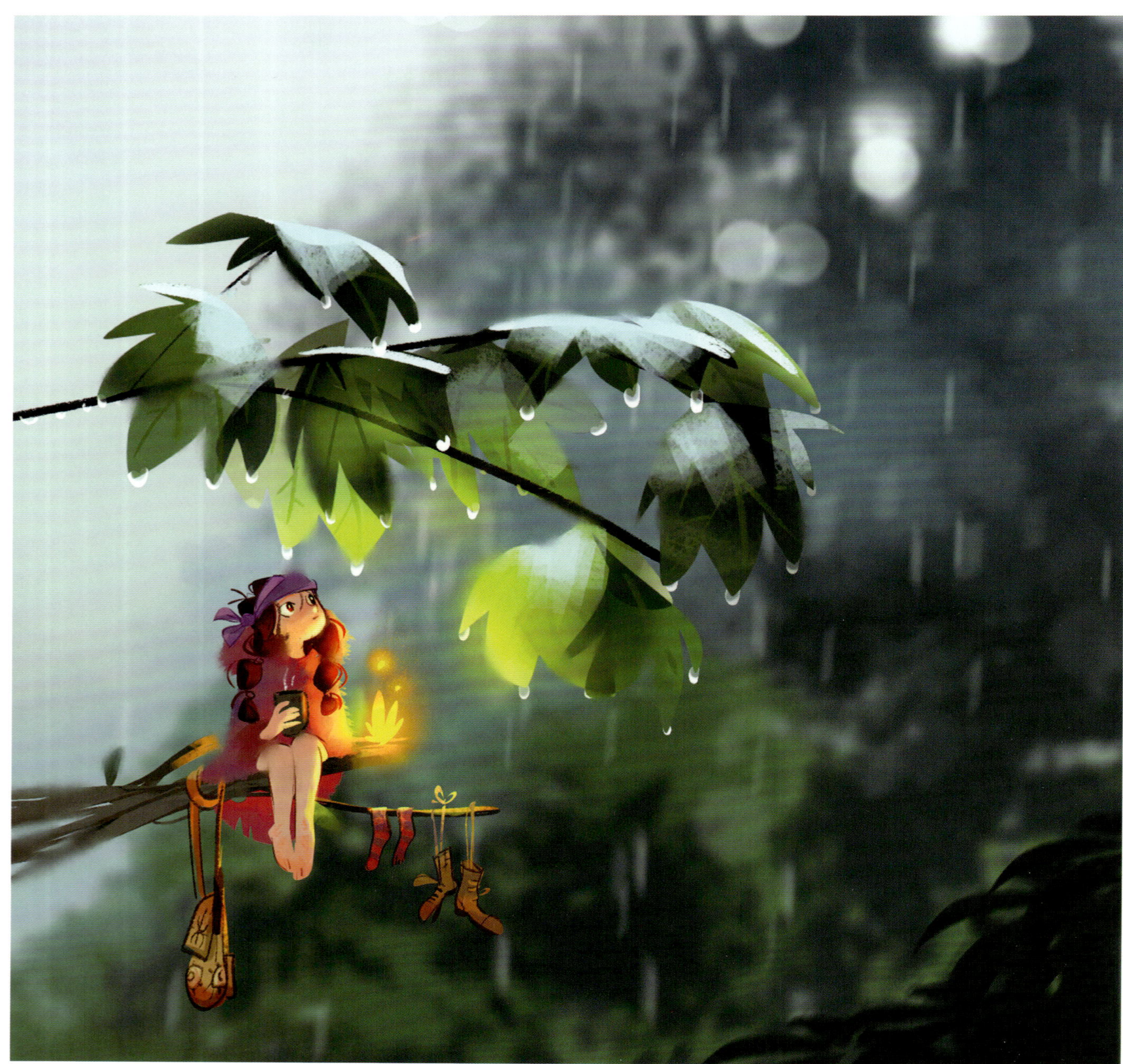

Over the years what kinds of inspiration have driven your designs?

I'm inspired by many different sources. I studied anime, specifically Studio Ghibli and the art of Disney and Pixar to form my style. I love French cartoonists, like Sempé, for their minimal lines and simple expressive style. I try to bring that knowledge to my work, too.

Nowadays, I treat social media like a never-ending art magazine – following my favorite artists and studying and analyzing how they do what they do.

Your designs are packed full of personality – do you develop individual backstories for your characters, or do they appear as part of the process?

For me, drawing a character is like acting. I can't bring a personality to life unless I understand and study it thoroughly. I add my personal emotions, imperfections, and humor, too, which I think makes it more believable. Artists can't help leaving fingerprints – every artist will inevitably appear in their work, it's up to you to decide what part of you will be in each character.

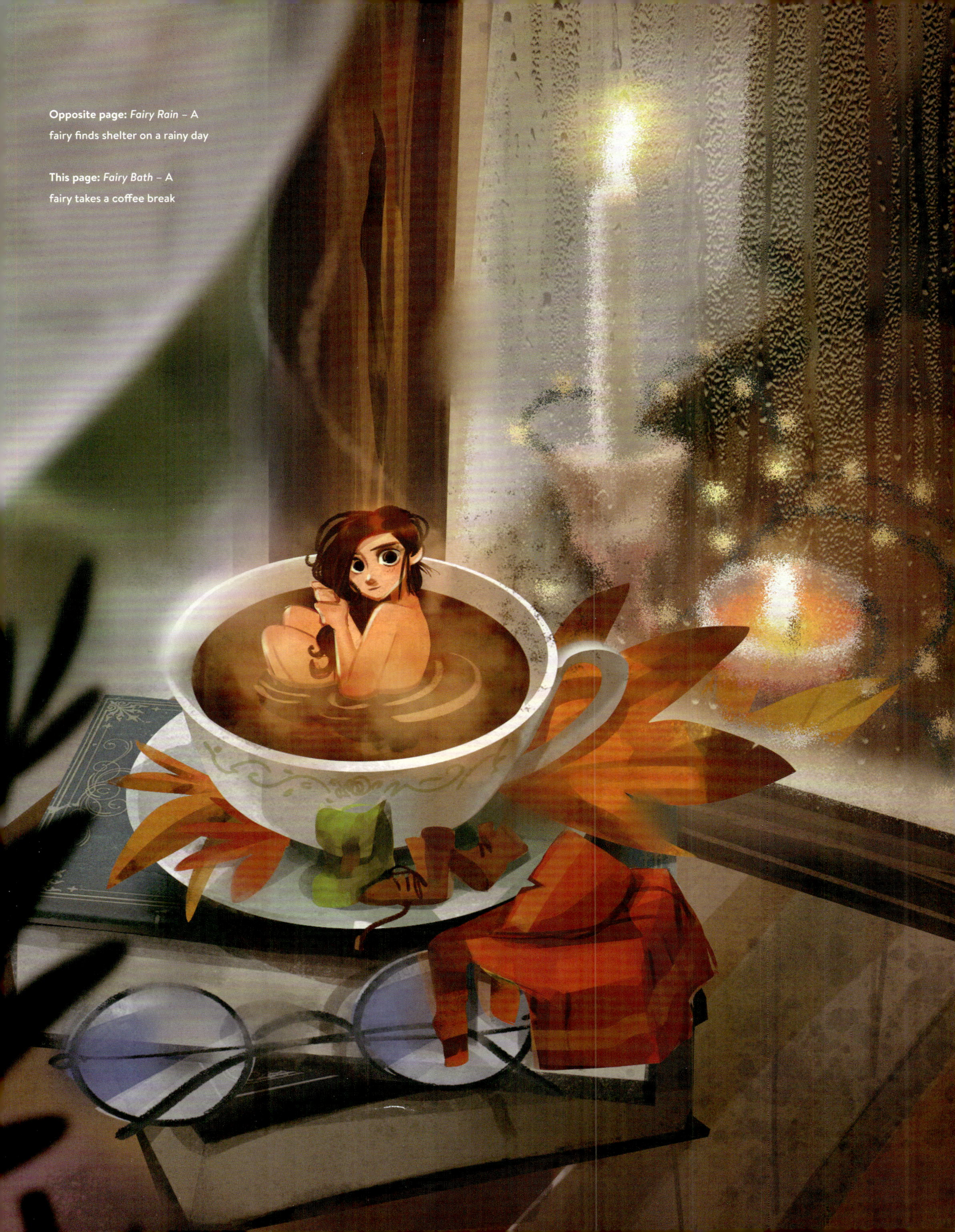

Opposite page: *Fairy Rain* – A
fairy finds shelter on a rainy day

This page: *Fairy Bath* – A
fairy takes a coffee break

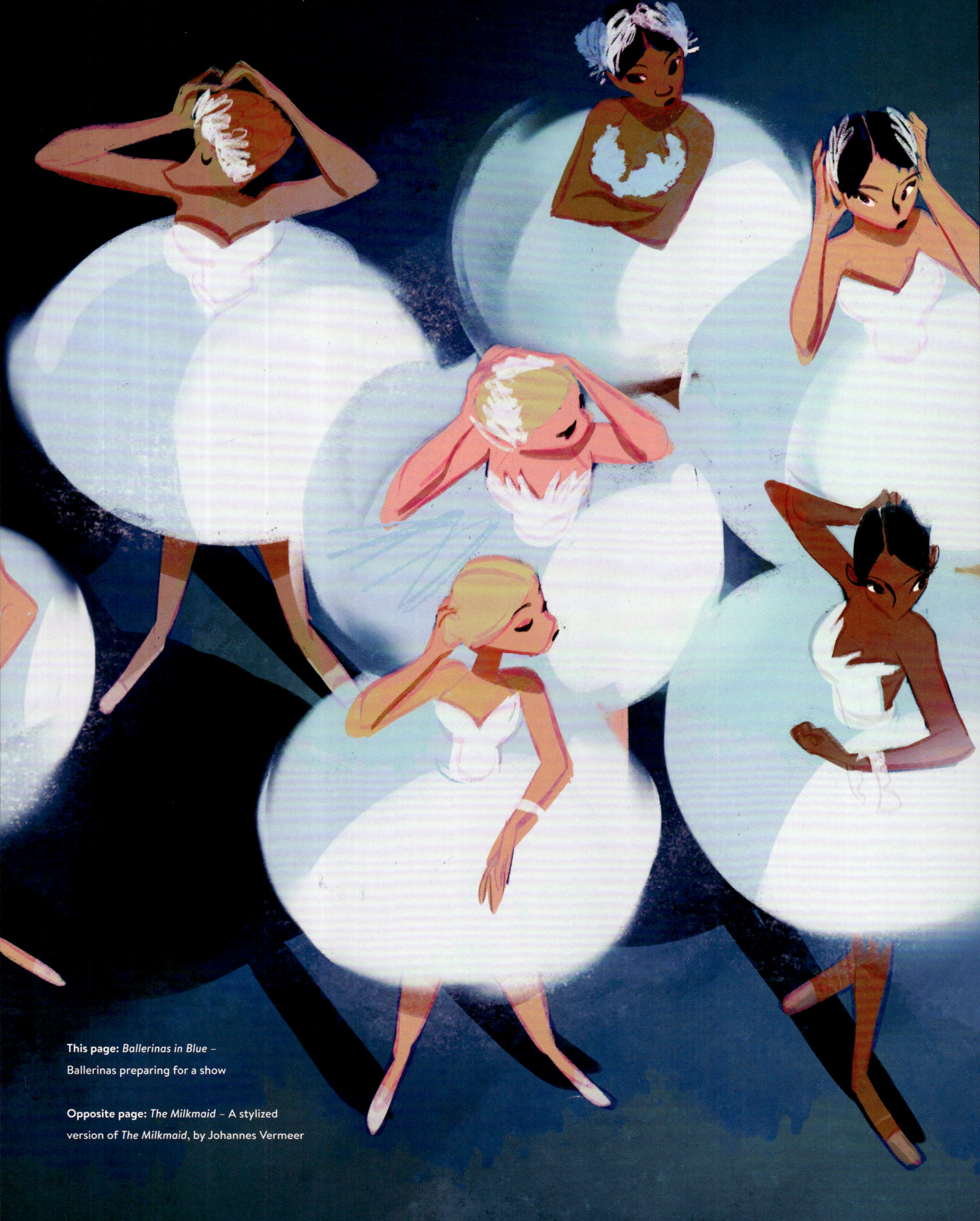

This page: Ballerinas in Blue –
Ballerinas preparing for a show

Opposite page: The Milkmaid – A stylized
version of The Milkmaid, by Johannes Vermeer

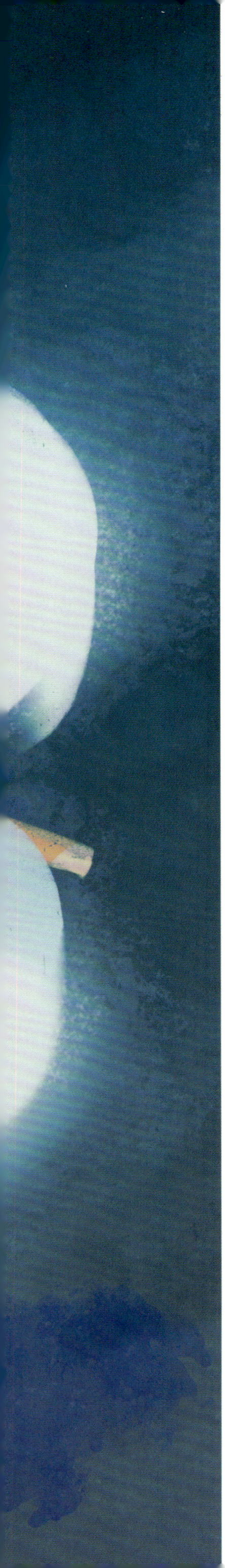

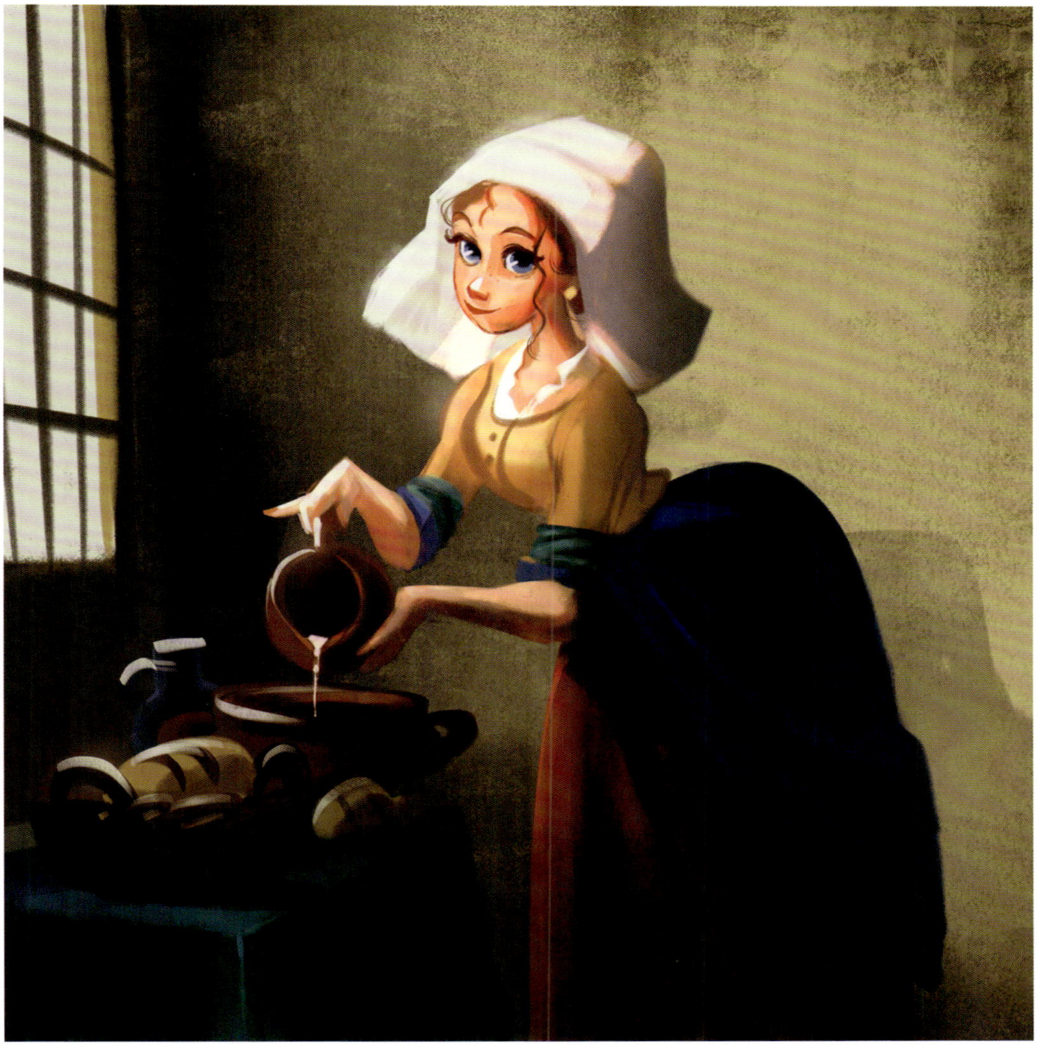

What different positions have you held in the art industry, and have you noticed a difference between certain fields, such as character design versus game design?

I have experience in graphic and motion design, illustration, game art, character and background art, and art direction. To be honest, every field feels like a different world! In animation and marketing, you have more creative freedom to work without boundaries. As an artist, your creativity will be appreciated more, but there is also a lot more pressure attached. Working in games, I have to limit my creativity, follow patterns, and learn more principles. But there is less pressure there, compared to other mediums.

What are the most enjoyable aspects of your job, and what advice would you give someone wanting to step into the industry?

The thrill of learning is what I enjoy most about art and animation. I am always excited to learn and grow and the more I know, the more I want to know! I would say to anyone who wants to join the industry, be open and passionate about your education. Ask questions, communicate, be proud to fail, and give yourself time to find your path. There is no shortcut to being a great artist, you must work at it!

Crafting the cover

When I was asked to make this issue's cover, I knew I had to make something eye-catching that conveys a feeling of joy, and fun. The image must cheer the viewer up, and make you want to grab the magazine!

We start the journey by looking for some inspirational resources and sketching some rough ideas. To begin, it's best to take your time to think about the ideal image you want to create, and imagine the feeling you want the piece to convey. I'll take you through each step from this first vague idea through to the finished piece. I'll be working with Photoshop, a Wacom Cintiq, and a laptop.

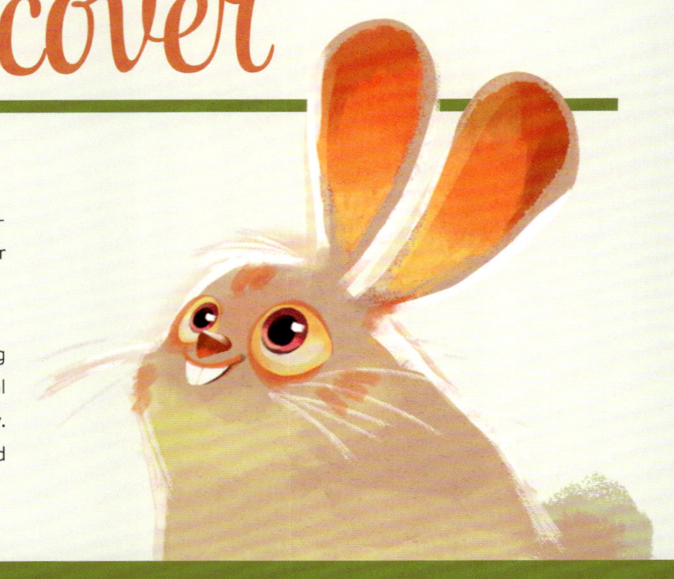

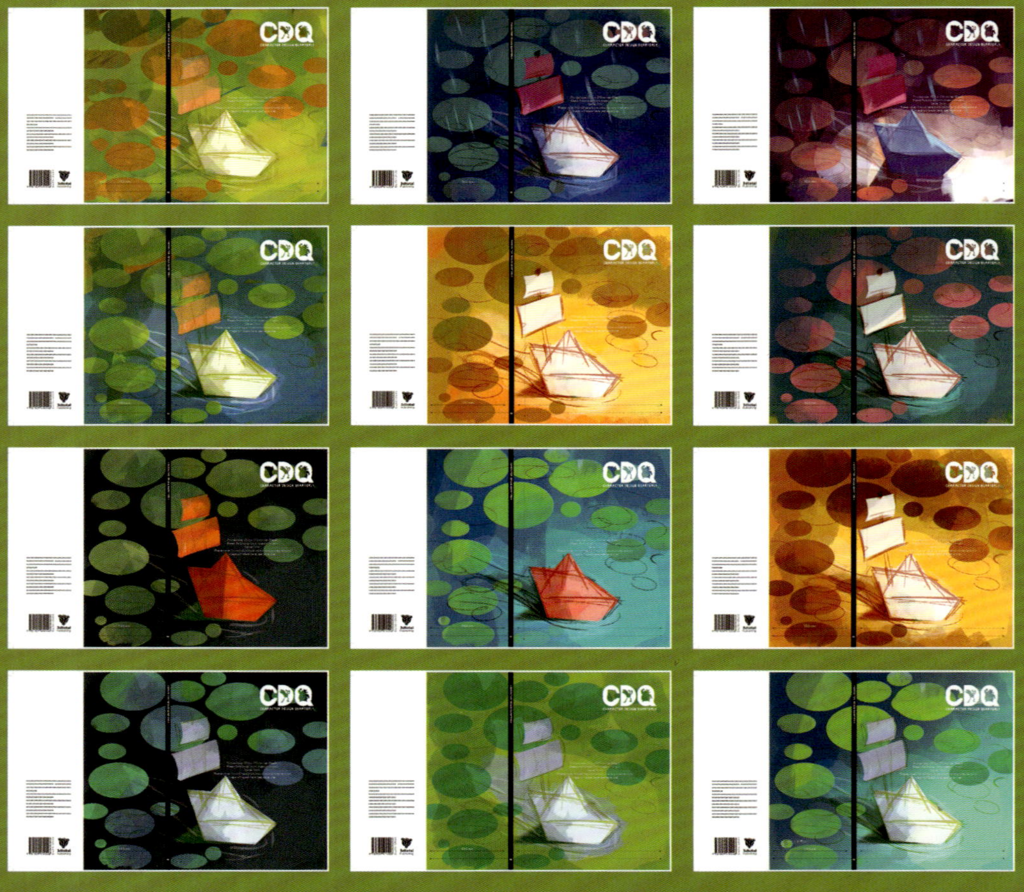

EARLY IDEAS

Let's start with the brief from the editors. The idea is to make an illustration with fairy characters, creating a magical moment in the real world. We can use elements which are already friendly and familiar to the audience to make the world feel more romantic. I draw a paper boat, a nostalgic element that connects us to our childhood feelings of adventure and simplicity. With the brief in mind, I make a composition to explore the mood and feeling of the image. Nothing is final at this stage, I'm just experimenting.

This page: Exploring the theme with thumbnails, rough colors, and lighting for the composition

CREATING WITHOUT BOUNDARIES

This first direction my drawing takes doesn't feel satisfying and eye catching enough for a cover, so I try something else. Sometimes it can be rewarding to forget about the limitations of a brief and, instead, do what you really love to do, and enjoy it! If you're struggling with an idea, retreat to your comfort zone and draw something familiar, something that always cheers you up!

LOOKING FROM A DIFFERENT ANGLE

Now, let's explore different angles of the same story. It's important not to immediately choose the first idea as the final image – by searching you can find the best possible visual outcome and develop it further from there. If you struggle to find references for some of the poses you want to try, then why not use a picture of yourself as a resource? It's really helpful to have a mirror or camera nearby while you work, so you can refer to your expressions and poses whenever needed and translate them onto your character.

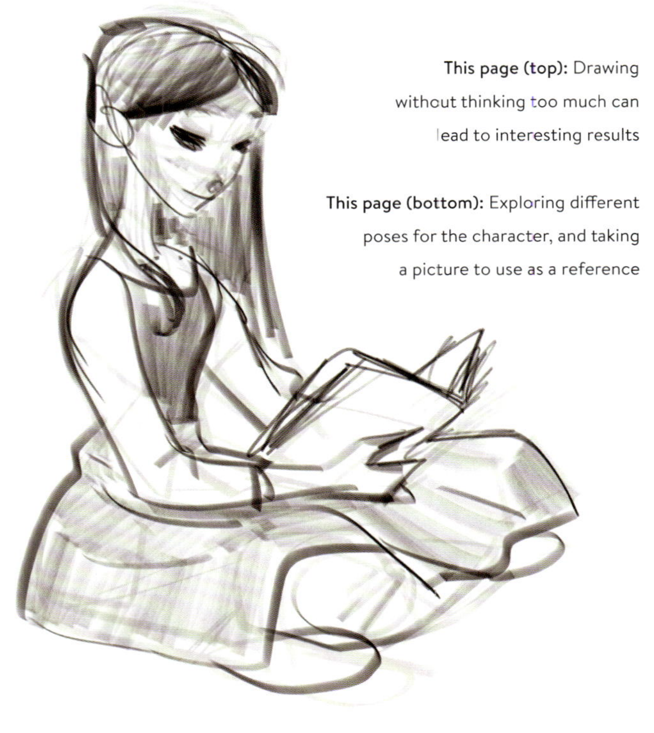

This page (top): Drawing without thinking too much can lead to interesting results

This page (bottom): Exploring different poses for the character, and taking a picture to use as a reference

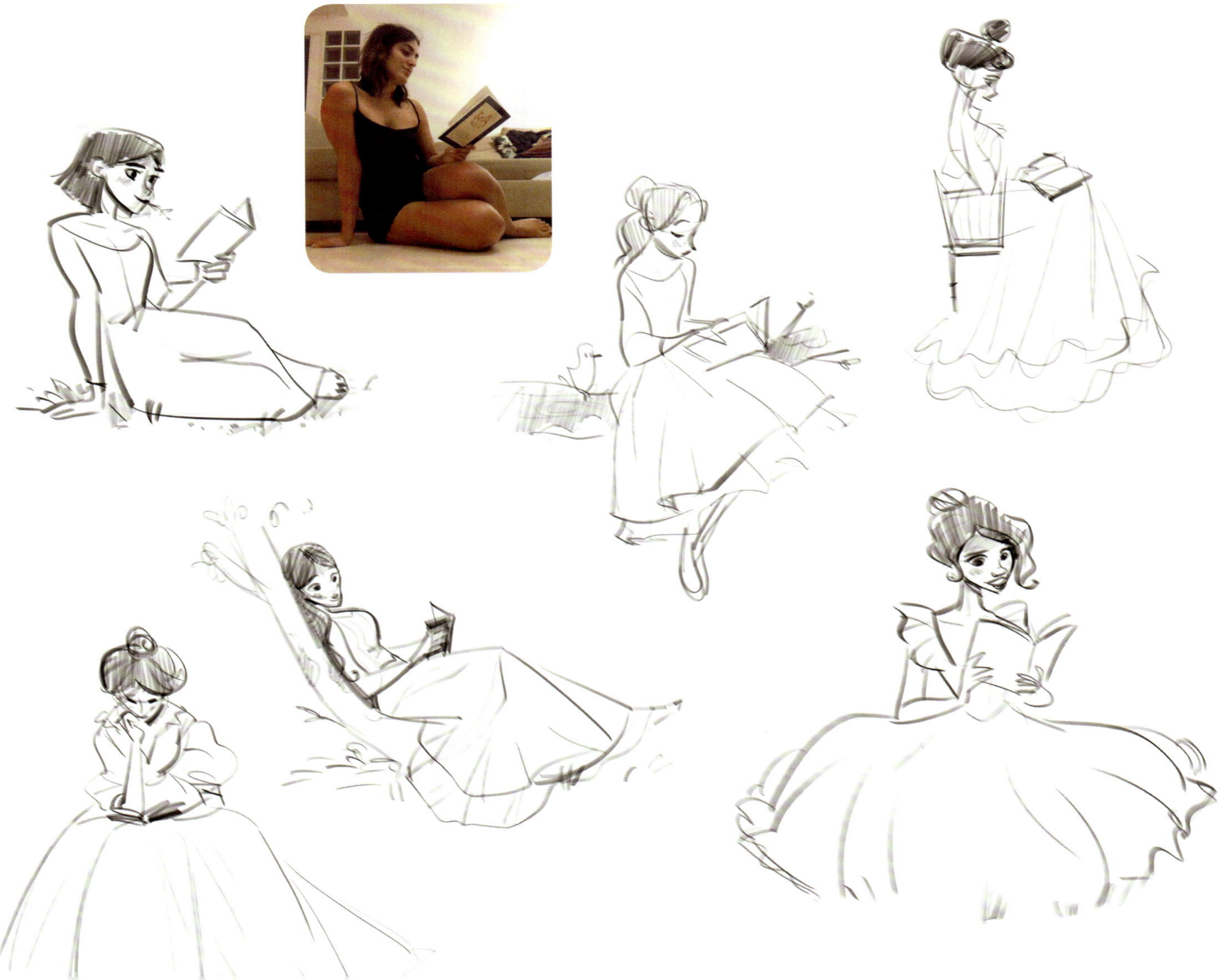

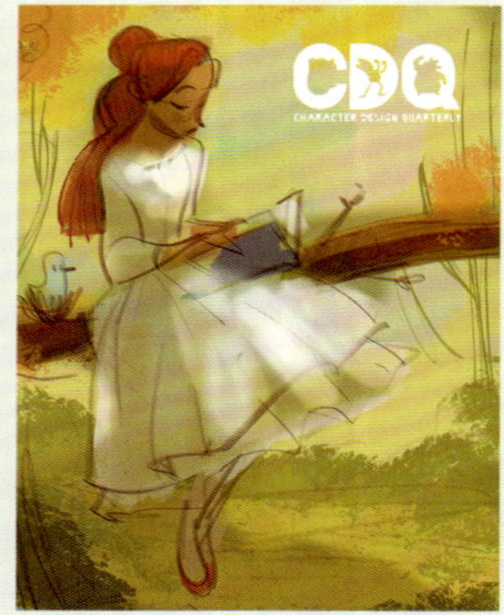
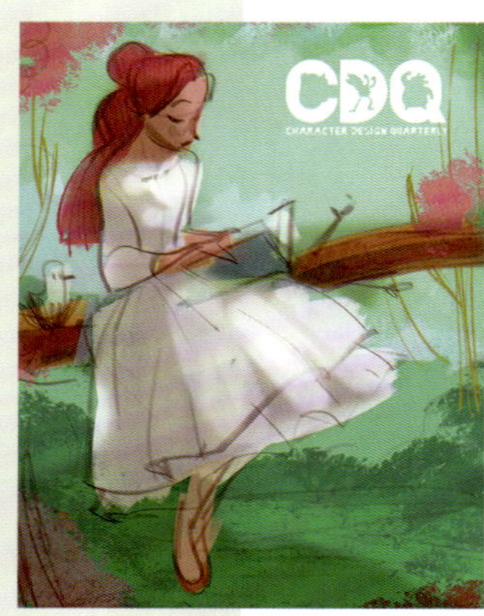
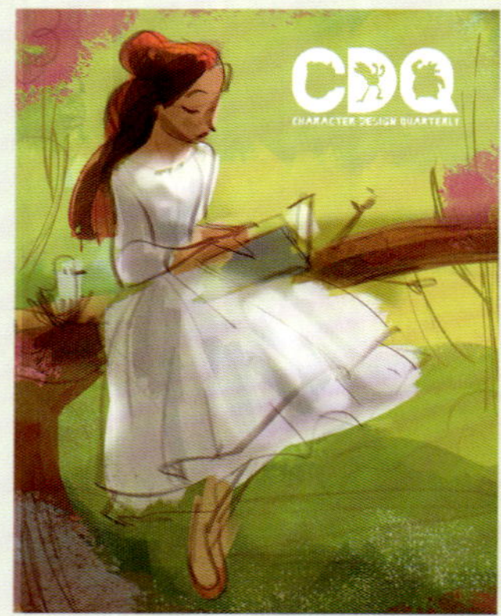
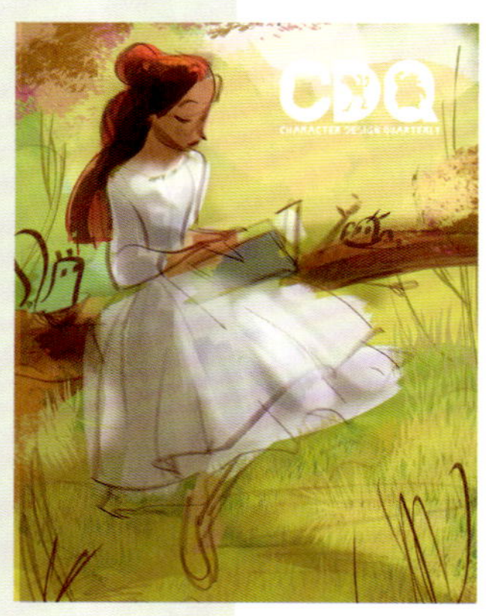
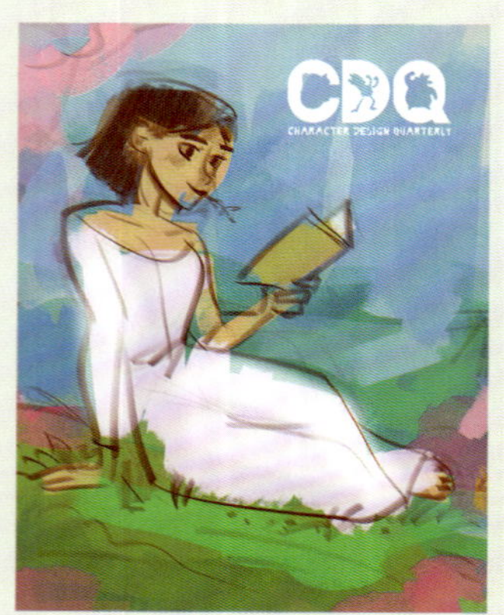
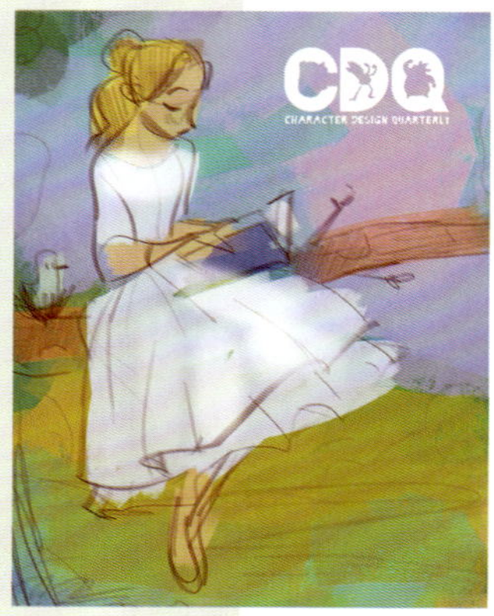
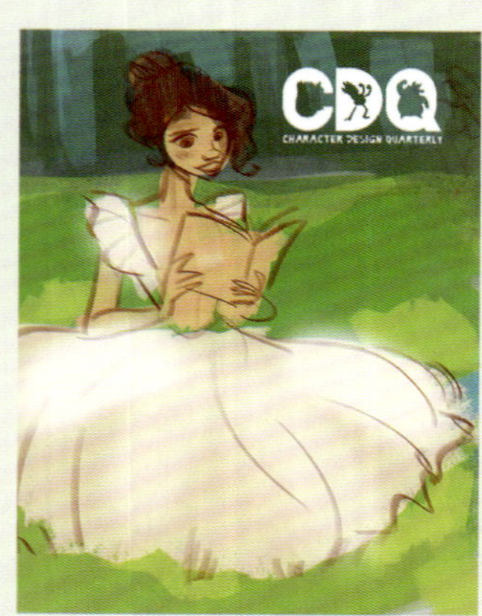
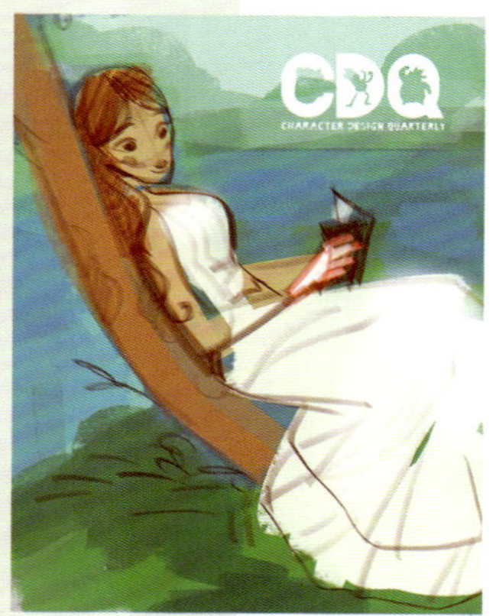

PICKING THE PERFECT PALETTE

I've picked my favorite pose, so now it's time to set up the camera and put the character into the environment. For this image, the surroundings need to be cheerful and bright, with a lot of air to breathe, and sun to make the image warm and inviting. Finding the right color palette is where we find the direction of the piece, so don't be afraid to experiment and work outside of your comfort zone. Try different colors, look for references, and be prepared to start from scratch if necessary.

LIGHTS, SHADOWS, ACTION!

To finalize the image I refine the shapes, create the first simple layering of foreground, midground, and background, and find the local colors (or base colors). Next, I add shadows, light, and then rim lights to the local colors, based on the light sources. It's important to study different materials for skin, hair, and fabric to be able to communicate enough differences in texture in the image, and show how light and shadow affects each surface.

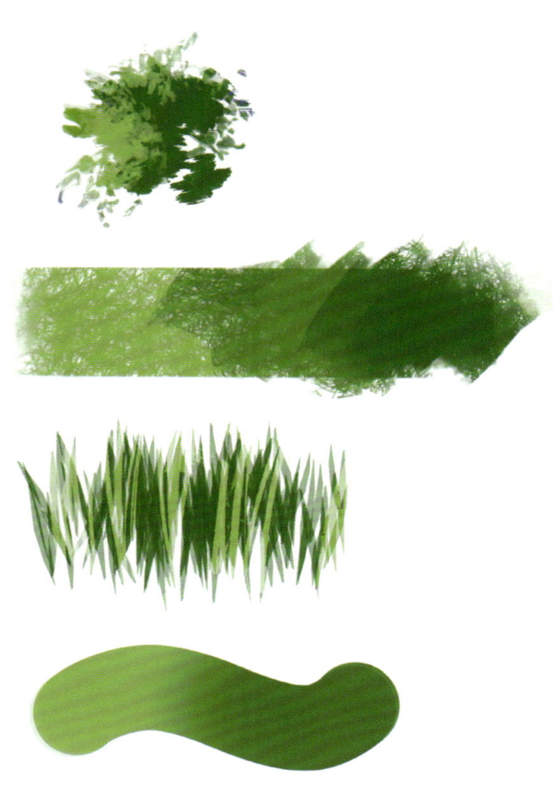

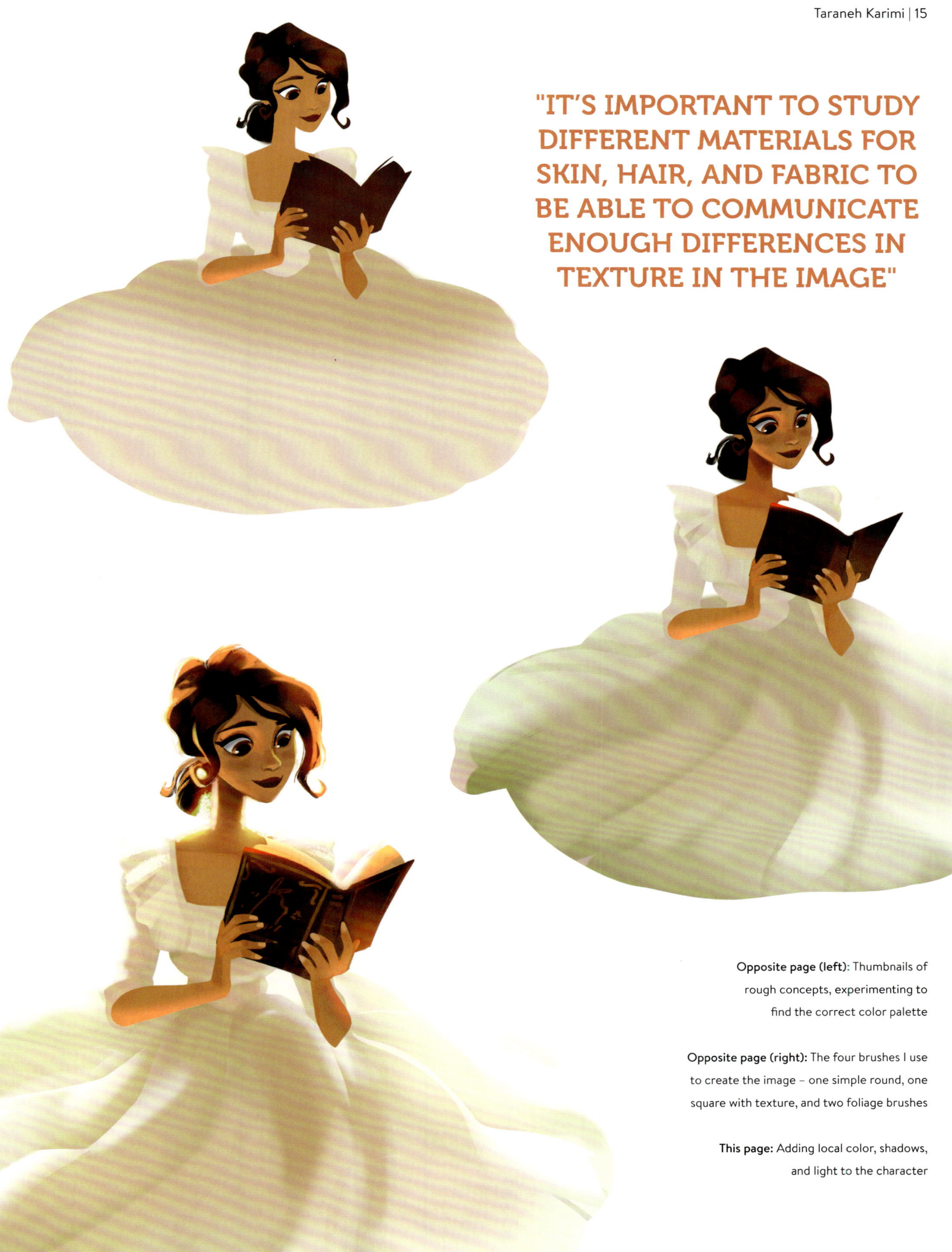

"IT'S IMPORTANT TO STUDY DIFFERENT MATERIALS FOR SKIN, HAIR, AND FABRIC TO BE ABLE TO COMMUNICATE ENOUGH DIFFERENCES IN TEXTURE IN THE IMAGE"

Opposite page (left): Thumbnails of rough concepts, experimenting to find the correct color palette

Opposite page (right): The four brushes I use to create the image – one simple round, one square with texture, and two foliage brushes

This page: Adding local color, shadows, and light to the character

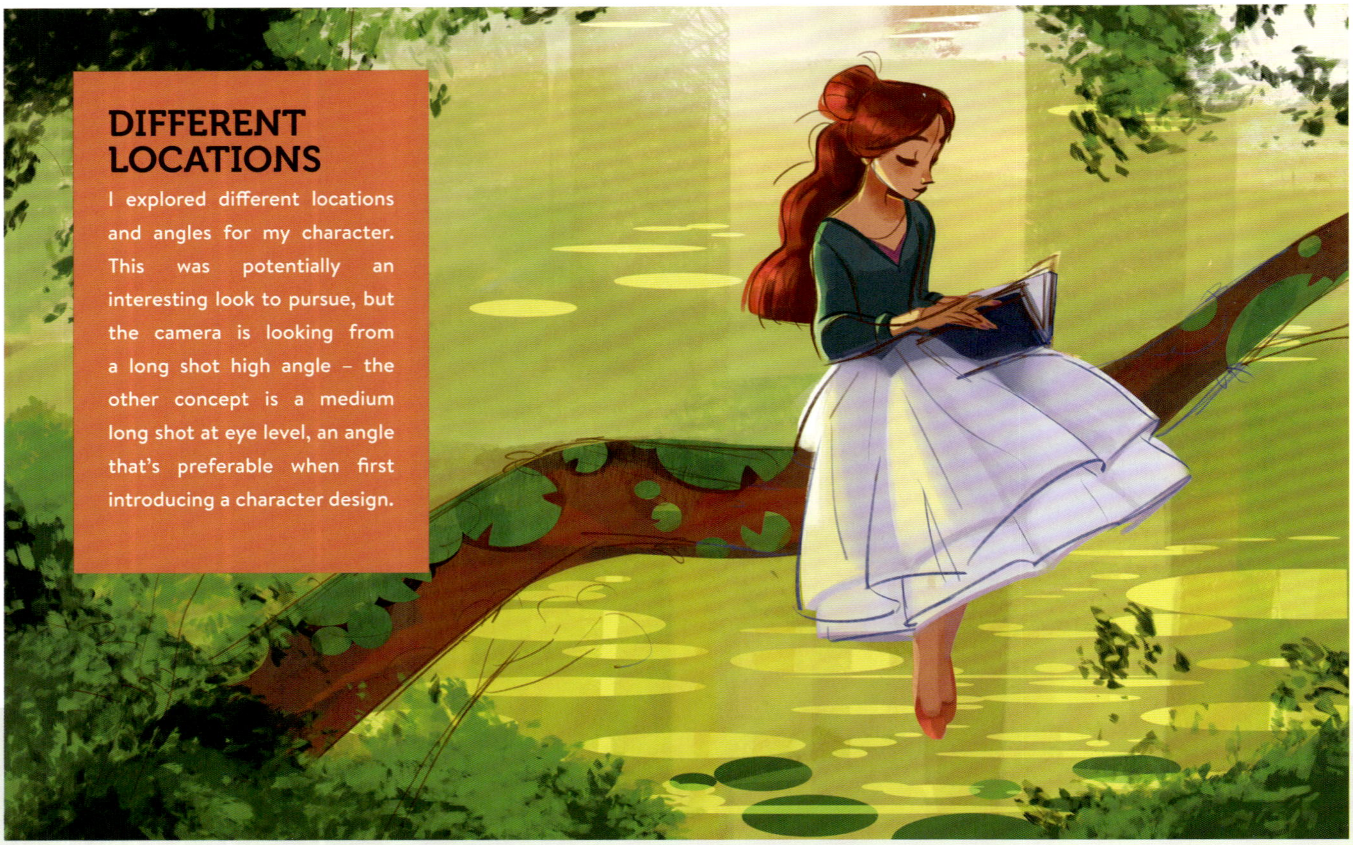

DIFFERENT LOCATIONS

I explored different locations and angles for my character. This was potentially an interesting look to pursue, but the camera is looking from a long shot high angle – the other concept is a medium long shot at eye level, an angle that's preferable when first introducing a character design.

THE FINISHING TOUCHES

It's never too late to add more spice to your story! With the main character finished, let's find something to make the image more magical – maybe some creatures, interesting plants, or more characters? Since we are adding extra elements to the image, we need to be careful about composition, finding the spots where extra details won't detract from the character as the focal point. We want the audience to enjoy discovering these elements, but not be distracted from the main story we are trying to tell. I add rabbits and a parasol to the background and the scene is complete, our character relaxes peacefully in the woods with a good book!

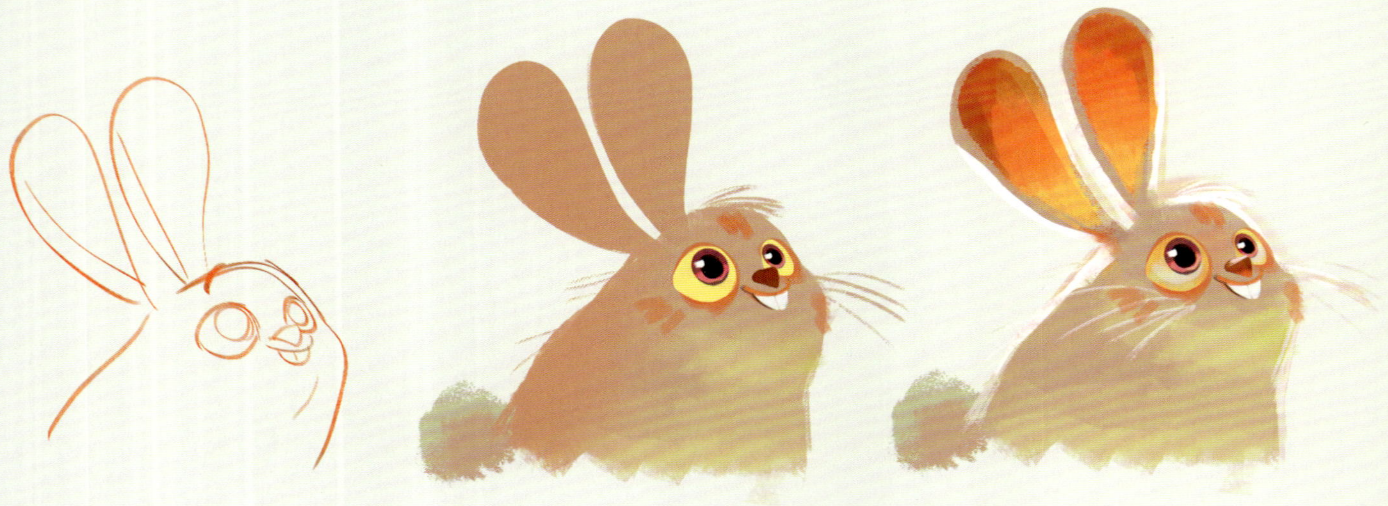

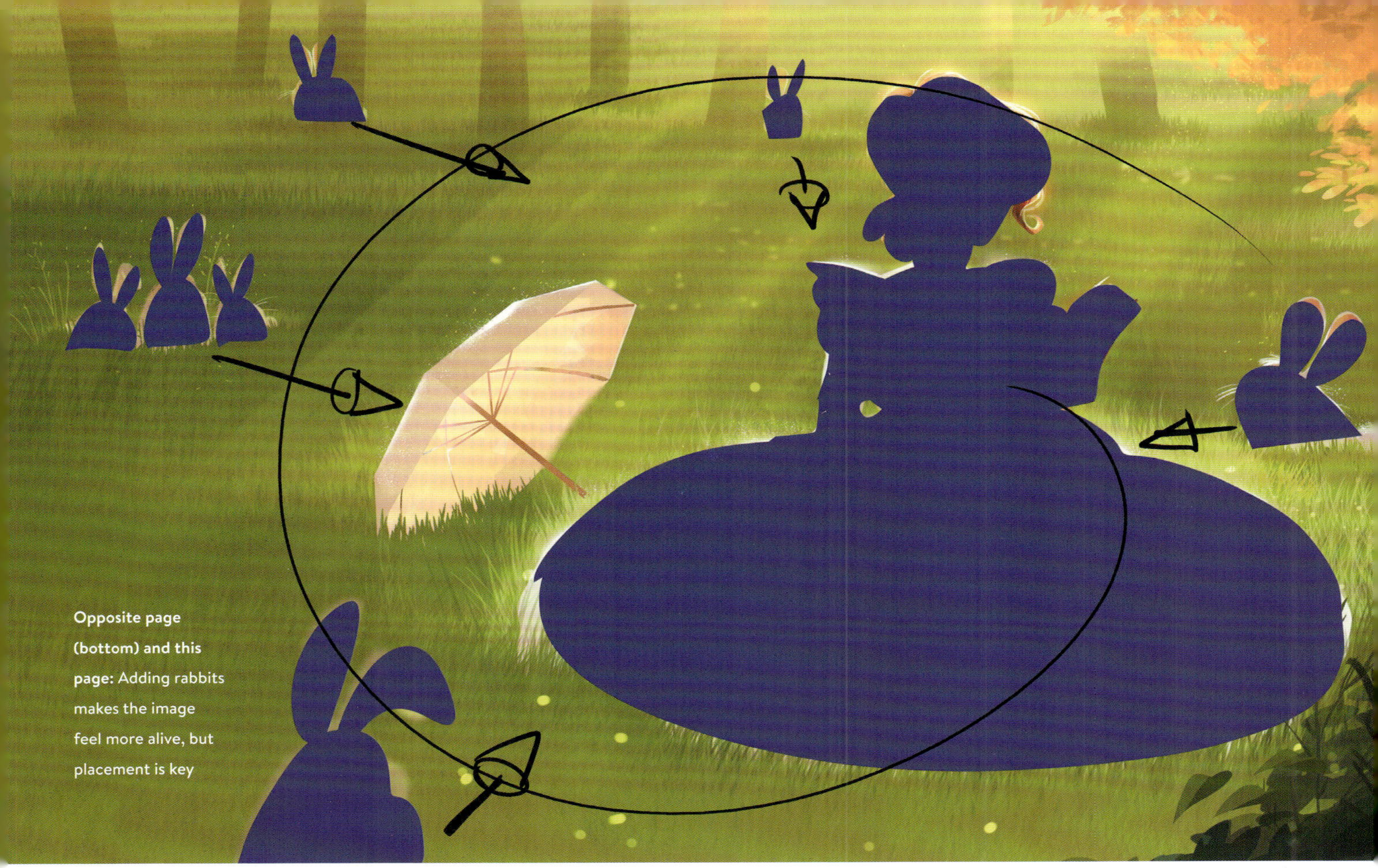

Opposite page (bottom) and this page: Adding rabbits makes the image feel more alive, but placement is key

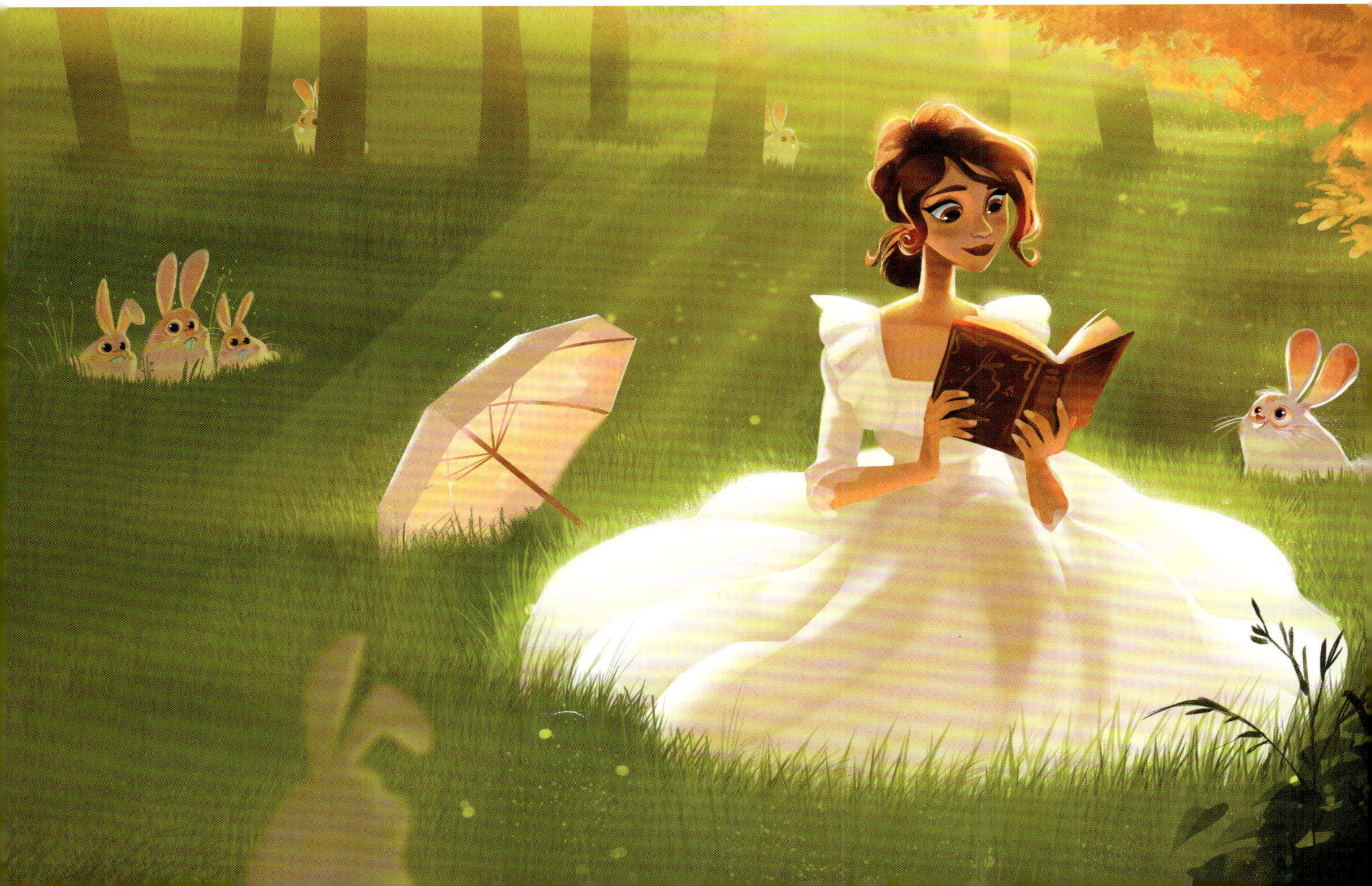

USING COLOR

HYUNA LEE

Color influences so much of how we consider a character. Whether it's telling us more about their personality, their mood, or even their surroundings, making sure that colors are appropriate and blend together is an important part of any piece of art. I'm going to start with a simple sketch and step by step add layers of color to end up with a finished character!

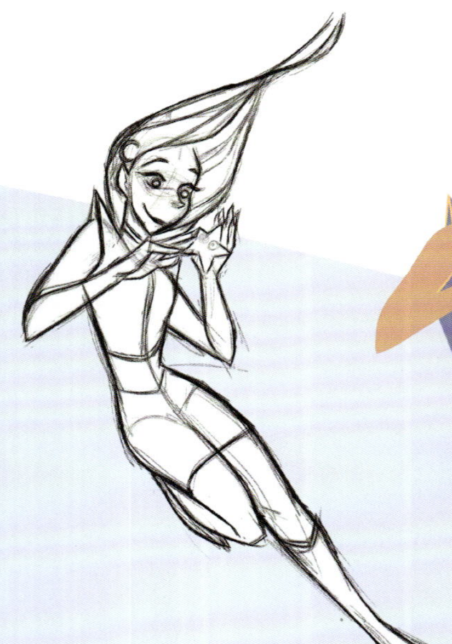

COLORING THE MOOD

When designing a character, the first thing to consider is their personality and mood. Ask yourself, what colors would suit the situation the character finds themselves in? First, I choose the base colors, and then experiment with different tones from there. If the character has a friendly personality, I will add warm tones. Likewise, if the character is colder and more distant, then cooler tones would be more appropriate. Feel free to boldly experiment with color choices, always referring back to the emotional truth of your character's personality.

All images © Hyuna Lee

LIGHTING THE WAY

When considering color, I spend a lot time studying cool and warm tones. I find observing and drawing fruit, or still life, a good way to experiment with how the environment can impact a subject's color. Try to look at the same object with several different light sources and try painting each. I also recommend studying the sky – there are so many colors in the sky!

FALLING STARS

Now we understand how we want to use color, let's go back a step – before adding color I will sketch out a design of the character I have in mind. It's at this stage that I'll try to nail down the character's personality and the general atmosphere of the piece. For this tutorial, I've drawn a character with long hair who is sad and crying. But let's make this more interesting – what if, as she cries, her tears turn into stars?

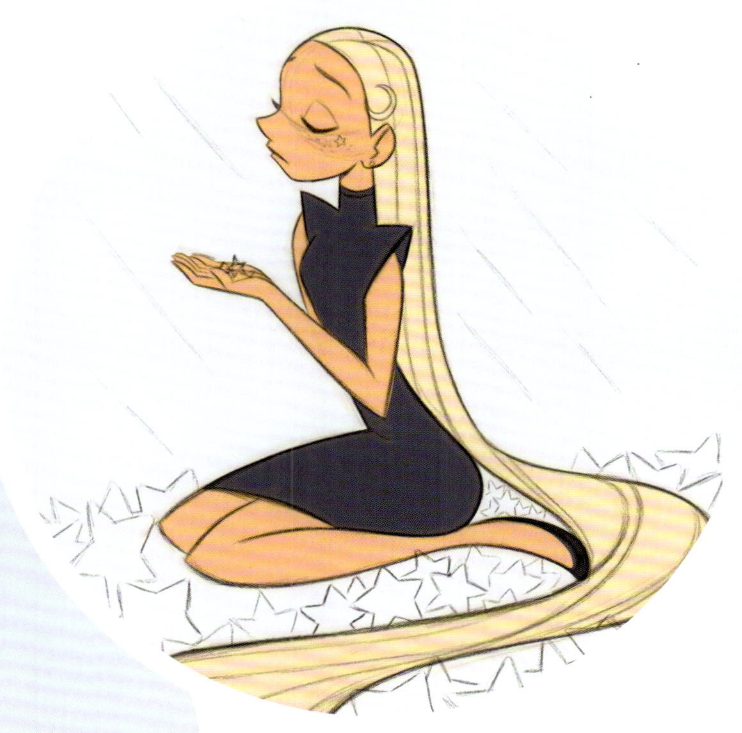

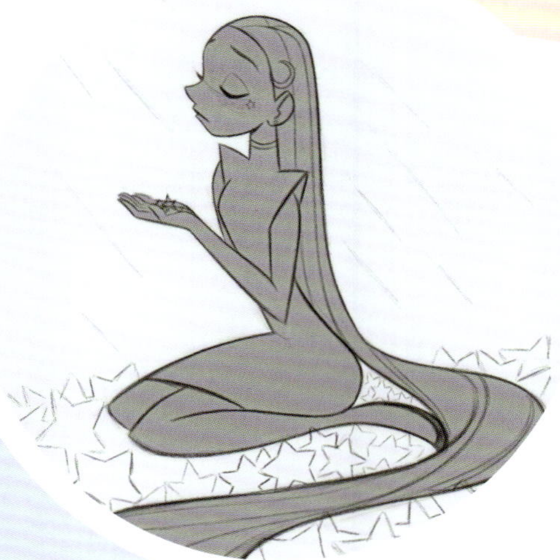

A CHARACTER'S NATURAL LOOK

With a basic sketch complete, it's time to start applying the colours we selected when considering the mood. With the character's silhouette defined, I add detail to distinguish their clothes, hair, and skin. Next, I add the character's natural color (or local color). I don't add lighting or contrast at this stage, I want to make sure the natural colors work first.

CHANGING THE TEMPERATURE

The first thing I consider when adding detail is where the main light source will be in the image. There are stars falling from our character, so we want a yellow light glowing from below. I want the background to be a rich blue like the night sky. This means the skin will need to show a blended transition of yellow light to rich blue on the skins surfaces that move away from the lightsource. I start with yellow and work through orange, red, and finally purple at the point where the effect of the light stops. The further away from the light, the more I try to mix blue and purple tones, and the closer, the warmer the colors should feel.

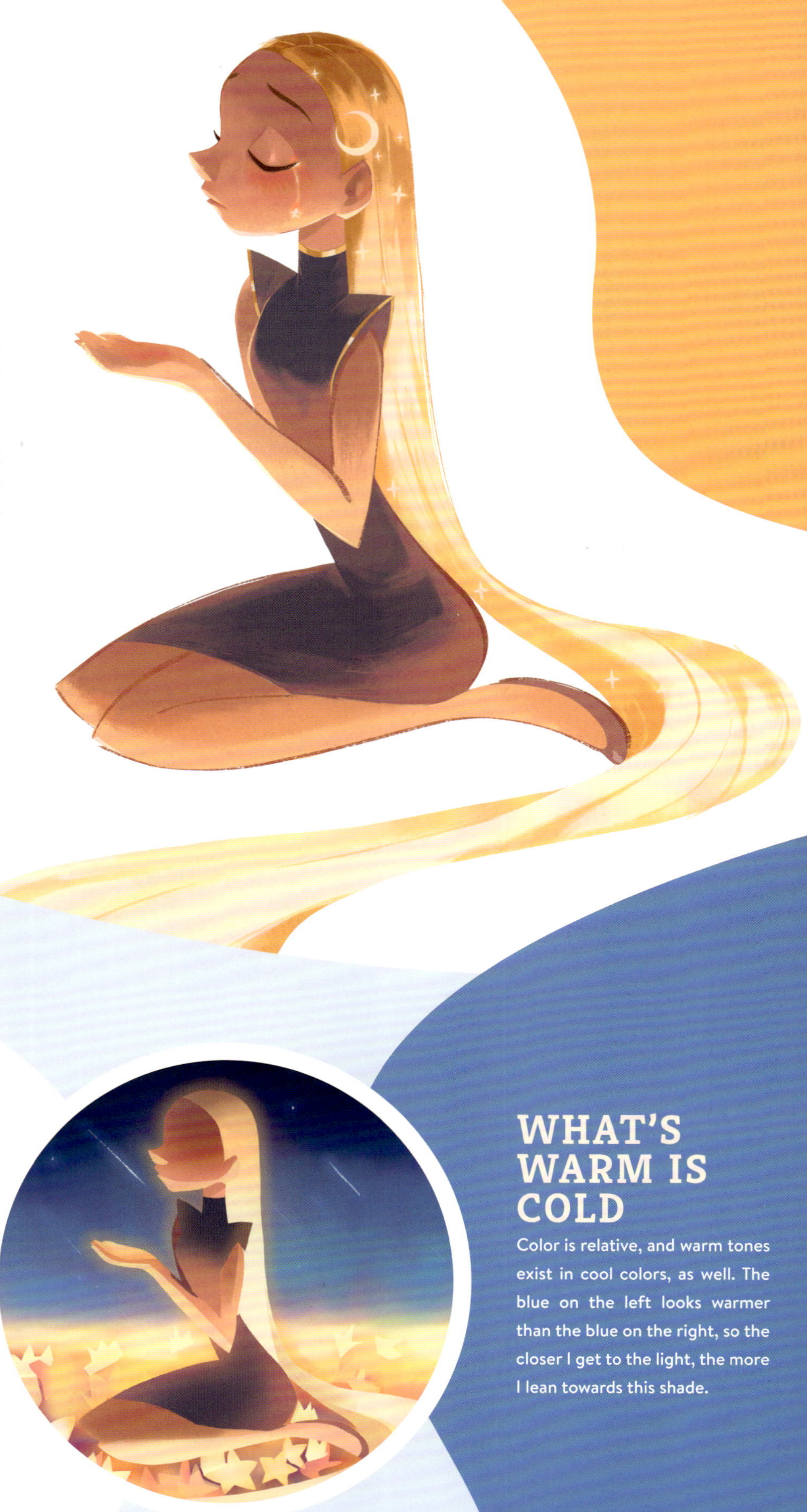

WHAT'S WARM IS COLD

Color is relative, and warm tones exist in cool colors, as well. The blue on the left looks warmer than the blue on the right, so the closer I get to the light, the more I lean towards this shade.

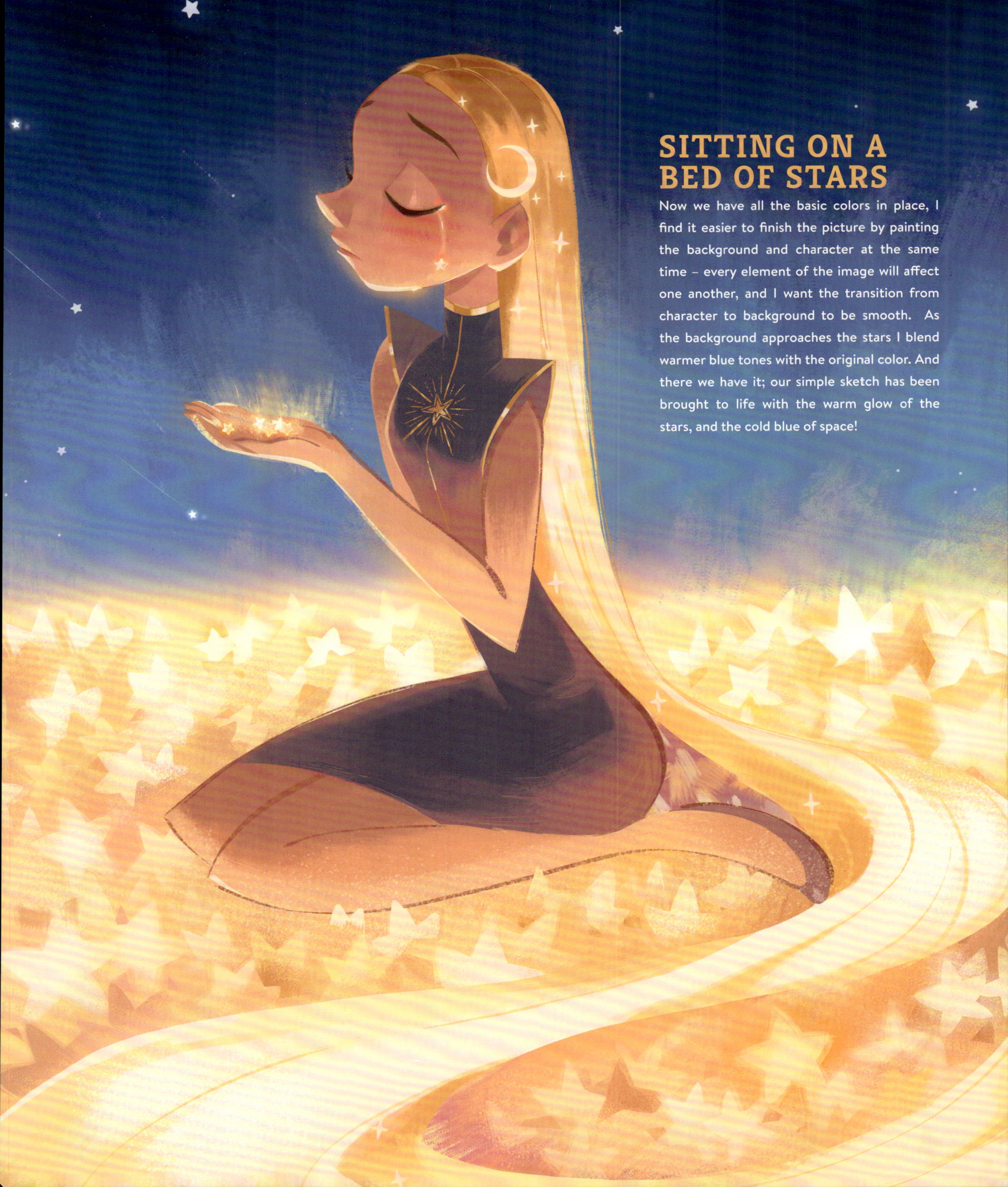

SITTING ON A BED OF STARS

Now we have all the basic colors in place, I find it easier to finish the picture by painting the background and character at the same time – every element of the image will affect one another, and I want the transition from character to background to be smooth. As the background approaches the stars I blend warmer blue tones with the original color. And there we have it; our simple sketch has been brought to life with the warm glow of the stars, and the cold blue of space!

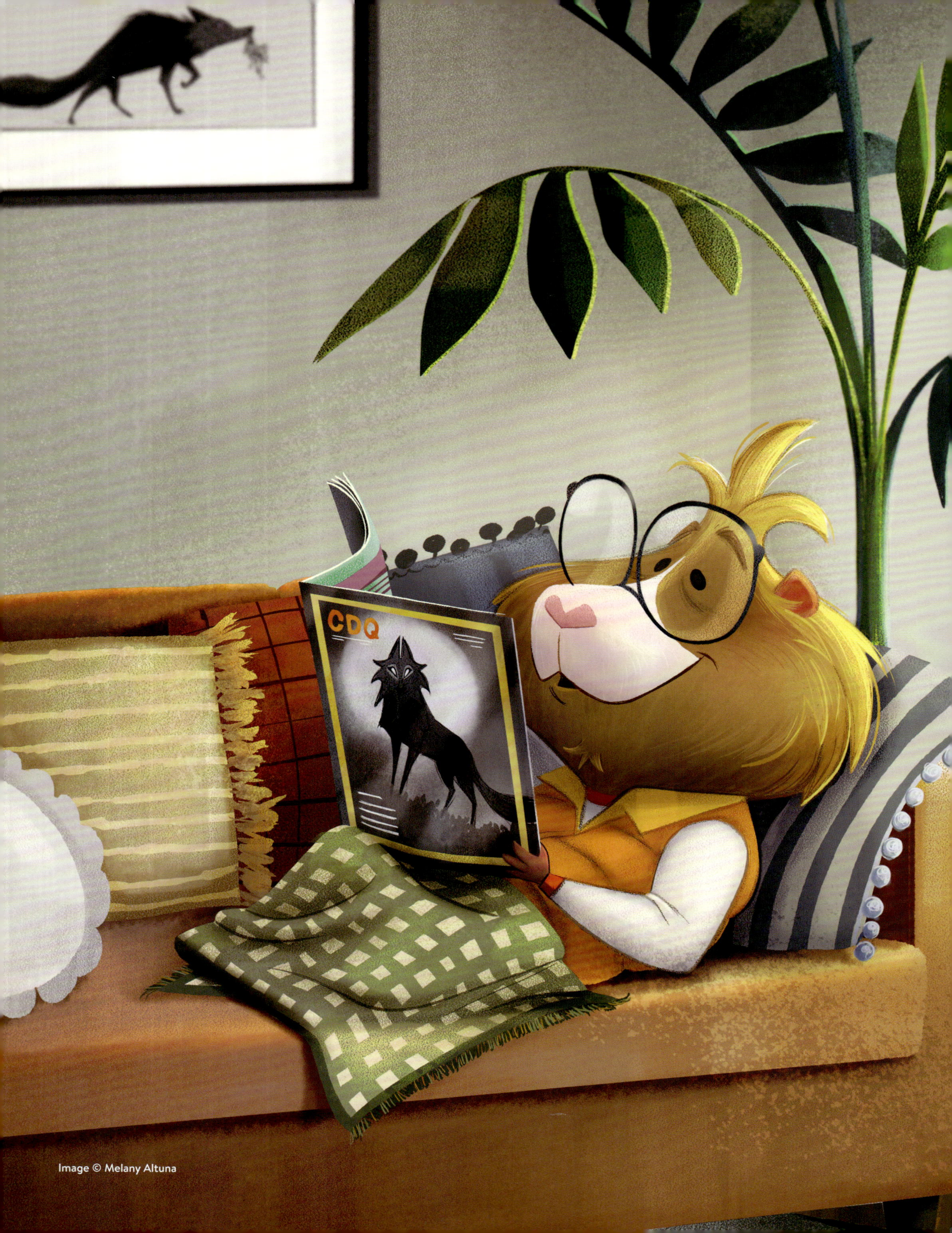
CDQ

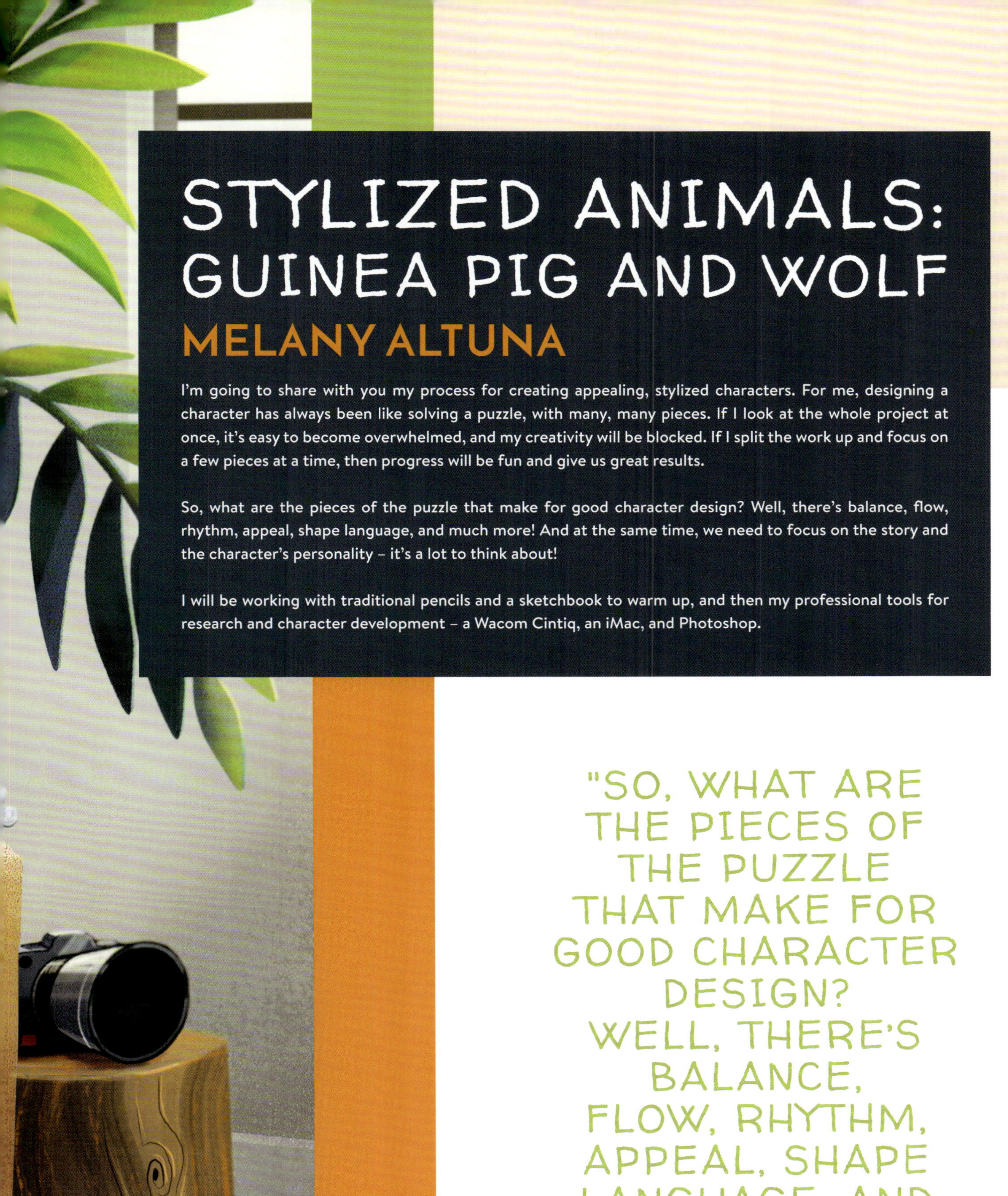

STYLIZED ANIMALS: GUINEA PIG AND WOLF

MELANY ALTUNA

I'm going to share with you my process for creating appealing, stylized characters. For me, designing a character has always been like solving a puzzle, with many, many pieces. If I look at the whole project at once, it's easy to become overwhelmed, and my creativity will be blocked. If I split the work up and focus on a few pieces at a time, then progress will be fun and give us great results.

So, what are the pieces of the puzzle that make for good character design? Well, there's balance, flow, rhythm, appeal, shape language, and much more! And at the same time, we need to focus on the story and the character's personality – it's a lot to think about!

I will be working with traditional pencils and a sketchbook to warm up, and then my professional tools for research and character development – a Wacom Cintiq, an iMac, and Photoshop.

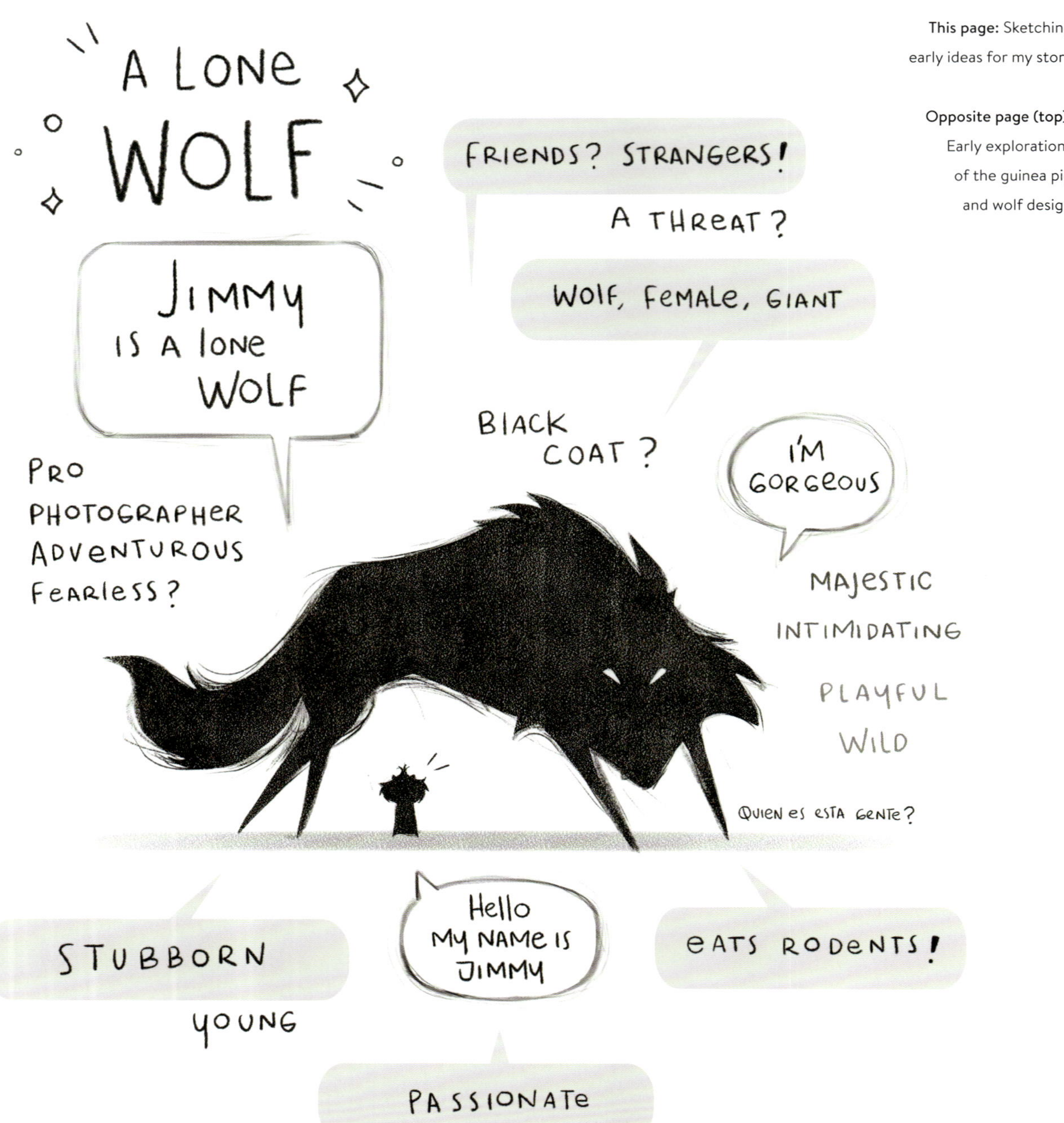

FINDING THE STORY

The brief for this project is very open – we will design two characters, a guinea pig and a wolf, and that's pretty much all we know about them. It's important we create a backstory for the characters first which will guide the rest of the process.

Looking online for references is a good starting point. Search for things that grab your interest and get your ideas flowing. Inspiration can come from anywhere. I was online shopping for outdoor clothing for my next camping trip before this project, and that sparked an idea. I want my main character to be a guinea pig and I want to focus the story on him. Let's call him Jimmy. Jimmy will be a professional photographer that has a unique encounter with a giant wolf. His job is to take the best picture of the wolf possible, but that might be easier said than done!

ASKING QUESTIONS

With our characters in place, now we need to get a better sense of the 5 Ws – Who are the characters, where are they located, what do they want, when is the story taking place, and why? These questions are a great place to start your research that will help you find all the visual elements needed to make your characters unique. I know this might seem like it takes quite a lot of time, but it's an important step in the process, and one you should never skip!

LET'S START SKETCHING!

When I draw animals, I like to start by sketching from photo references. I go online and collect lots of pictures of wolves and guinea pigs of all shapes, sizes, and colors. This helps me get a feel for the shapes that make this animal unique. Don't worry too much about making anything pretty at this point – just try to experiment, learn, and pay attention to the proportions and characteristics. You never need to show this step to anyone if you don't want to. Keep that in mind and the pressure is off – enjoy the process!

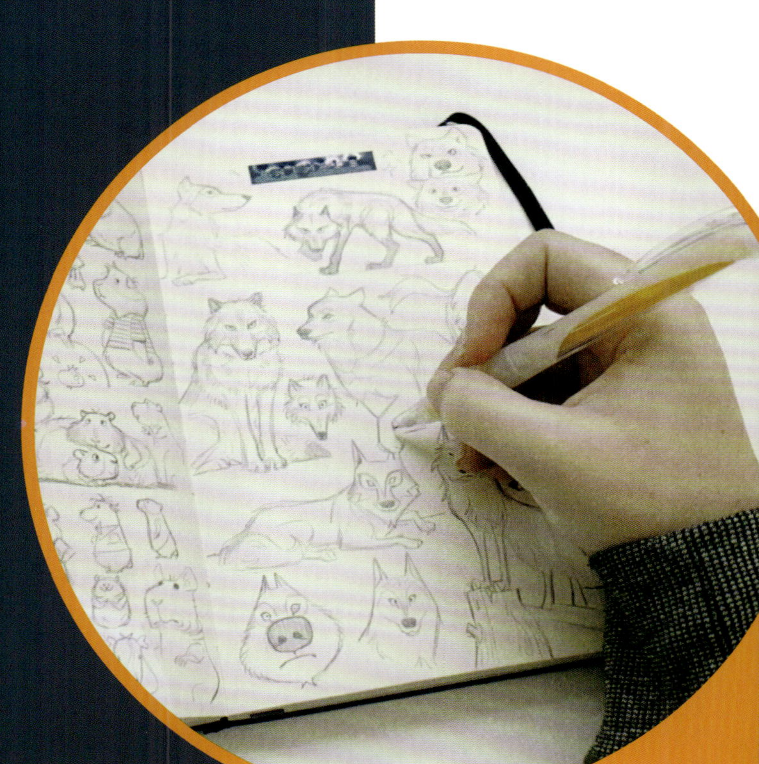

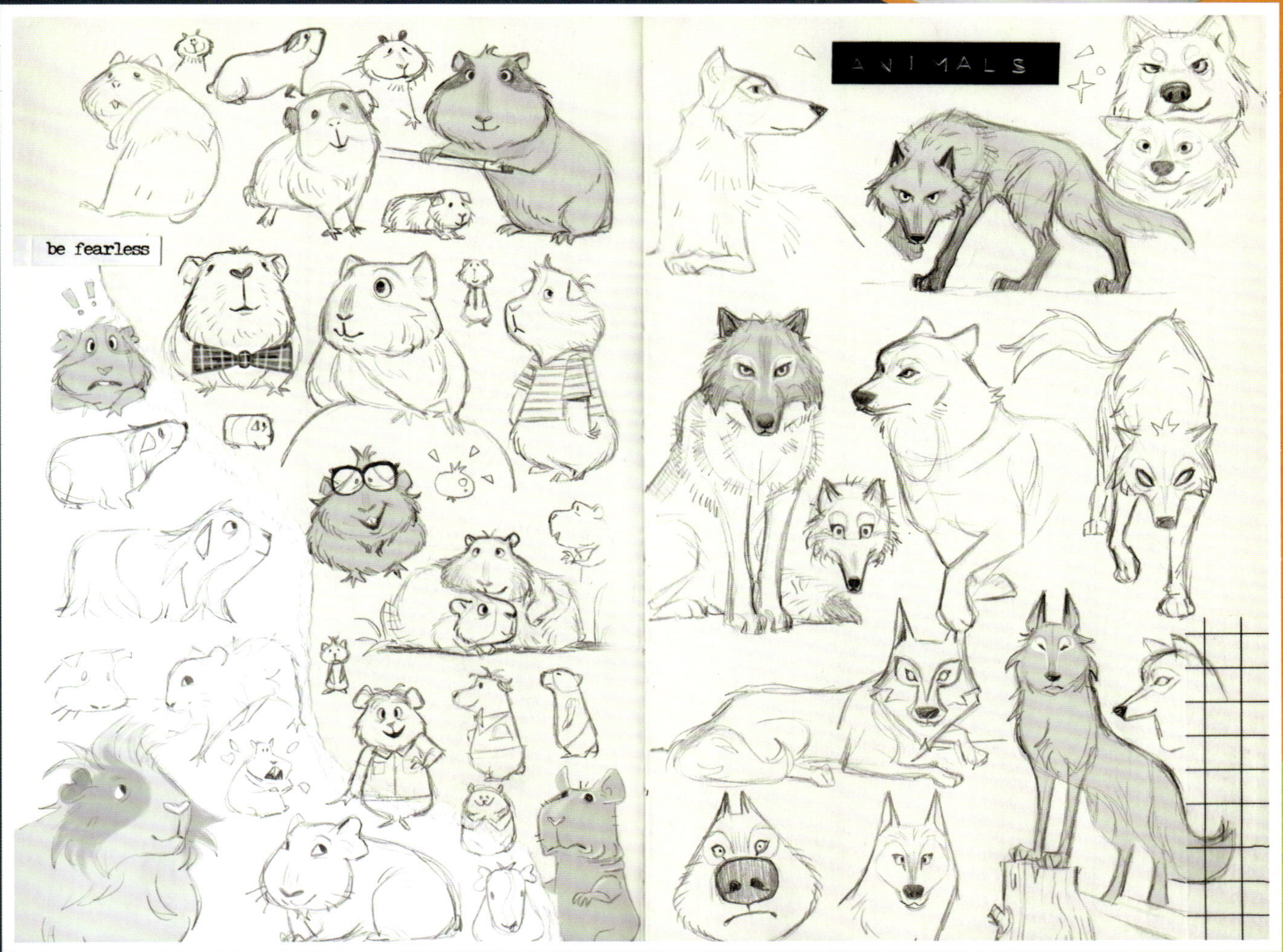

"I CONSIDER THE BALANCE BETWEEN THE BODY AND FACE AND HOW LARGE, MEDIUM, AND SMALL SHAPES CAN AFFECT THE DESIGN"

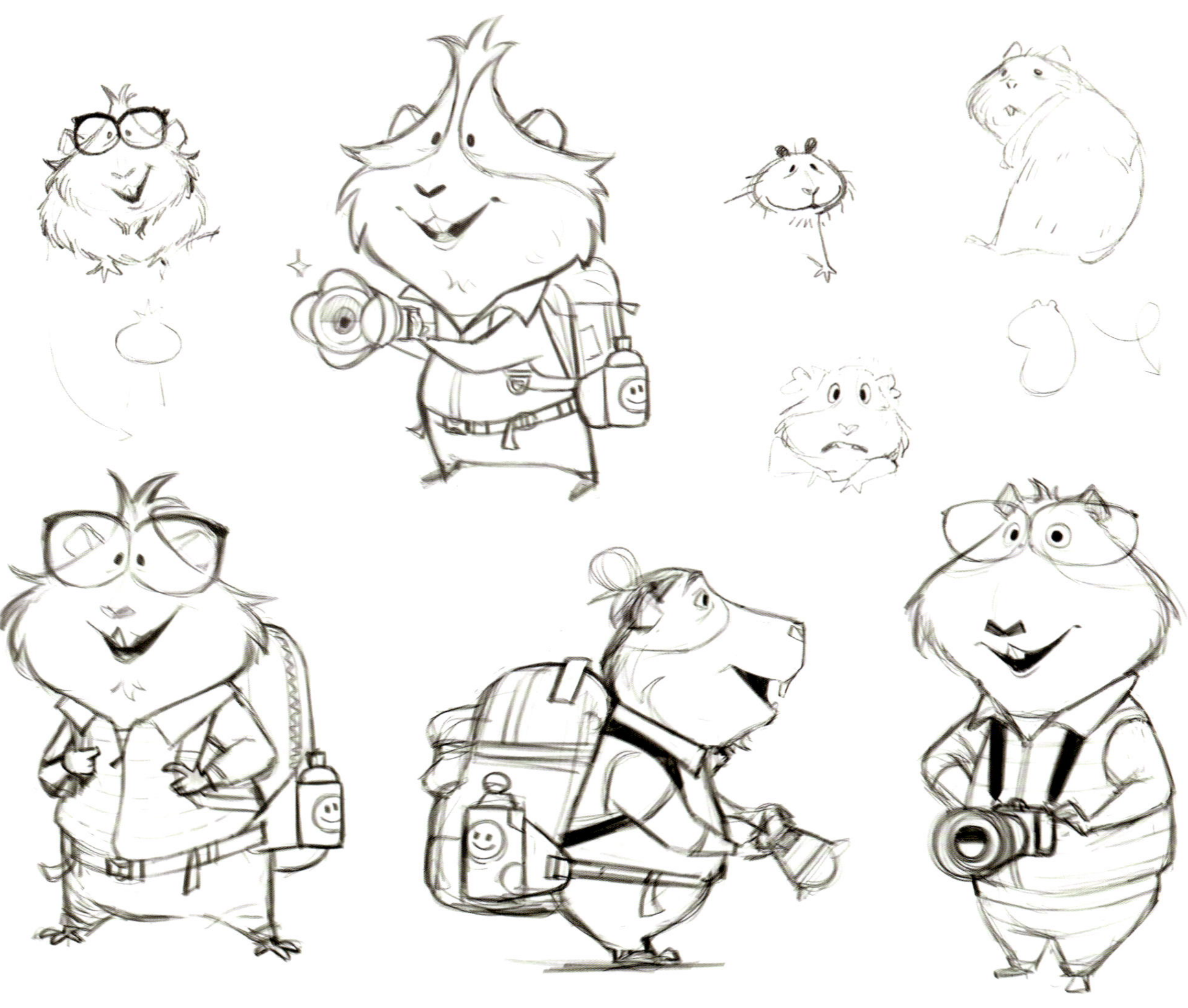

SHIFTING SHAPES

After warming up in the sketchbook I like to look at all the drawings and find a few that I really like, then start playing around with the face and how large, medium, and small shapes can affect the design. I push the shapes and play with size to find an appealing look.

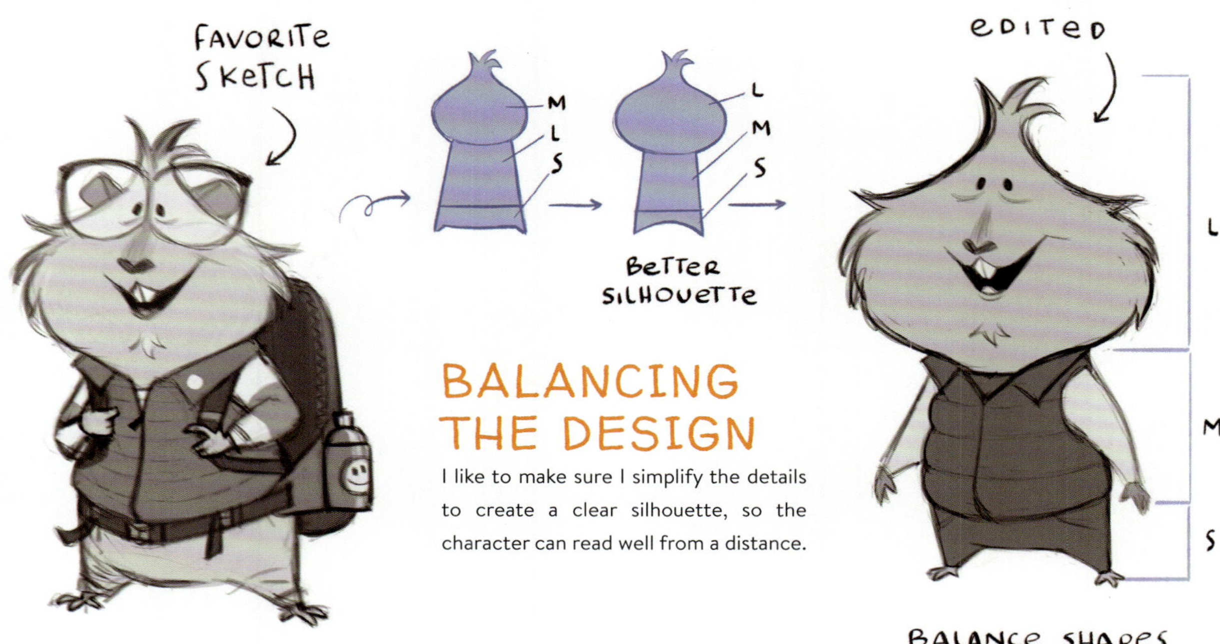

BALANCING THE DESIGN

I like to make sure I simplify the details to create a clear silhouette, so the character can read well from a distance.

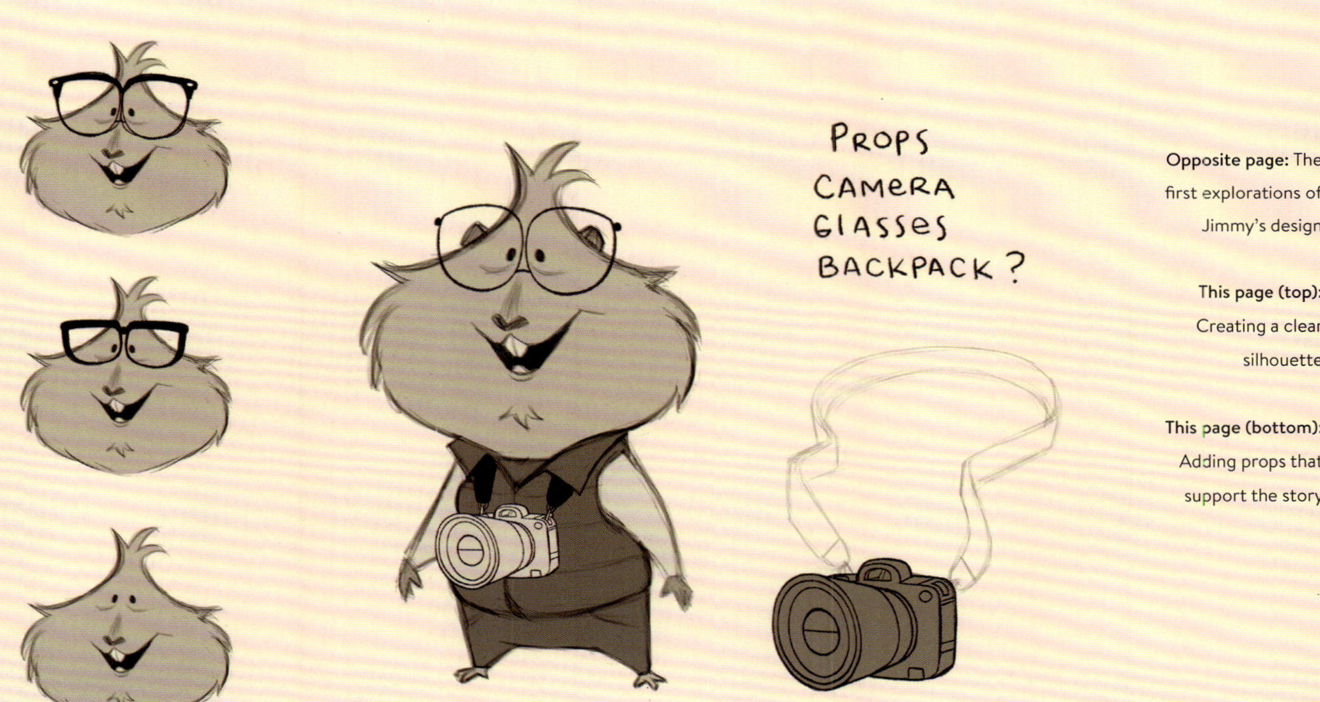

Opposite page: The first explorations of Jimmy's design

This page (top): Creating a clear silhouette

This page (bottom): Adding props that support the story

PROPPING UP THE STORY

Adding props to a character can help express a little more about their personality. In this case, we need to make it obvious that Jimmy is a photographer on a mission, maybe by adding a camera or backpack. I also give him some glasses to compensate for his tiny dot eyes and to help the audience understand who he is right away.

Working on this step I notice that people may mistake Jimmy for a tourist, and that's not the look I want for this character. I need to make sure I stay away from anything that suggests "tourist" when moving on to color and poses.

COMPLETING THE JIGSAW

Previously, I mentioned how I view the process of designing a character like putting a puzzle together – the more you practice, the faster your brain will start to put the pieces together all by itself. And just like with a jigsaw or puzzle, if you get stuck then the best thing you can do is take a break! Go for a short walk, clear your mind, and when you come back try a different approach.

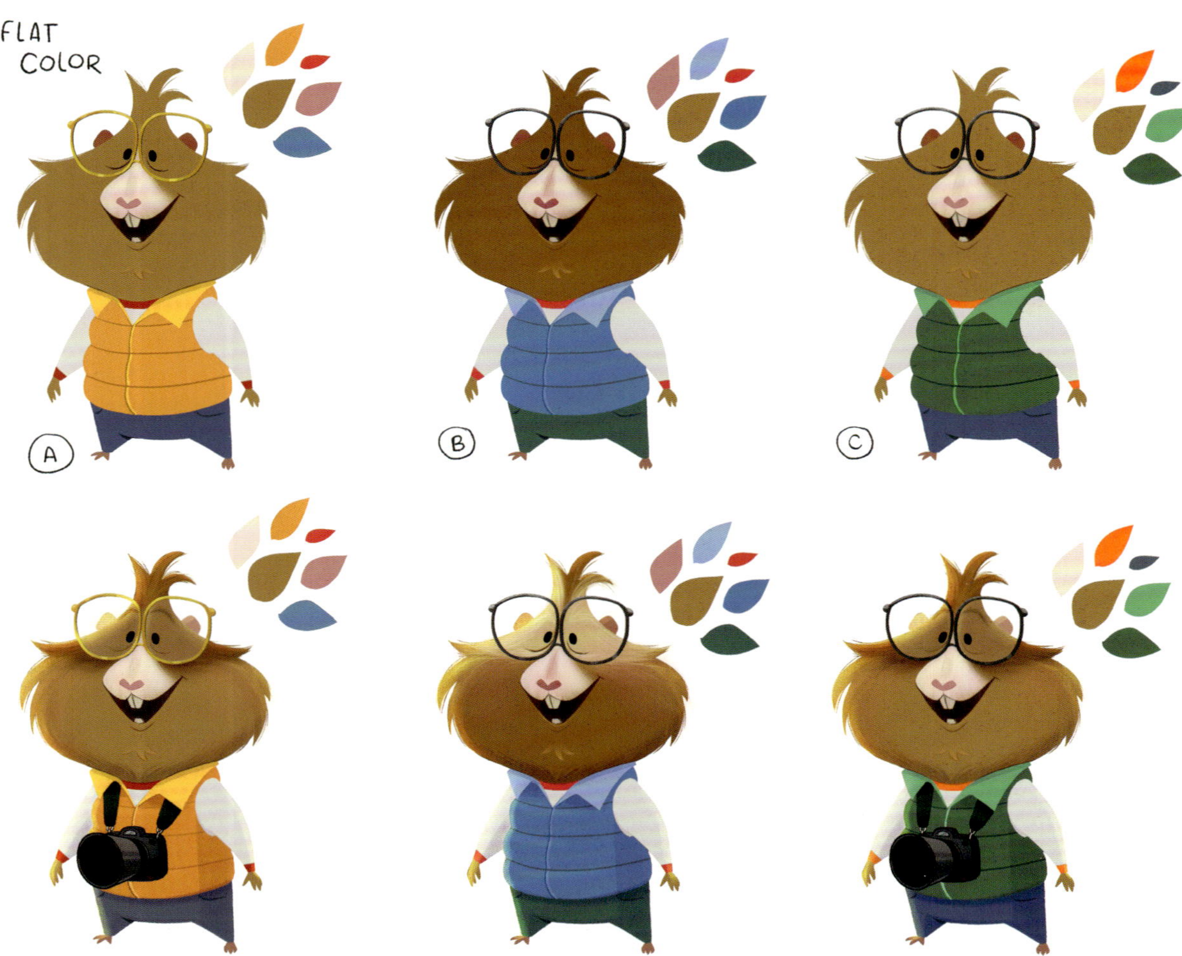

DRESSING JIMMY FOR THE JOB

Time for color! At this point I go back to my references and look for consistent colors in their clothing. Looking at online stores helps you know what's on trend at the moment and what look could stand out. It might even help you to find a more unique color combination than you originally imagined.

I want Jimmy to have warm colors in his hair – a mix of medium browns will look really pretty. We can then use the hair as a base and choose colors for his outfit that complement him. While working through different variations I start to notice that certain color combinations will make Jimmy look older than I want. Keep in mind the story you are trying to tell at every step of the process – every visual element influences what the audience will take from your design.

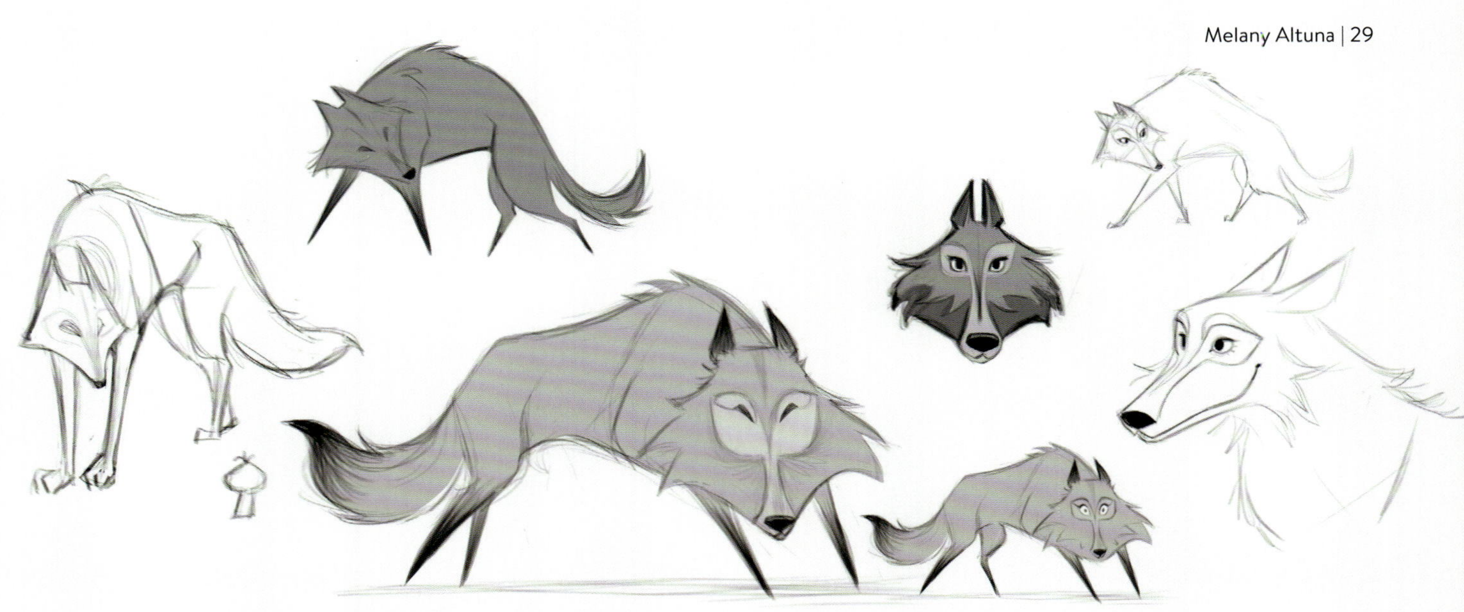

THE WOLF AT THE DOOR

Now, let's start working on the wolf. Again, I pick my favorite early sketches and start pushing shapes to create a good balance. I want the wolf to feel big and elegant – I'm looking for a rhythm that flows from the tip of her foot to the last hair on her tail. I'm imagining the final design as almost a full silhouette, with bright eyes and lots of texture, so I focus on poses that read easily.

Keeping a small silhouette of the other characters in your scene close to hand can help build contrasting shapes and keep a nice sense of scale.

STEPPING AWAY

To be honest, I wasn't happy with how any of my first sketches of the wolf turned out, so I take a break and go back to it the next day. Stepping away from a project can sometimes help with your perspective – when you go back to it you can see it with fresh eyes. I start thinking of the overall shape and pose, and drawing the wolf starts to become easier. Thinking about straight vs curve, line of action, and simple vs complex helps me get a better silhouette for the wolf. When I'm happy with the overall shape, I start getting into the face and hair details.

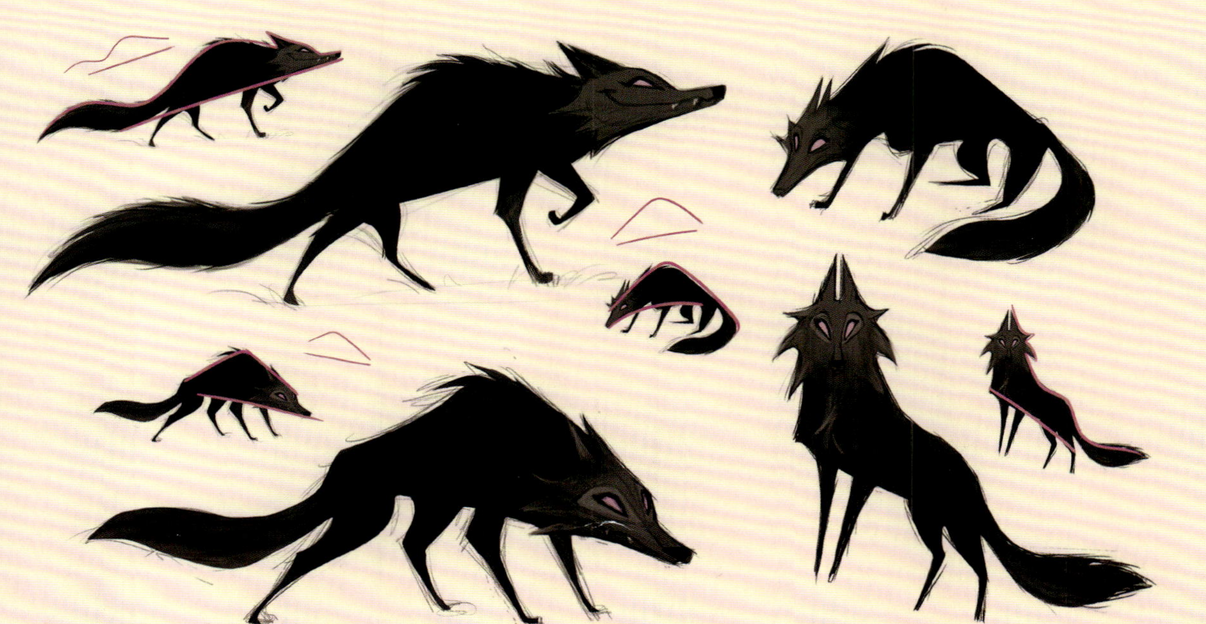

Opposite page:
Finding a color palette that's right for the story I want to tell

This page (top):
Exploring the design of the wolf

This page (bottom):
Finding a nice silhouette

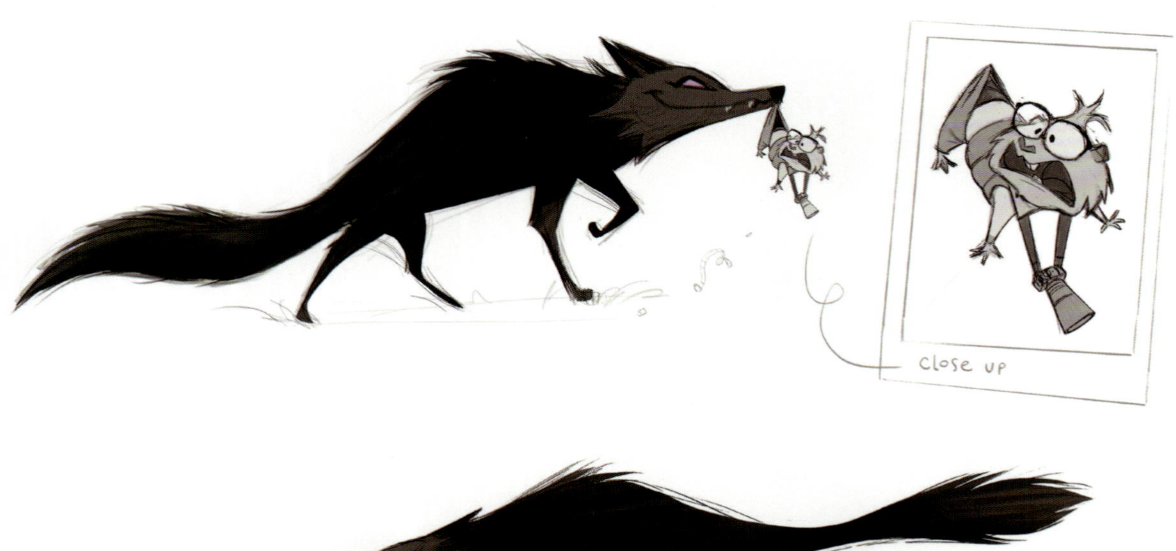

CLOSE UP

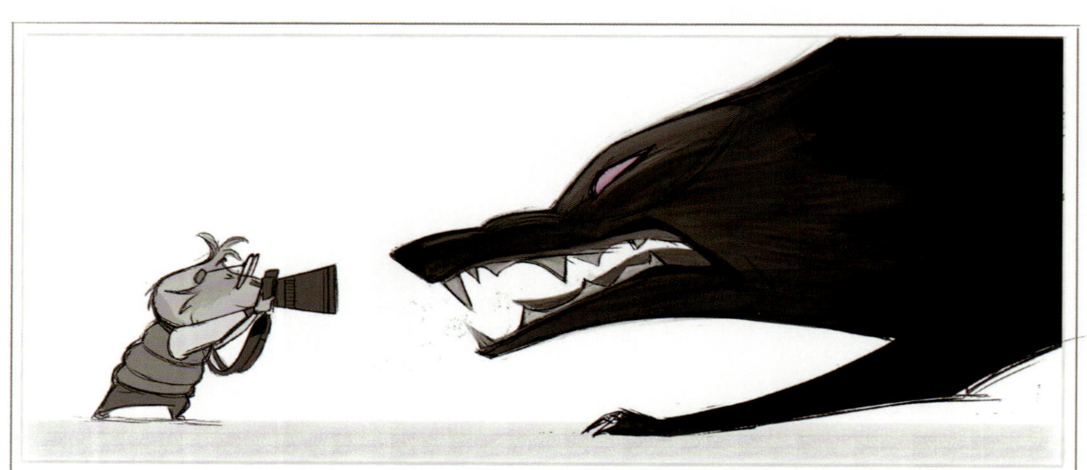

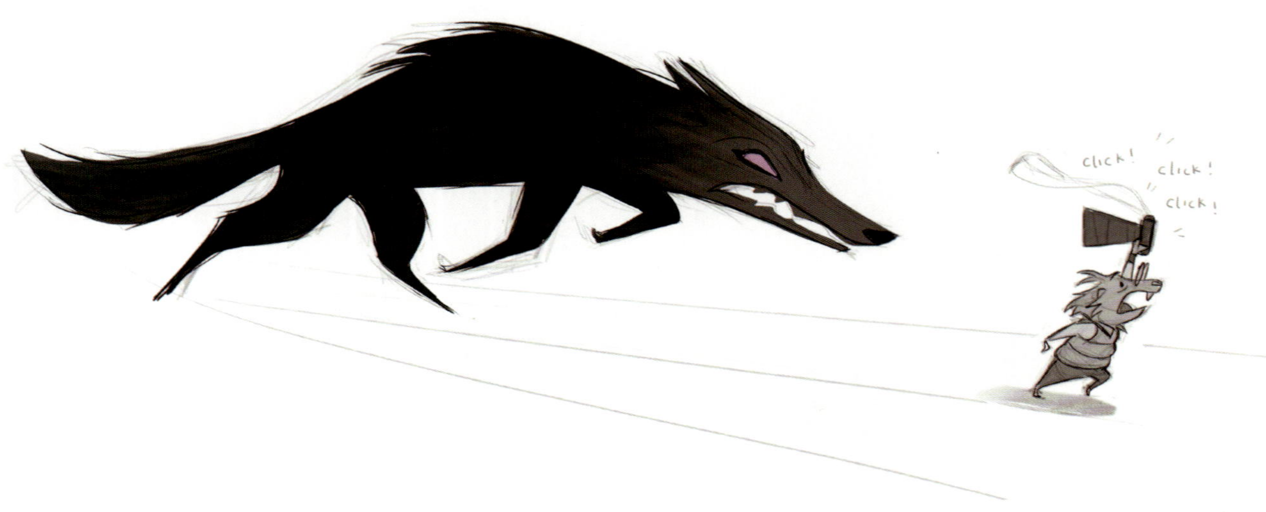

click!
click!
click!

"WHEN CLEANING THE LINES, WE WANT TO MAKE SURE THE ENERGY AND OVERALL FEELING OF THE SKETCH DOESN'T GET LOST"

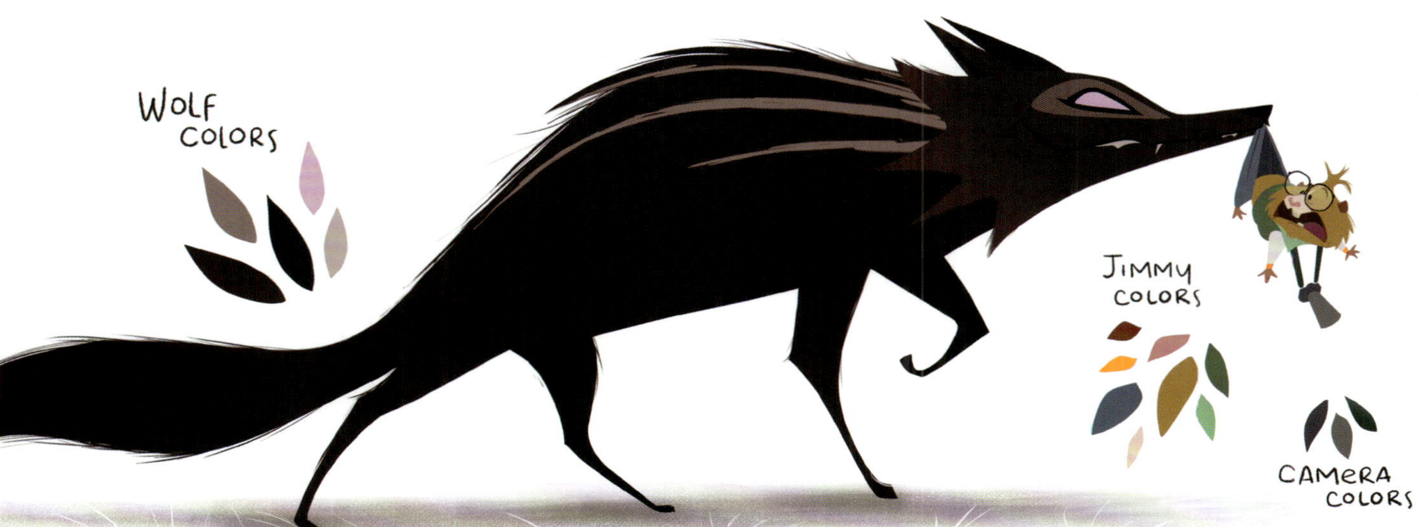

TELLING THE STORY

Now we know how both characters look, we can start playing with posing them. I want the poses to show who they are and what's going on in the story. Try to start this step really loose – think about the energy and the story moments more than technicalities right now. I decide on a few poses to show – I want the characters face to face. I want to see how they look running from one another, and I want the wolf to catch Jimmy! Just feel free to play with different ideas, keeping in mind who the characters are and what they would do in any given situation.

You can take this step as far as you like, making as many poses as you want and picking your favorites. You can even clean them up and color them, but this step isn't about creating anything clean and perfect – you just want to tell the story and keep the characters on model.

It's important to remember that character design should always be in support of the story. Without a story, a design can look good, but it won't be a real character.

CLEANING UP AND COLORING

When cleaning the lines, we want to make sure the energy and overall feeling of the sketch doesn't get lost. It can be hard, and a bit frustrating, but if you make sure you keep the important pieces, you can make it work. You can do the clean-up with just basic shapes to prep for the render, or with line art.

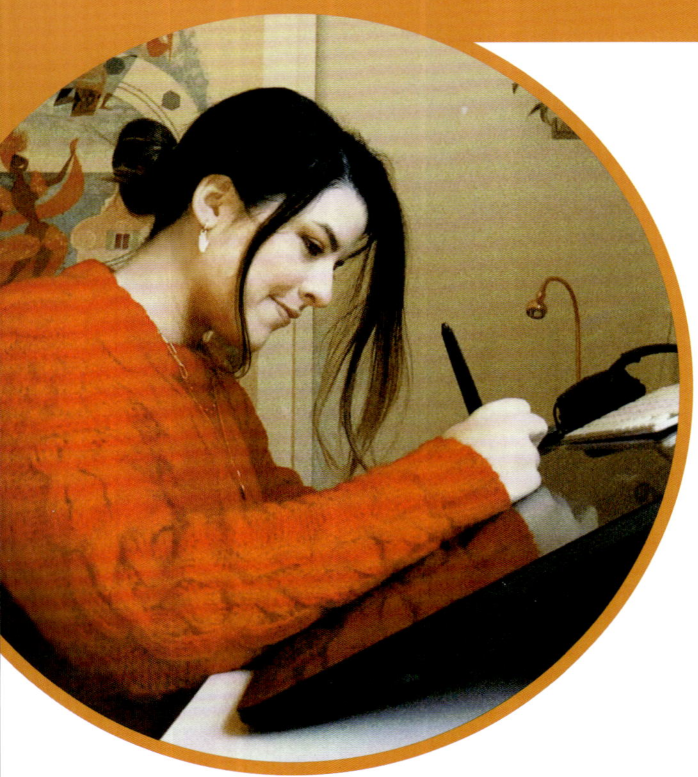

A COLORFUL ENCOUNTER

Once we're happy with the flat color shapes, we can start adding textures, detail lines, and shadow and light. I like to keep it simple and not get too crazy with the rendering when the shapes and expressions are already reading well. I add a close-up of Jimmy so the audience can see him better, without losing the contrast in size between him and the wolf.

And that's pretty much it! I love the story and characters I've come up with and will continue drawing them and see where the story ends. I hope Jimmy makes it out of the situation and manages to deliver his work on time!

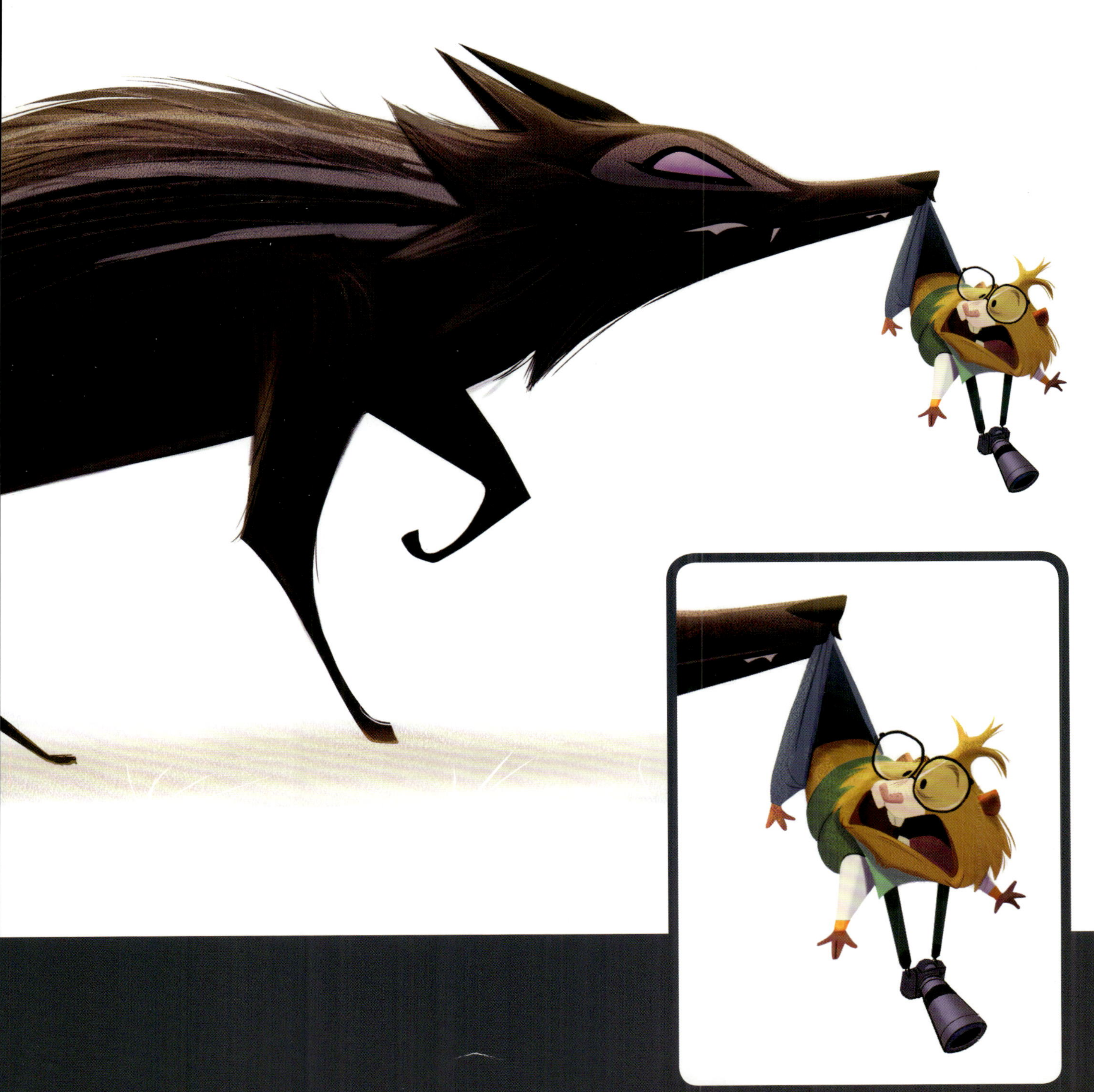

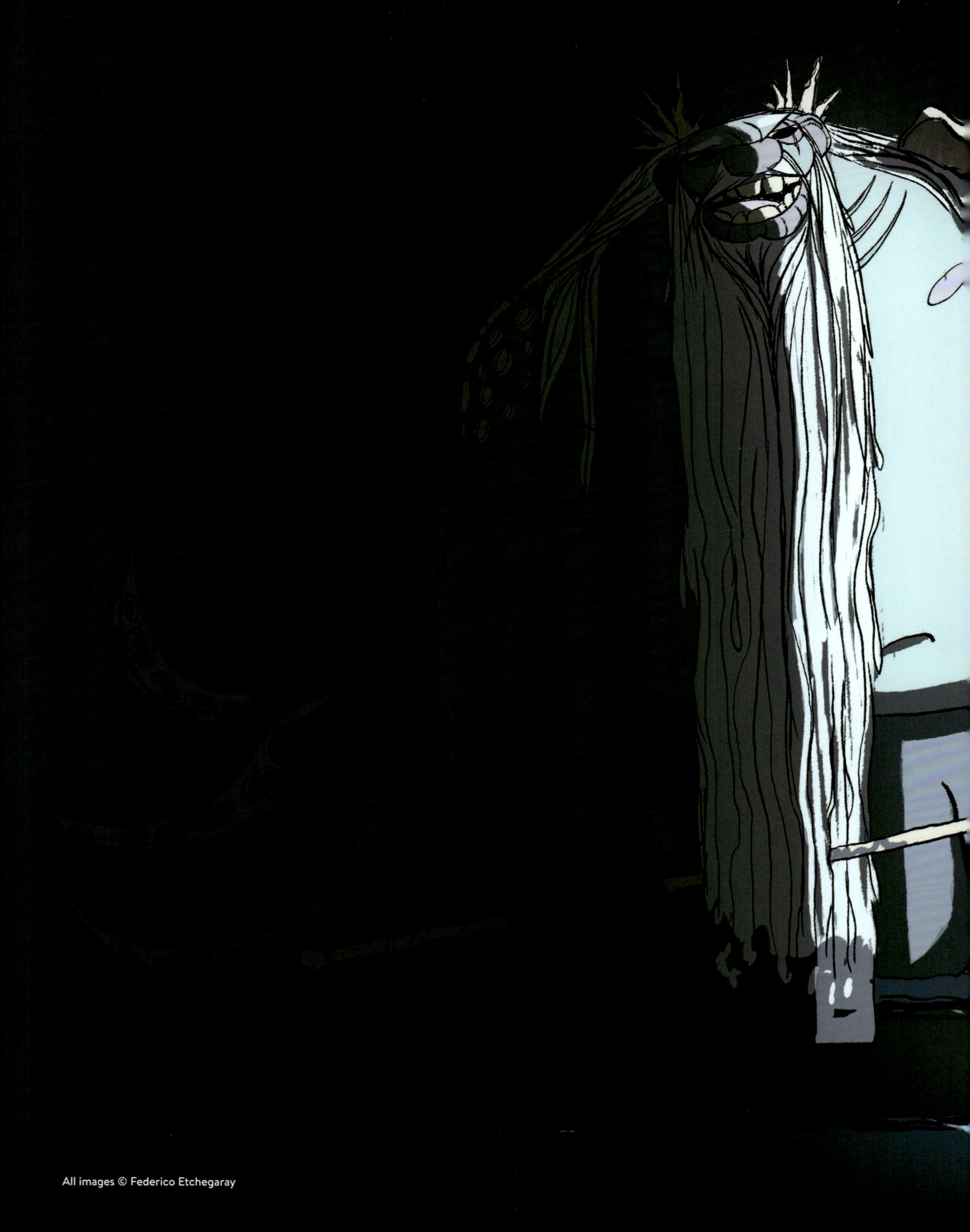

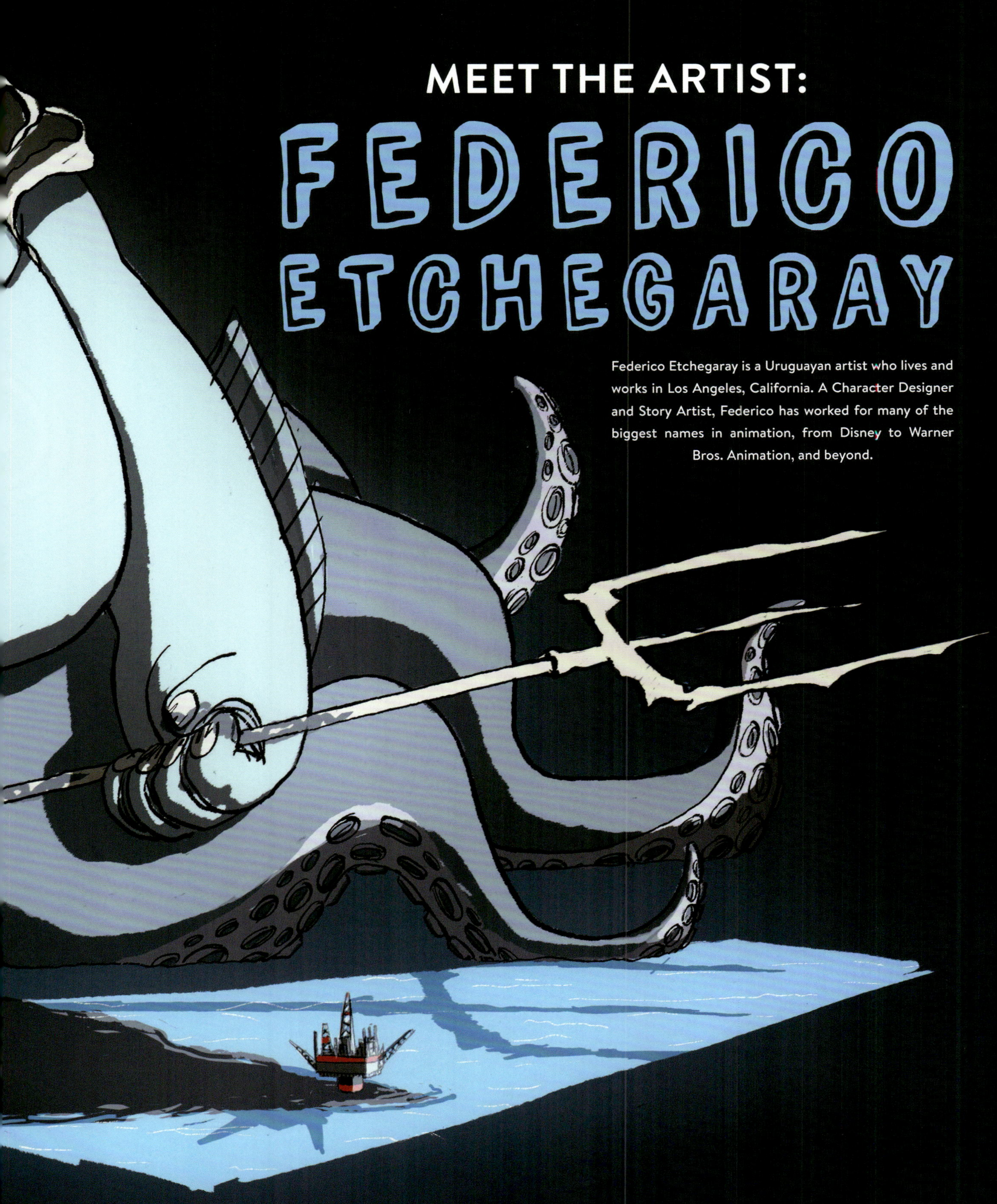

MEET THE ARTIST: FEDERICO ETCHEGARAY

Federico Etchegaray is a Uruguayan artist who lives and works in Los Angeles, California. A Character Designer and Story Artist, Federico has worked for many of the biggest names in animation, from Disney to Warner Bros. Animation, and beyond.

I first got into character design at a really young age. I started by drawing and copying my favorite characters' designs. You could say that was the beginning of my training – copying designs from the masters, and then creating my own! I was fascinated by the way character designs looked – the simplicity, the style, and how different and yet similar they were from their real-life counterparts. There is something about simplifying the real world, while still retaining the essence of the original that will never cease to amaze me. Finding that essence and pushing it forward is what character design is all about for me.

That fascination faded through my teen years, until two great films brought it all back. I was eighteen, watching TV, when I saw a copy of _The Incredibles_ on top of the DVD player. For some reason I put it on and it was one of the most entertaining movies I'd ever seen! It brought all the passion for character design flooding back! It wasn't until I saw another Pixar film, _Ratatouille_, that my mind was made up – this was what I wanted to do. _Ratatouille_ blew me away – the design, story, animation, music, and most of all, the theme. The film's message, that "anybody can cook" really spoke to me, coming from a small country where it was impossible to even study animation!

From then on, I worked hard night and day to make my dream come true. Two years later, I was accepted for a scholarship at SCAD and off I went to the US! Once I'd finished my four years of study, I flew right to LA where I was able to work for some great studios, such as Disney TV, DreamEast, and Warner Bros.

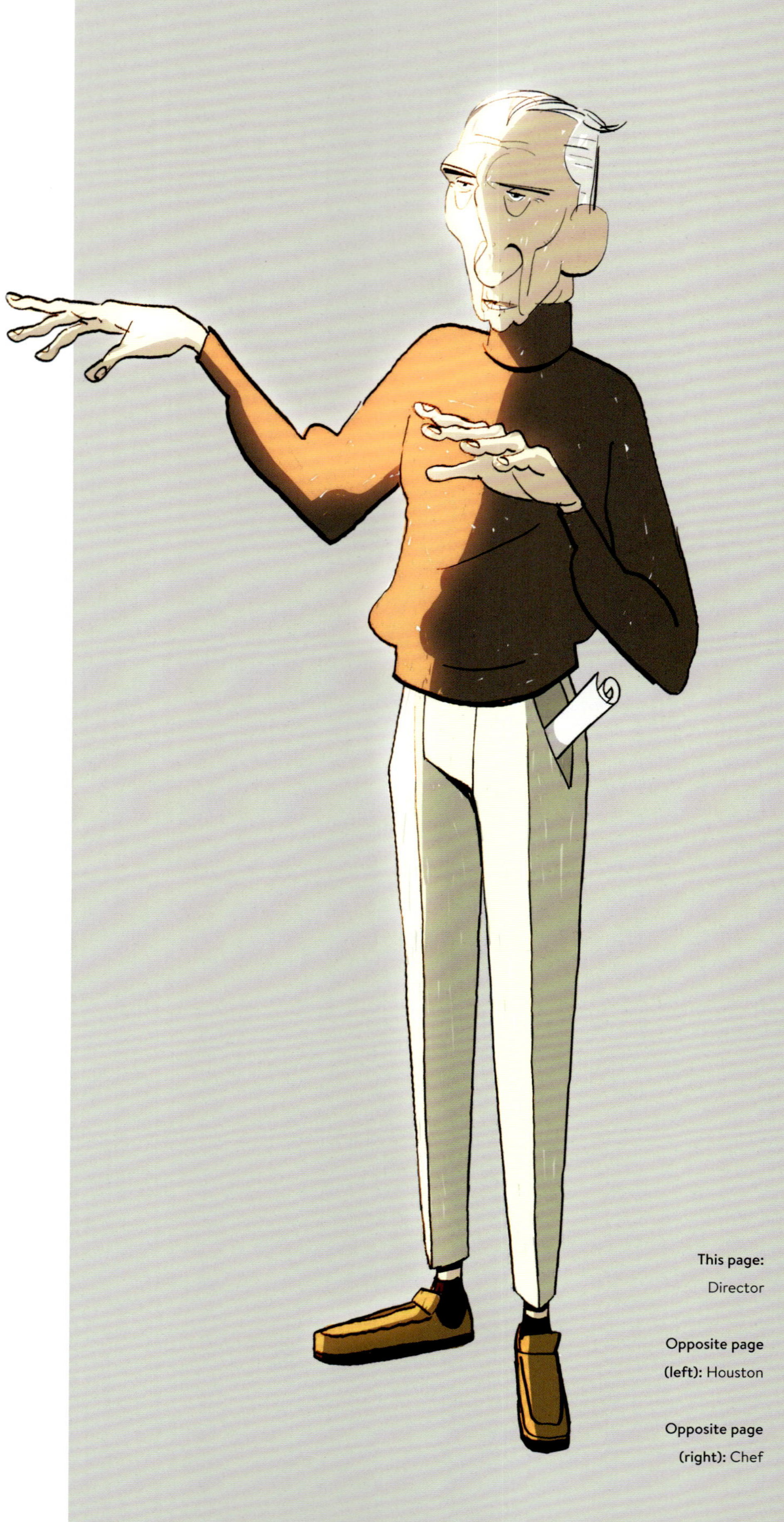

This page:

Director

Opposite page
(left): Houston

Opposite page
(right): Chef

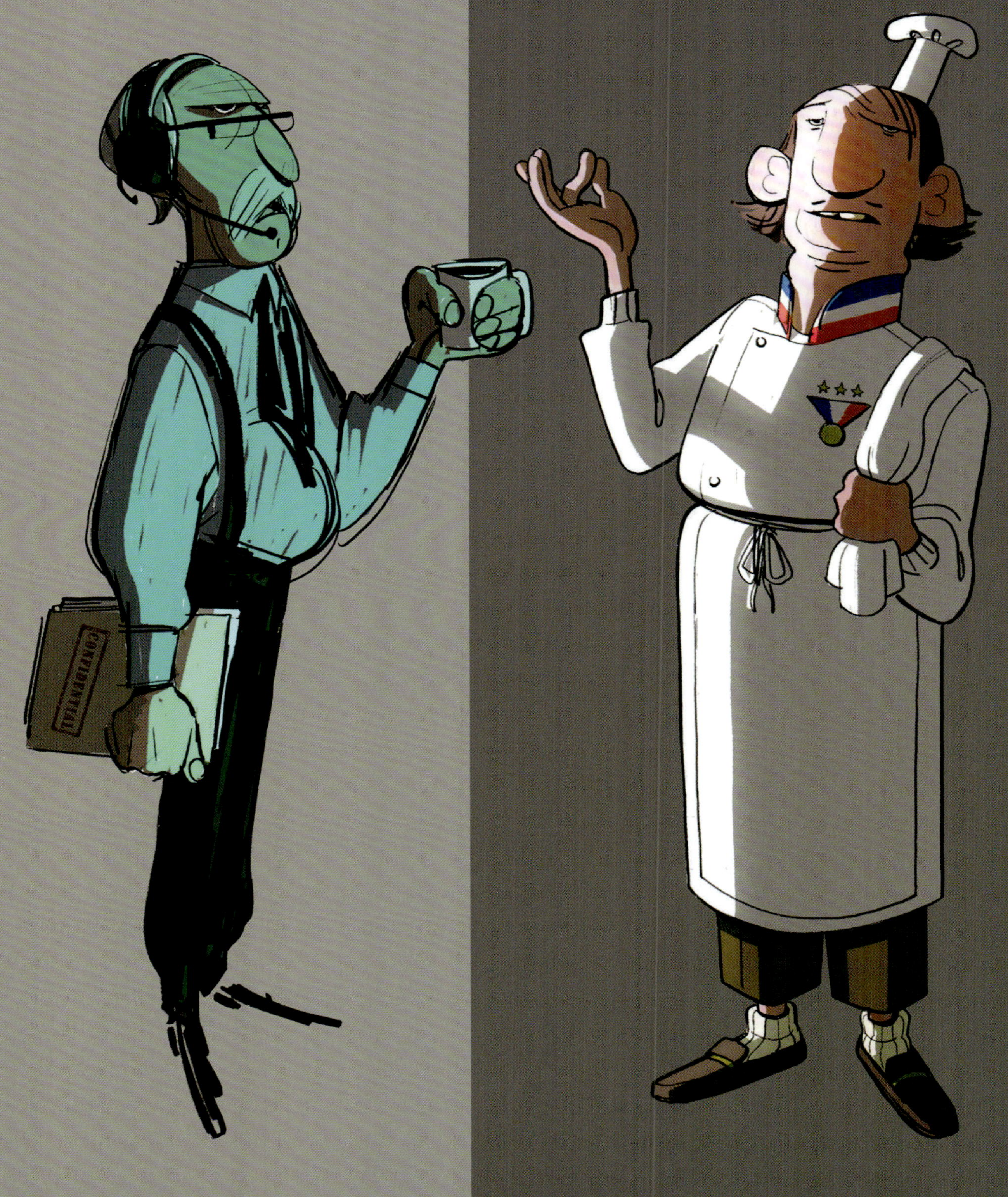
CONFIDENTIAL

"EACH AND EVERY STUDIO IS A DIFFERENT BEAST AND EVEN INSIDE THE SAME STUDIO PROJECTS CAN OPERATE COMPLETELY DIFFERENTLY FROM ONE ANOTHER"

This page:

Cowboy

Opposite page (left):

The Lumberjack

Opposite page (right):

El Conquistador

What do you feel you have learned from your experience working at these different studios? Do you believe that each place has impacted your working style in some way?

I've learned a whole lot! Working at a studio forces you to adapt really quickly to different design and storytelling styles. Tight TV deadlines pressure you to be quick and efficient – you need to stop the perfectionist inside from slowing you down. Studio culture also introduces the iterative production process. Instead of banging your head against the wall trying to nail a design or sequence in one go, you're encouraged to fail and fail fast! Then you work on top of those failures, until you find what the director is looking for. Your job is to adapt to the director's sensibilities and try and give them what they were envisioning. It's definitely a big jump from working to your own deadlines and vision at school.

Each and every studio is a different beast and even inside the same studio projects can operate completely differently from one another.

For example, a 2D show has completely different requirements than a CG show. As a TV Designer, or Story Artist, you need to be able to jump between them, and have a clear idea of the strengths and limitations of each. Another big challenge of studio work is keeping your creative juices flowing. Productions can be really demanding creatively, asking you to be "on" all the time, no matter if it's a good or bad day for you. I found that in order to avoid creative burnout, artists have to be constantly feeding themselves new content that inspires them. This can be anything – live action movies, TV shows, comics, manga, video games, but the input has to be greater than the output!

Last, but not least – know when to stop. I constantly struggle with this! The industry encourages you to work really long hours and even practice in your off hours. It's easy to fall into this trap, because animation is our passion and we love doing it, but it's really important to have a life outside of work. See friends, family, whatever it takes to have much needed downtime from work.

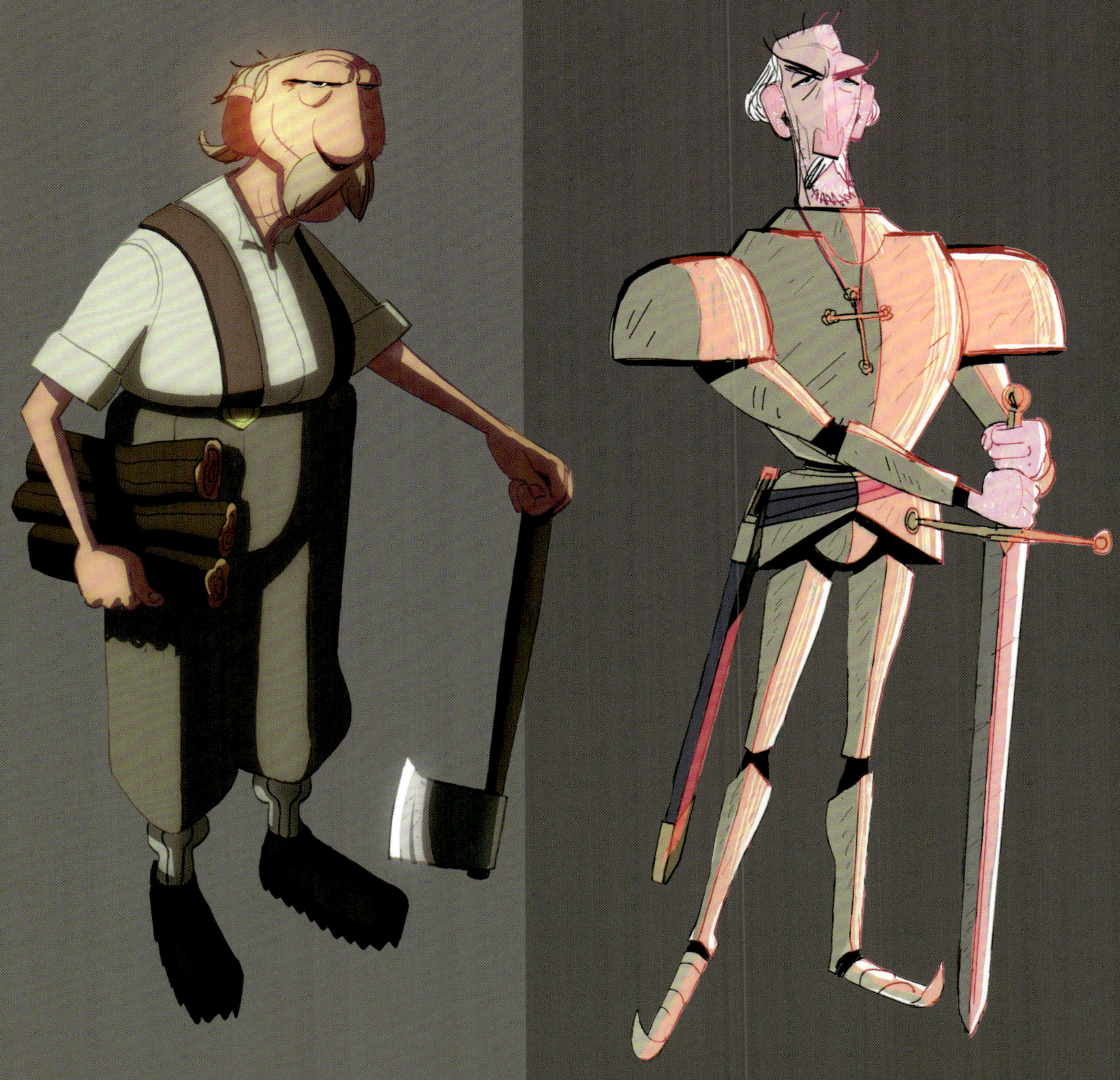

This page:
Mermaid

Opposite page:
Calaca

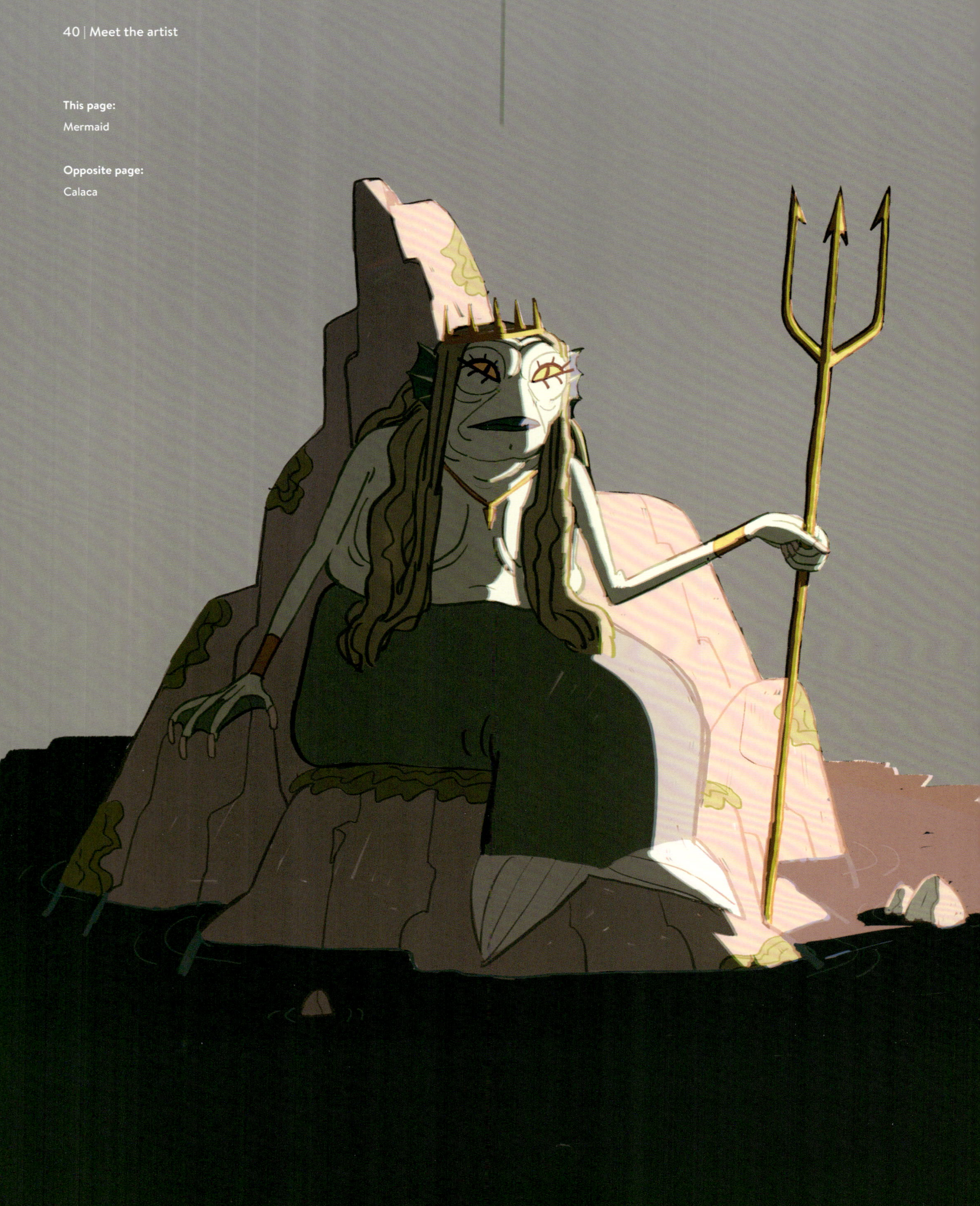

"IT WAS REALLY IMPORTANT FOR THE DESIGNS TO FEEL REAL AND FITTING FOR THE TIME"

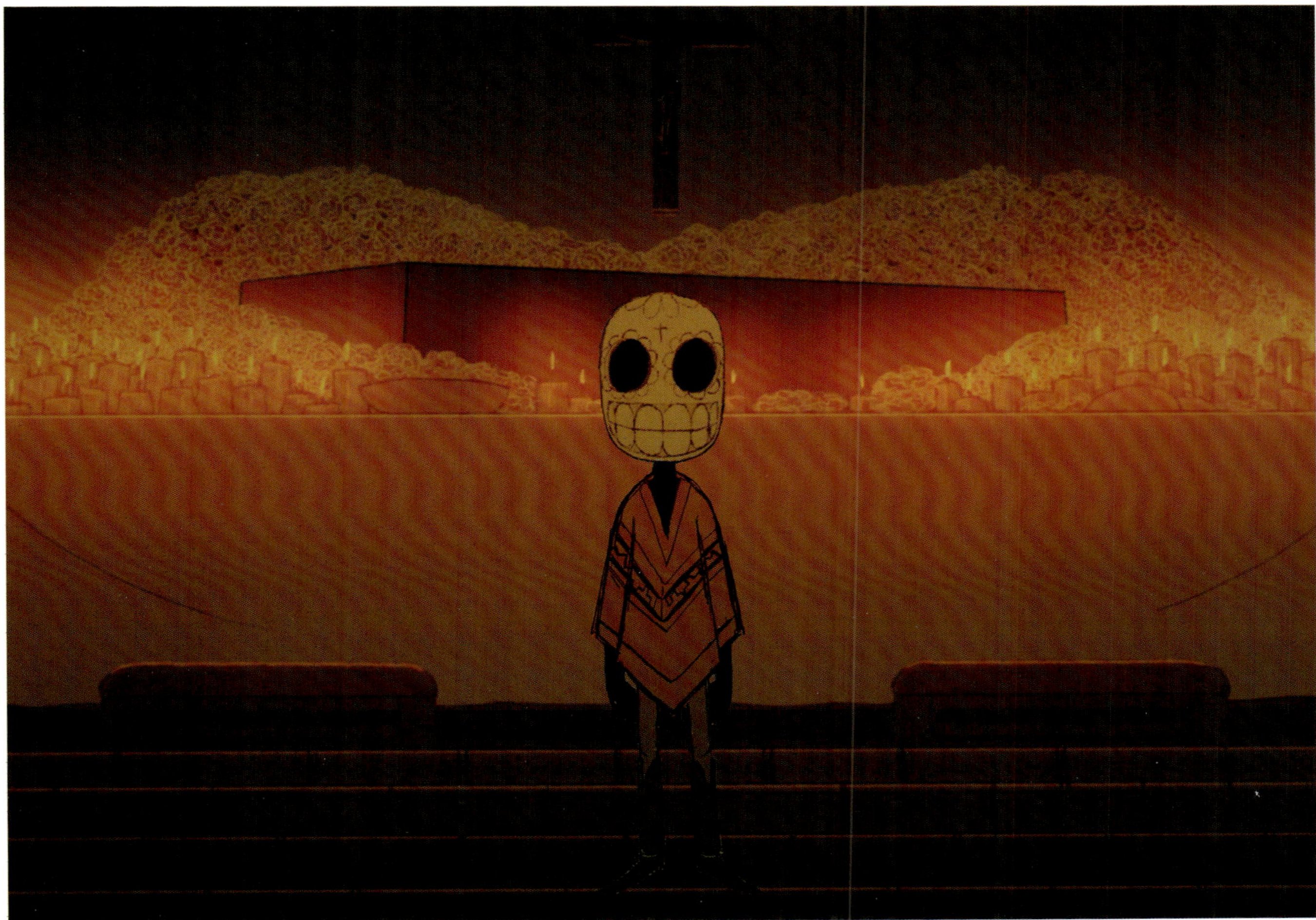

What was the inspiration behind your mesmerizing story *Calaca*, and how did you devise the characters to work as a whole cast?

Calaca was a personal story inspired by the sudden loss of my grandmother that I developed while I was a student at SCAD. She was, and still is, one of the most important people in my life, so having lost her while I was far away affected me deeply. *Calaca* explores the idea of confronting a personified Death for a chance to get see your loved ones again, even if it means giving years of your own life in return. That was a really tough year for me, so exploring what I was feeling through writing and storytelling allowed me to cope with my sadness and the whole grieving process.

I've always been inspired by Latin folklore, so it was important for me to set the story in colonial times, when most Latin folkloric stories were born. I invented a small, colonial town in New Mexico where my story would take place. The main characters are a maize farmer, his daughter, the town doctor, and Death, personified as a quirky masked child who fetches the souls of the dead. It was really important for the designs to feel real and fitting for the time. Death was especially tricky to design, because we are so used to seeing the "grim reaper" version of him. I wanted a more magical realist take, more ambiguous and less evil looking.

Yes, it is deliberate! I love the look of pencil or ink on paper and the looseness of sketchy work. For me, it's important to see work that has clearly been drawn by hand with all its flaws, instead of the sterile perfection of the computer. I started my studies by drawing exclusively on paper and later had to transition to using a Wacom tablet and pen. It was tough, because even though the technology has got better and more precise, you still don't get the same quality of line control that you will when putting pencil to paper. So, I try to imitate that look and draw as loosely as I can to try and find new shapes and proportions for the characters I design. It's easy to fall into the trap of stiff drawing and lose that sketchy exploration phase. I try to push the exploration as far as I can before I commit to a design and do turnarounds, expressions, and poses. Knowing when to stop isn't an exact science – I just keep drawing until it feels finished. Of course, there are minimum requirements, finishing all the features of a character with the right proportions, expression, and pose, but I try to avoid overworking a design. Excessive cleanup or overdrawing can both end up killing a good design.

When you see the work of a master, like Nico Marlet, you can see his whole process in one single drawing. You can usually see his orange colored under-sketch, his final line work in graphite, markers on top for shading, and sometimes paint to fill in opaque colors. You see his exploration, where he committed a shape and a line, and his final render; it's all there for the audience to see. Every single one of his drawings is a sight to behold!

Carter Goodrich is another master whose designs are loose and sketchy, and full of life. You can see that he really studies his characters – their personality, their idiosyncrasies, their clothing, and the environment they live in. He takes the stereotype a character is supposed to be, and then he flips it on its head and gives you something unique. He clearly explores line and shapes a lot with his graphite pencil, and that's why his designs feel so alive.

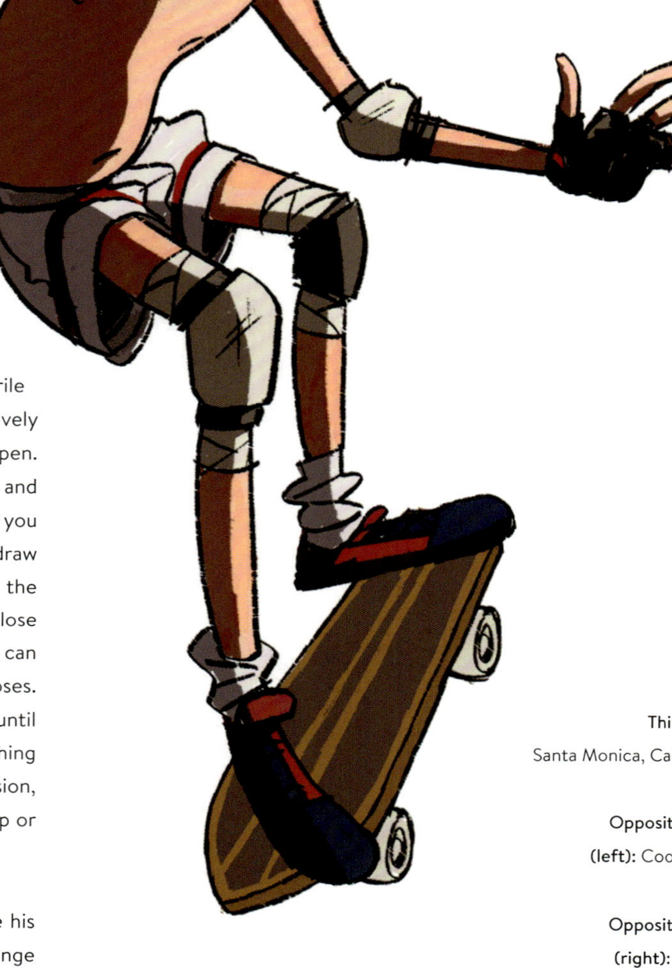

This page:
Santa Monica, California

Opposite page
(left): Cool Dude

Opposite page
(right): Skater

Thank you! I do love dramatic lighting. I think my preference for that type of lighting came from studying the masters in art history. The famous chiaroscuro paintings by Caravaggio and Rembrandt always strike me as dramatic and interesting to look at. Using this type of lighting on flat drawings also has the benefit of adding a 3D effect, without the need to render them.

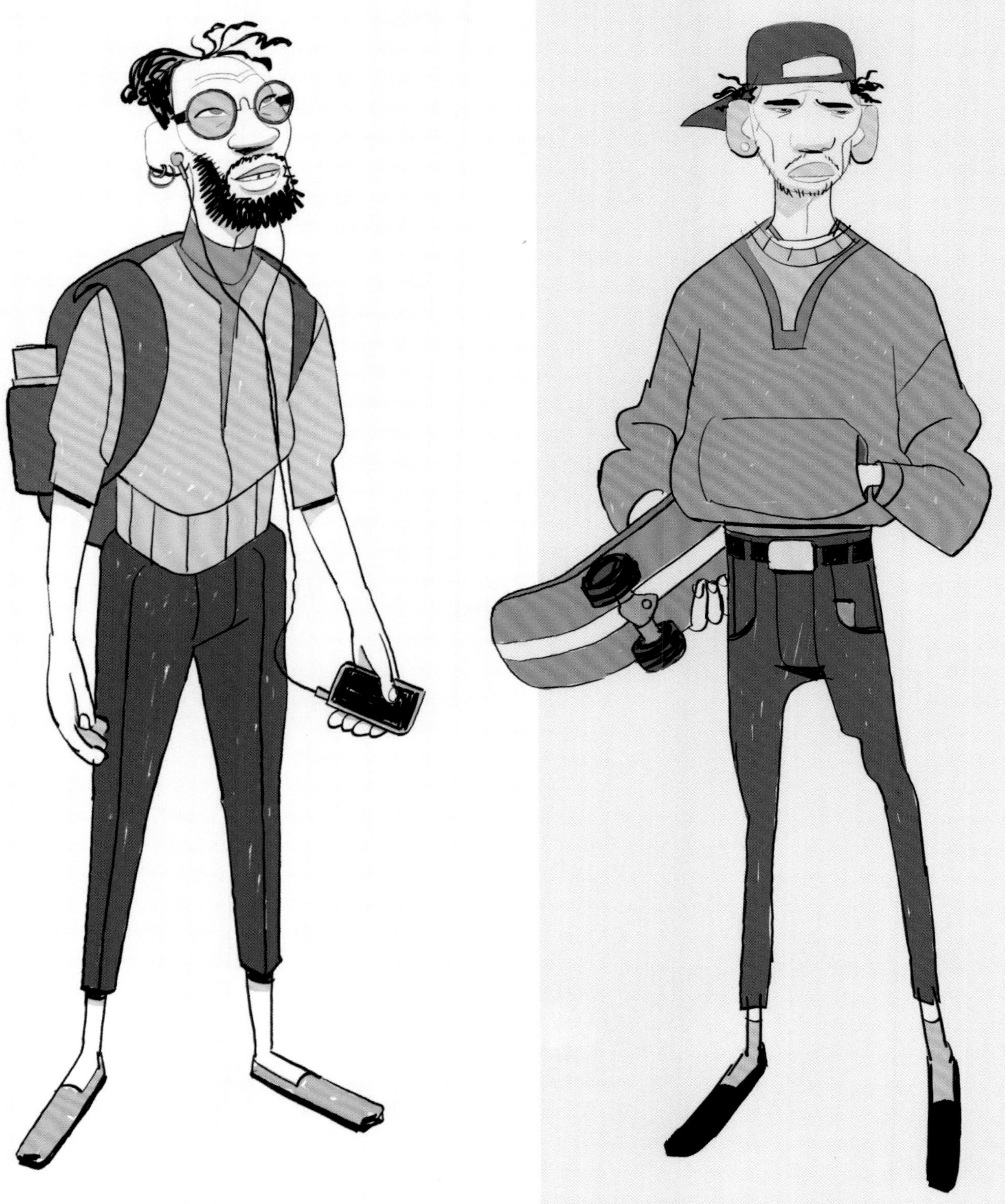

expressing emotions:
TRUST AND FEAR

FELIPE RODRIGUEZ

To explore the emotions of characters, you must first understand the shapes the design is composed of and modify and break them according to the intensity of the feeling. In animation, each character plays a specific role, so each must have their own way of expressing themselves – your main character's fears may be different than your villain's. The tone of each emotion is also important – feeling trusted and arrogant can be different from feeling trusted and relaxed.

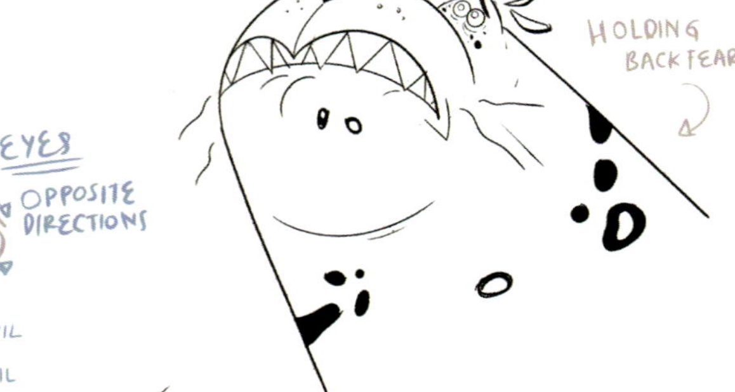

FEAR

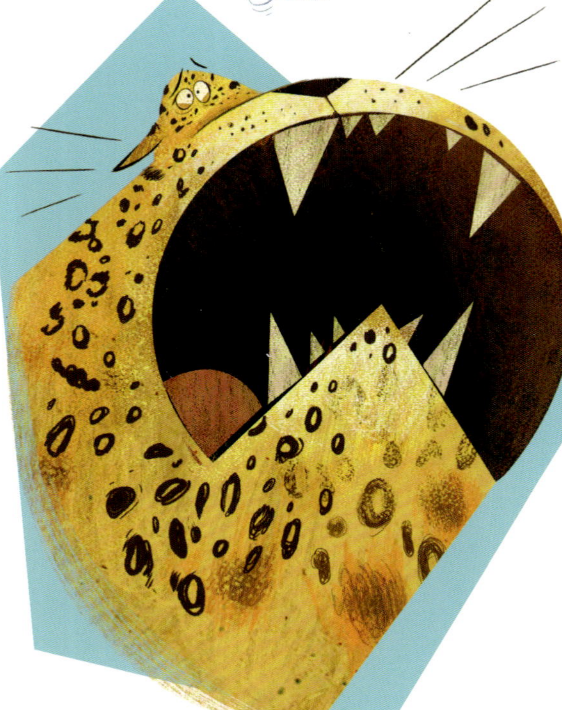

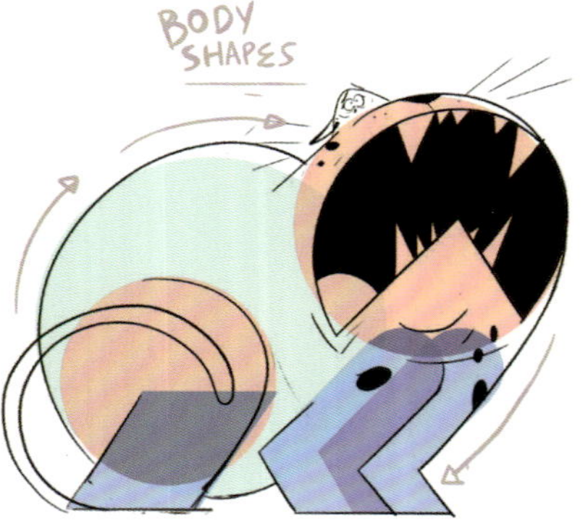

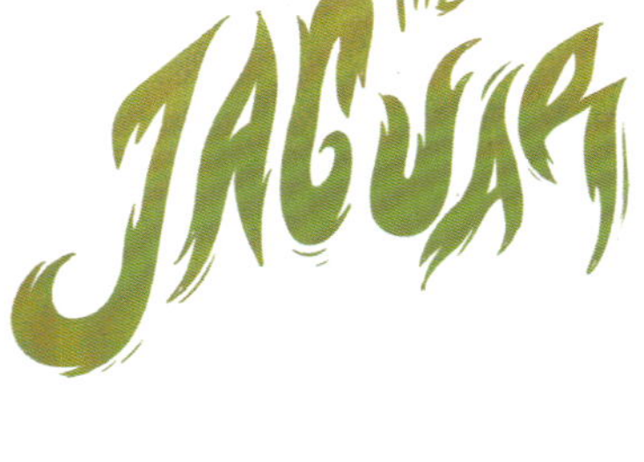

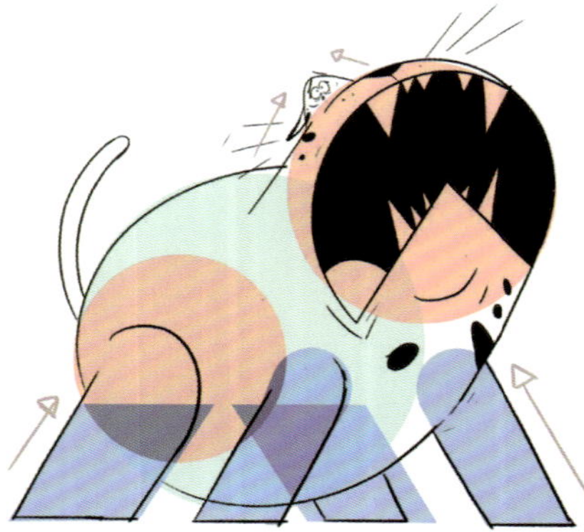

RECOGNIZE THE MAIN SHAPES

Start by analyzing the shapes that make up your design in its simplest form and combine them according to expression. If you have triangles and circles as your main shapes, use them repeatedly in both facial and body expressions.

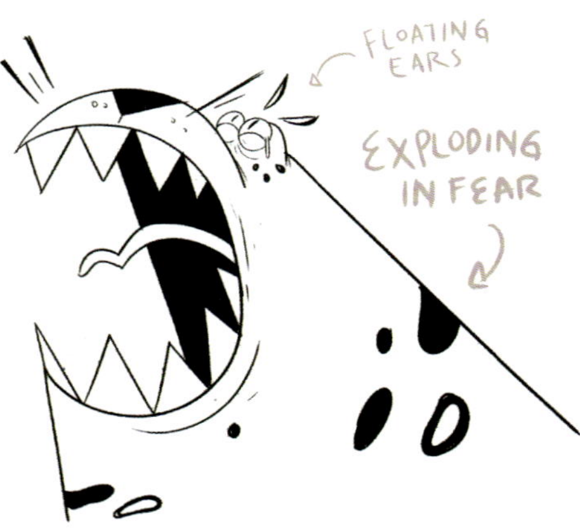

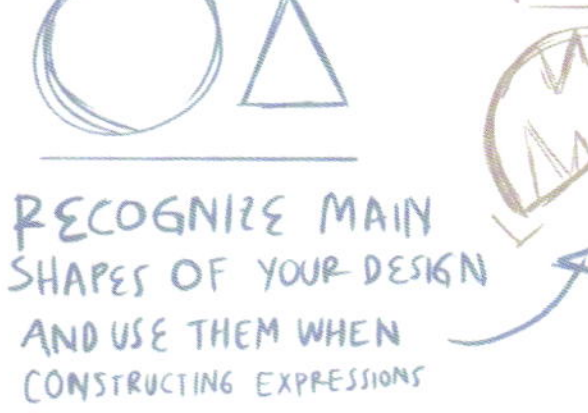

FEAR

THINK ABOUT THE SITUATION

To recognize the different tones of an emotion, imagine the situation and the moment of reaction. Your character's expression of fear may be different when they are anxious something bad might happen, from when that bad thing is actually happening!

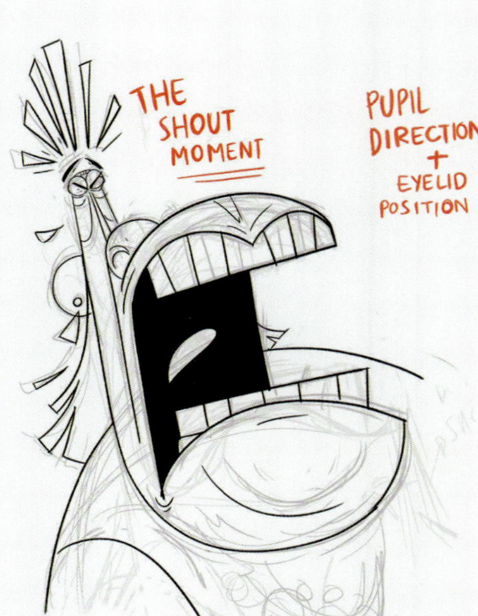

LEARN FROM FILM

One of the main resources for understanding how characters act is cinema. Look for actors and actresses that relate to the personality of your character and extract from them ways to express emotions. Film language can also help you understand how to place your character in front of the camera.

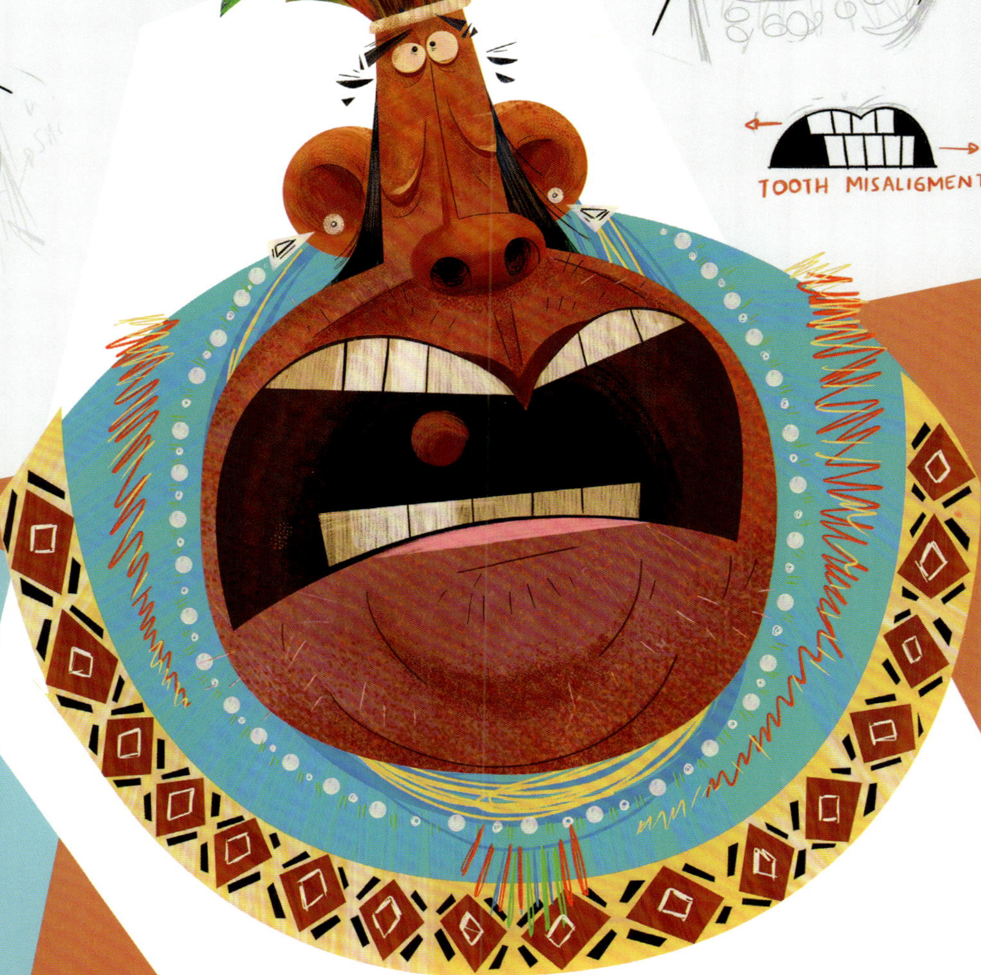

THE photographER

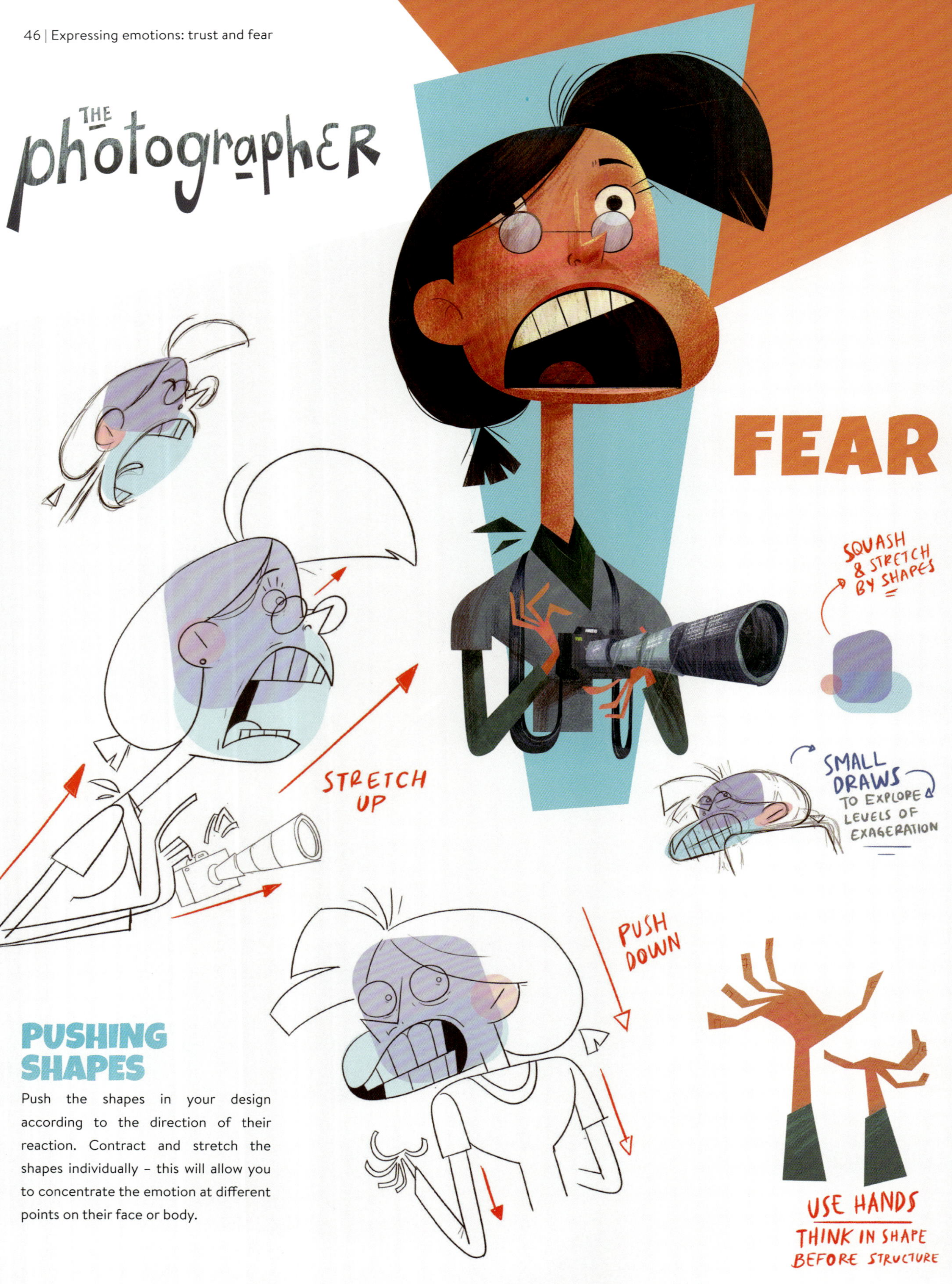

PUSHING SHAPES

Push the shapes in your design according to the direction of their reaction. Contract and stretch the shapes individually – this will allow you to concentrate the emotion at different points on their face or body.

THINK THE EMOTION IN MOVEMENT

HOW IS THE CHARACTER BEHAVIOR?

EMOTION THROUGH MOVEMENT

Understand how emotion would affect your character's behaviour and movements. Even the way they walk can tell the audience a lot about how a character feels.

THINK SIMPLE

Start with simple shapes that express the emotion you want your character to feel. Once you have this essence of the emotion in place, then add layers of complexity. It can be useful to make miniature drawings very quickly to find the emotion that's right.

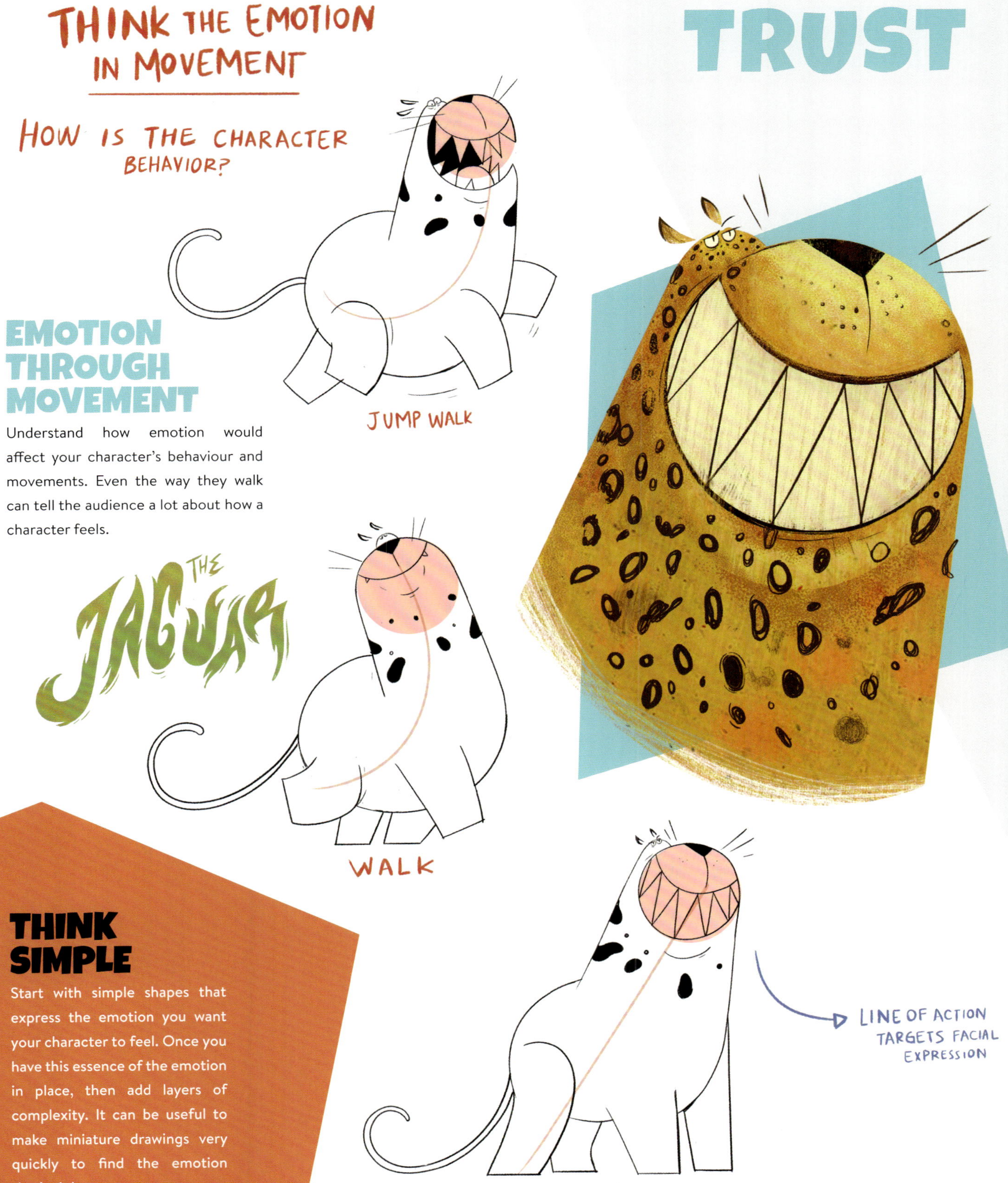

TRUST

COMBINING EMOTIONS

Blend several emotions together to find new ways for characters to express themselves. Tilting the head and shoulders can add different tones to emotions.

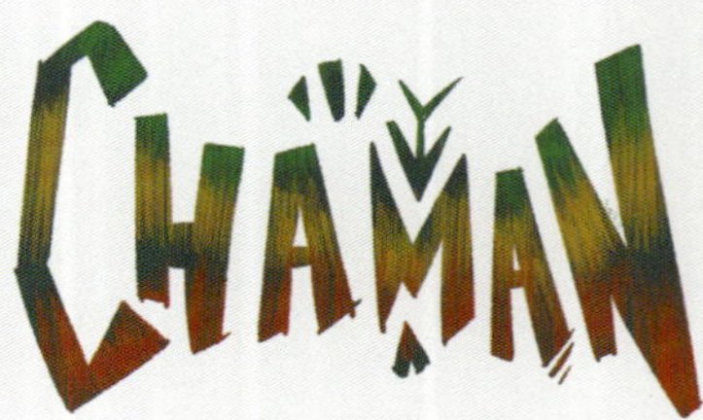

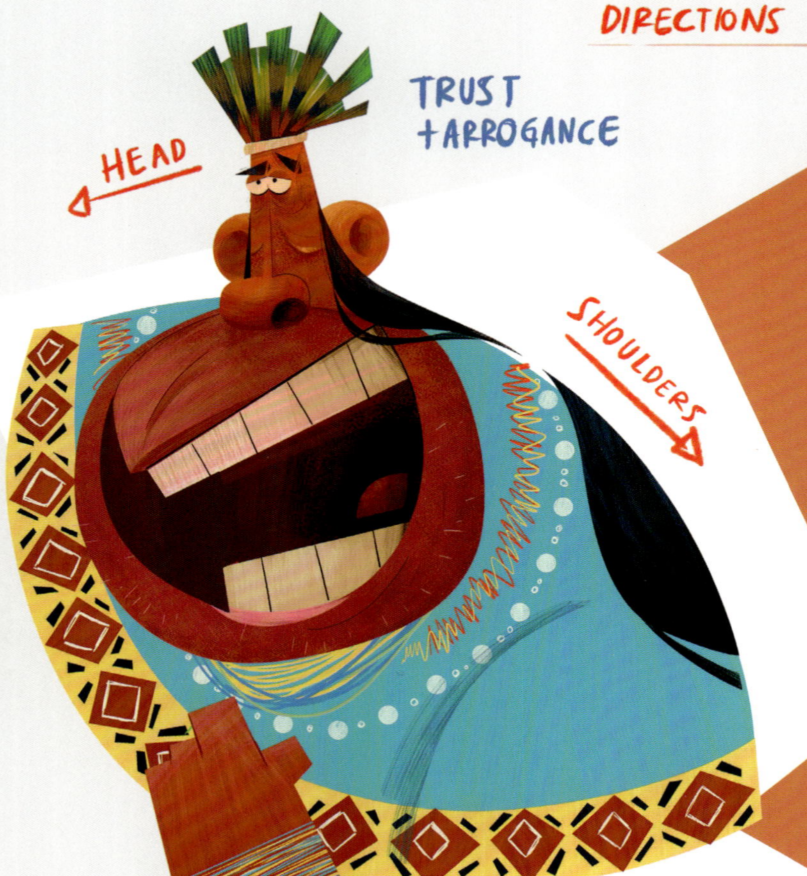

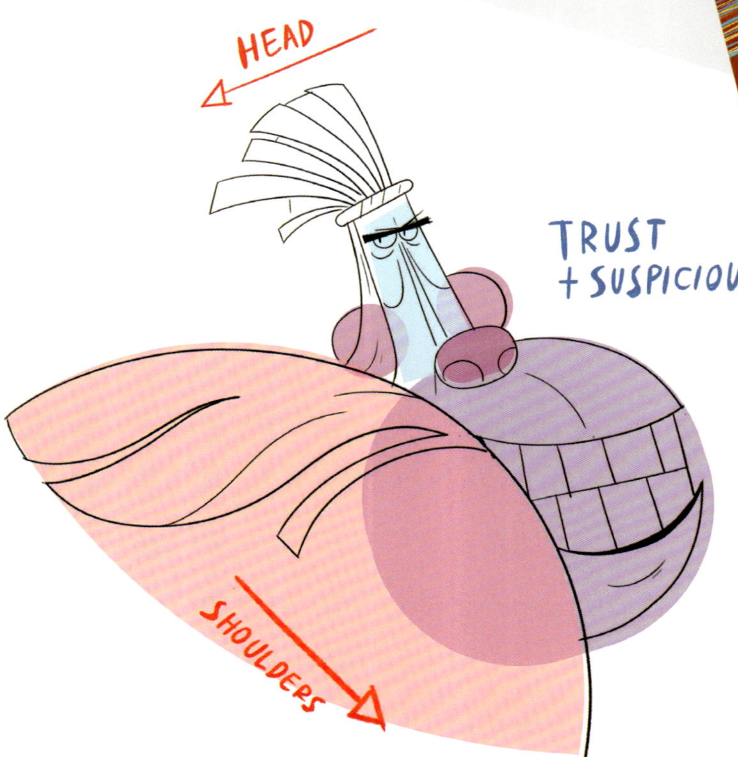

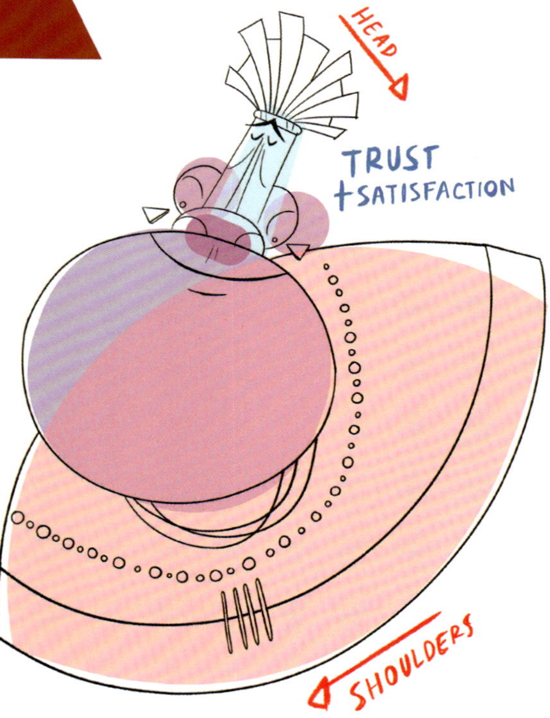

THE phoTogrAphER

TRUST

SHAPES, SHAPES AND MORE SHAPES

When your character needs to react with a more extreme emotion you can reiterate shapes in the design to exaggerate their expressions. Don't forget, your character is part of a story and the shapes that are part of their design represent their unique role and help them stand out.

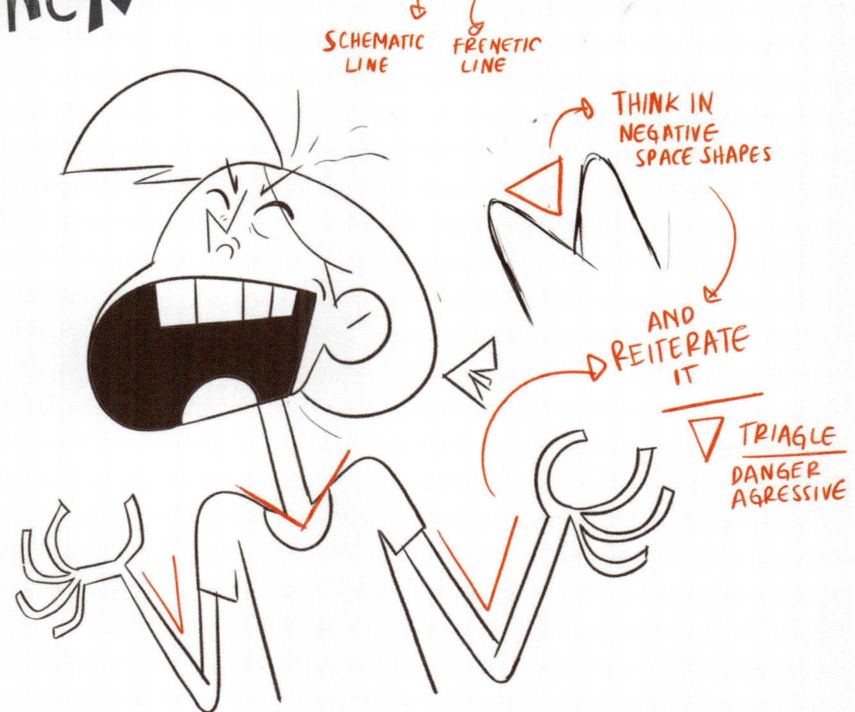

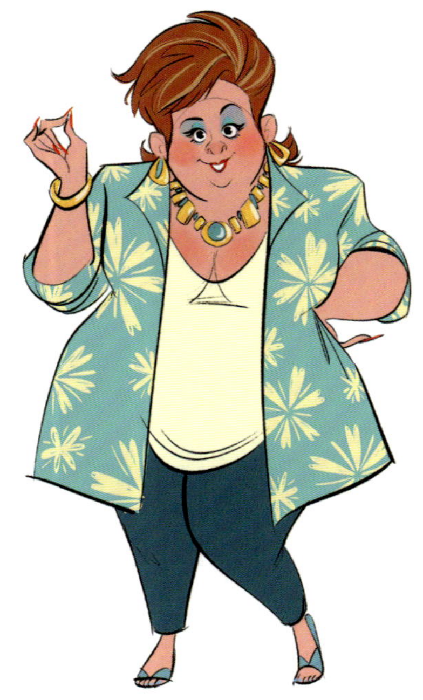

MEET THE ARTIST:
CHRIS ABLES

Chris Ables is a professional illustrator and visual development artist. With over ten years' experience in the industry, creating characters for Walt Disney, Netflix, Nickelodeon, and many more. We caught up with Chris to find how he started out, and how his career has developed.

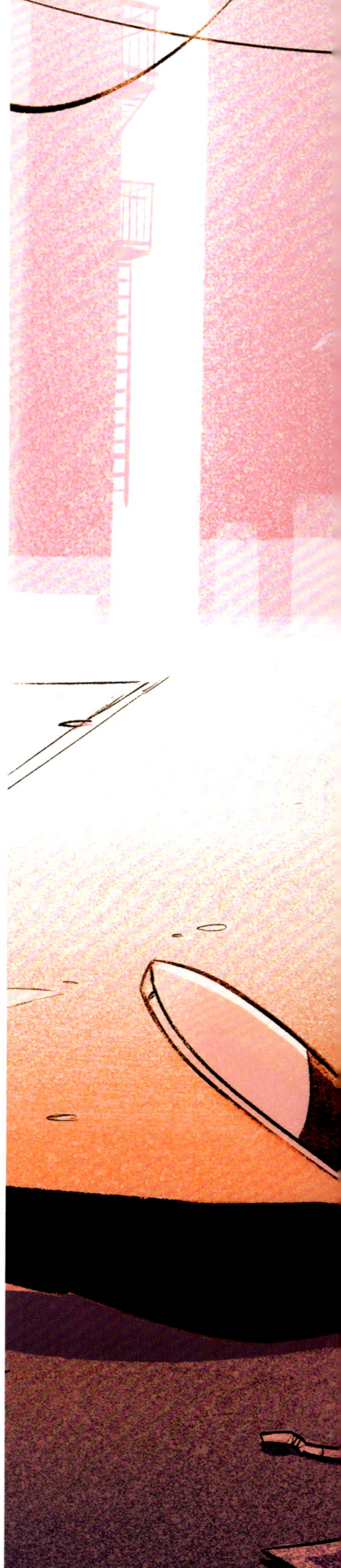

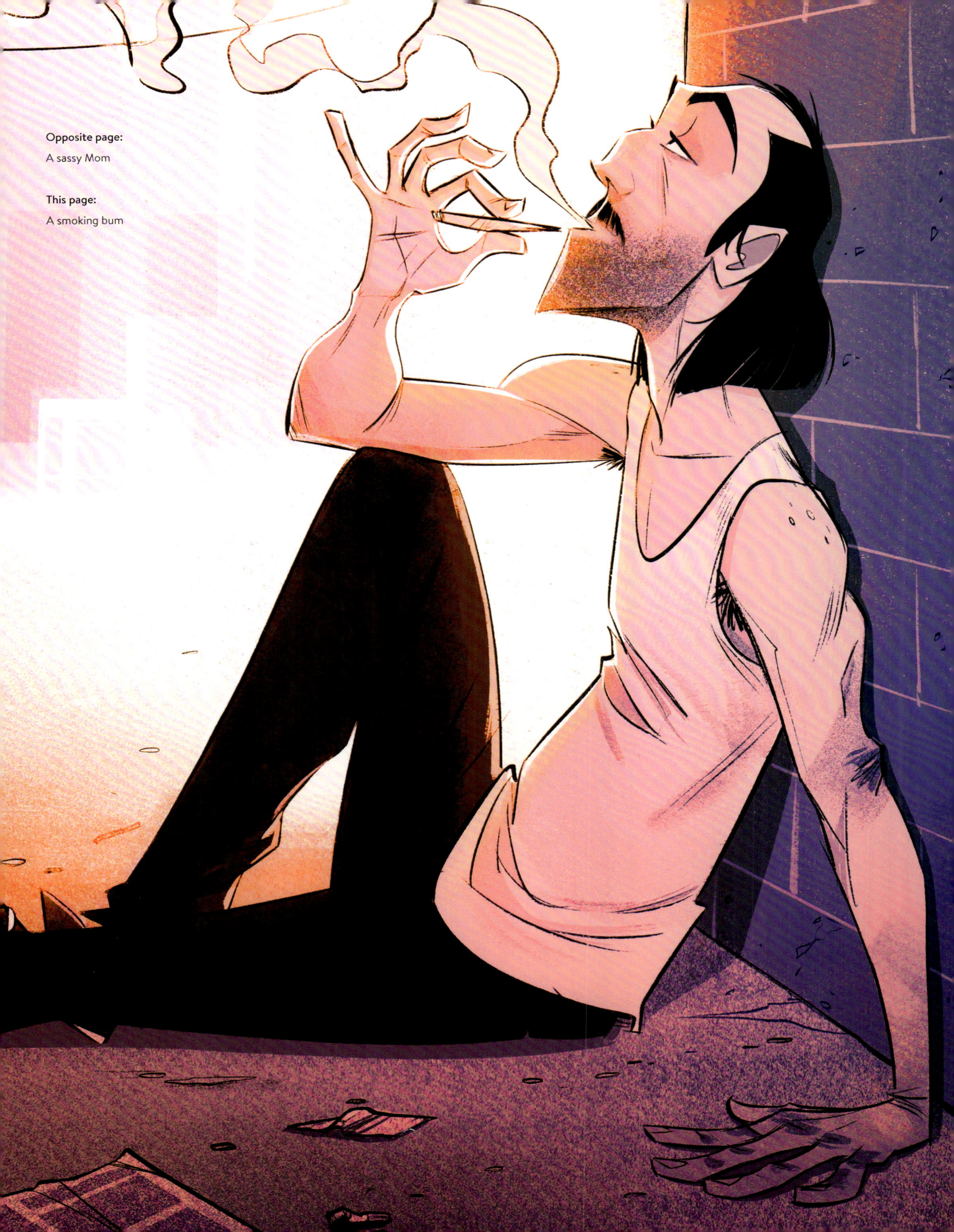

Opposite page:
A sassy Mom

This page:
A smoking bum

Hi Chris, it's fantastic to talk to you. Could you introduce yourself to our readers?

Of course, thank you for inviting me to speak with you! I'm a character designer, illustrator, and visual development artist. I've been working for over 10 years within the entertainment arts industries.

How did you initially break into the industry?

I've been asked this question several times before, and to be honest, I don't quite know the answer! I think young artists, or those just starting out, often ask this question in the hope of using my answer as a template for themselves. I worked hard, I was constantly drawing, and taking chances by applying to jobs I felt I was qualified for, putting my work out there for people to see. Of course, many times my work was rejected, but gradually I started getting studio and agency jobs, and my work started getting noticed. As I began to receive more job offers and opportunities, these in turn led to more work further down the line.

"I WORKED HARD, I WAS CONSTANTLY DRAWING, AND TAKING CHANCES BY APPLYING TO JOBS I FELT I WAS QUALIFIED FOR"

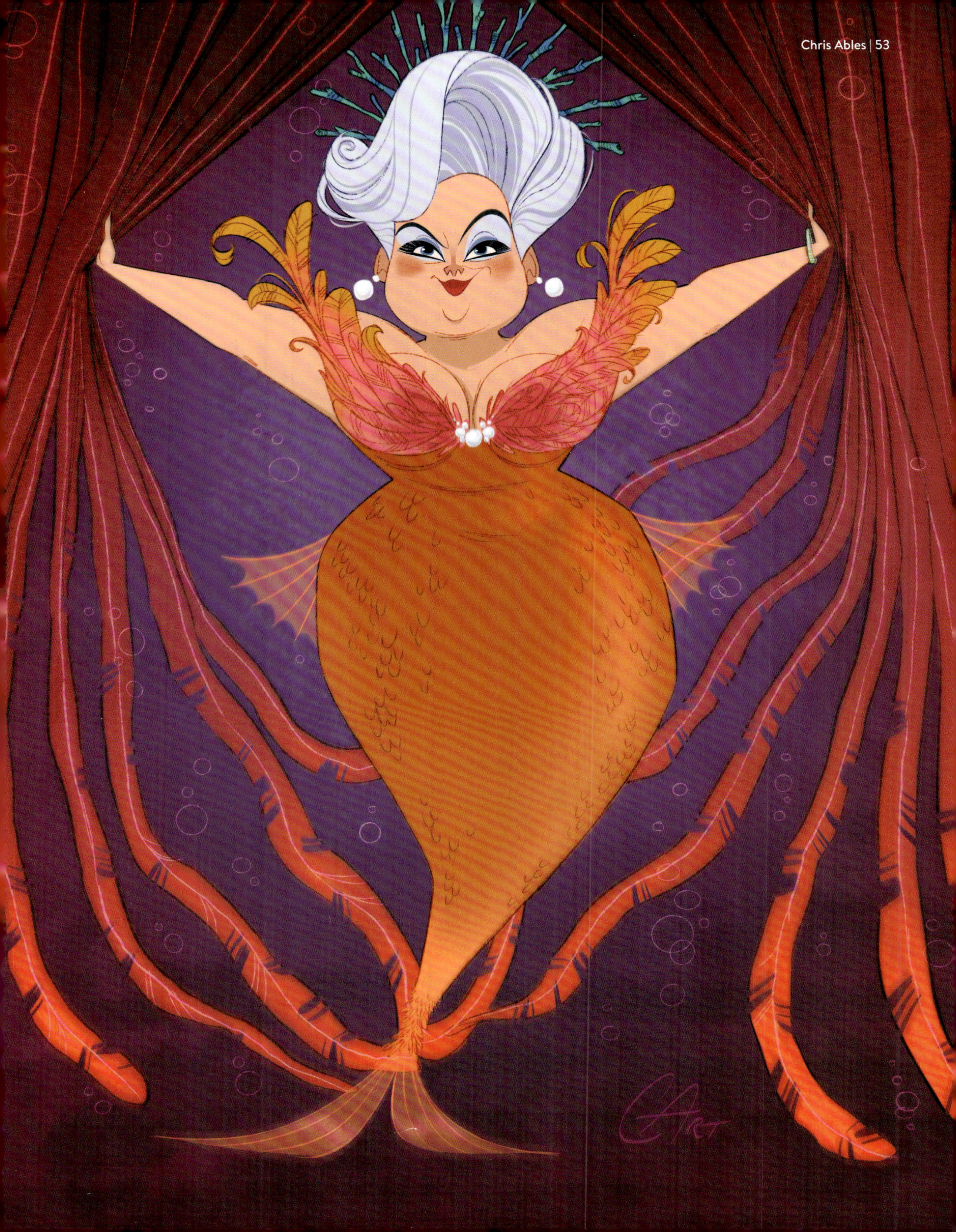

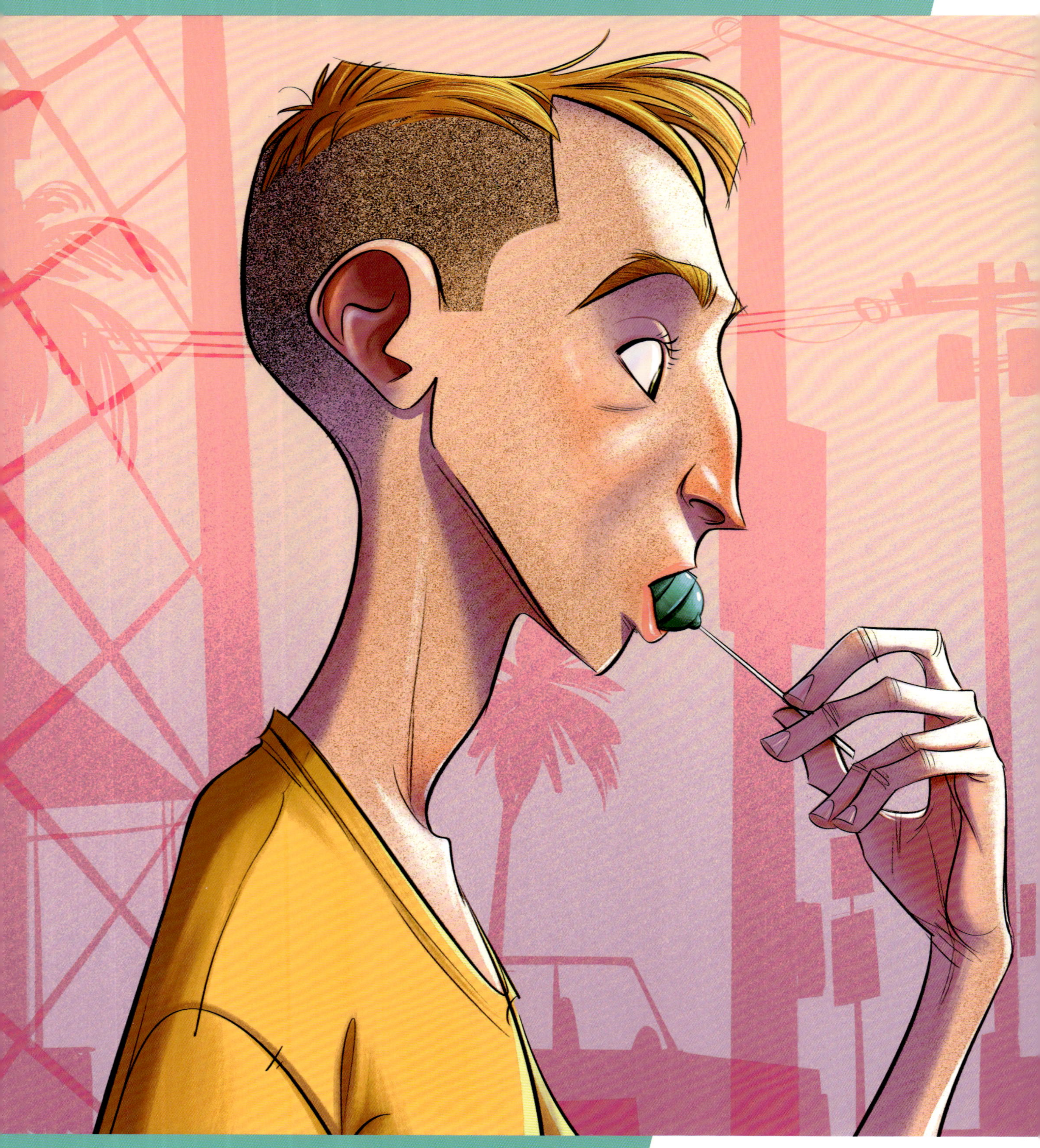

Did you always know you wanted to become a character designer, and if so, what attracted you to the profession?

I didn't always know I specifically wanted be a character designer, but I knew I wanted to be a professional artist. I've been drawing pretty much non-stop since I was two or three, according to my family. Much of my youth was spent drawing beloved characters from my favourite '80s and '90s cartoons, as well as Disney animated films, which I love above all else. From there, I began to immerse myself in the art of animation and moved forwards with plans to pursue a career as an animator. It wasn't until I entered college that I realized that, as much as I love animation, the actual process of animating didn't feel as rewarding as the illustrative and design process of creating characters did.

This epiphany triggered a bit of an identity crisis, as I had planned for years to become an animator! Thankfully, over time, and with a lot of practice, setbacks, and hardships, some wonderful opportunities came along, and I steered my career to where it is today.

When you began your career, what steps did you take toward being able to create industry-level art? Did you go into formal education, or are you self-taught?

I've taken numerous art classes over the years, even when I was back in grade school. I pursued a formal education by attending art school, which I strongly recommend, because frankly, there's a certain level of experience and knowledge that can only be obtained through formal training. A solid figure or life-drawing course can teach you rules that will apply to all your work in the future. That said, a lot of my knowledge, which still has plenty of room for refinement and growth, came from me just doing the work on my own time. I draw almost daily! I use figure drawing books, concept art books, and the work of artists I admire, as both resources and inspiration for my work.

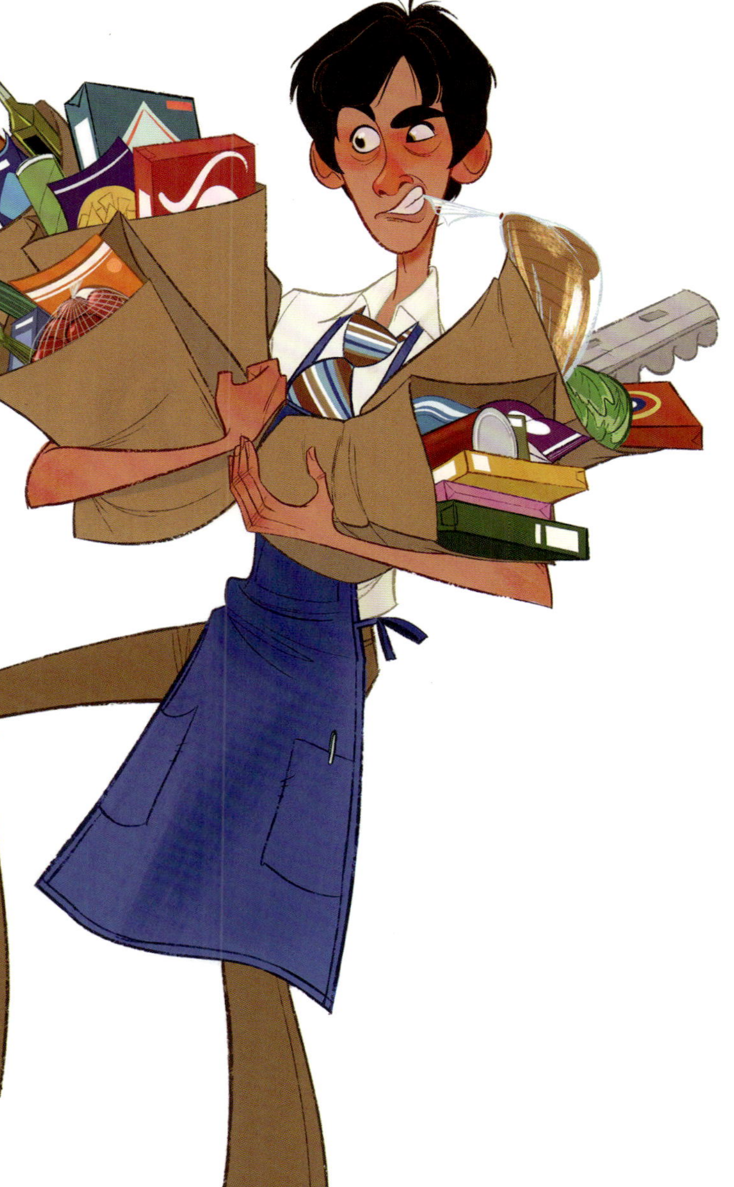

Opposite page:

A street kid

This page:

Grocery store bagger

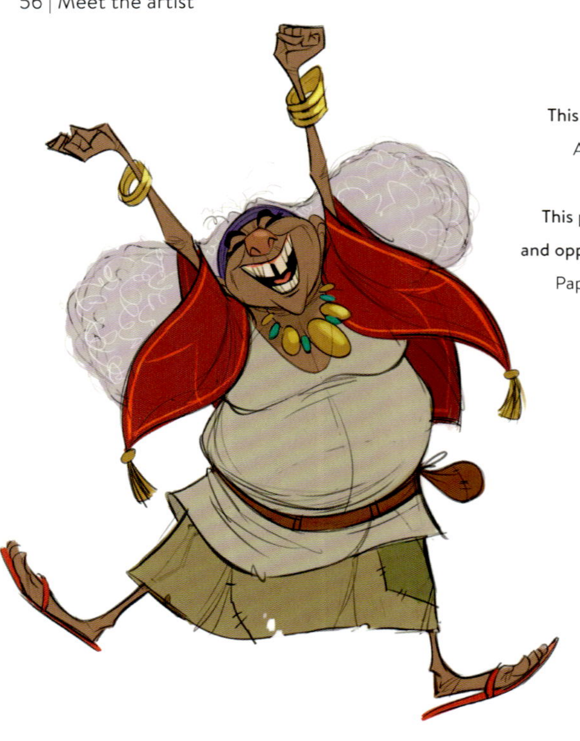

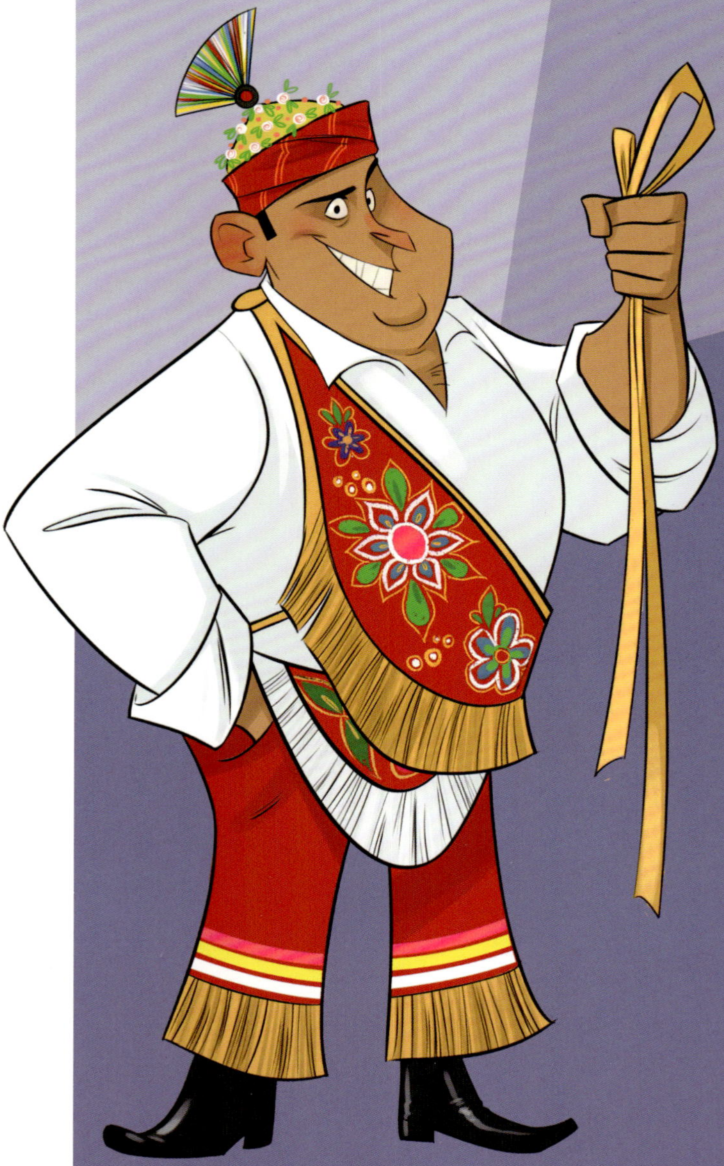

You feature a long list of high-profile clients on your website – do you remember which job it was that made you think, "I've made it?"

I will admit that some of the clients and jobs I've landed have definitely been exciting stepping stone moments for me, but I still think I haven't "made it" just yet!

What do you think has got you noticed in the world of character design?

Over the last two or three years, social media has led to an increase in attention, and hopefully a genuine appreciation for my work. The art ultimately has to speak for itself, but through platforms such as Instagram, or sites such as ArtStation, I've been able to reach more and more people.

When and how did you come up with the idea to set up your own illustration workshops? How have they been received?

Setting up an illustration workshop was something I had been thinking about doing for a while and I was approached by La Galeria Roja, an art gallery in Seville, Spain, to do just that! They have conducted workshops with illustrators and various artists, many whom I look up to or admire. My workshop, which was a three-day online course, was a success. In fact, the gallery have told me the students were so pleased with it that they would like me to do a second workshop!

"OVER THE LAST TWO OR THREE YEARS,SOCIAL MEDIA HAS LED TO AN INCREASE IN ATTENTION, AND HOPEFULLY A GENUINE APPRECIATION FOR MY WORK"

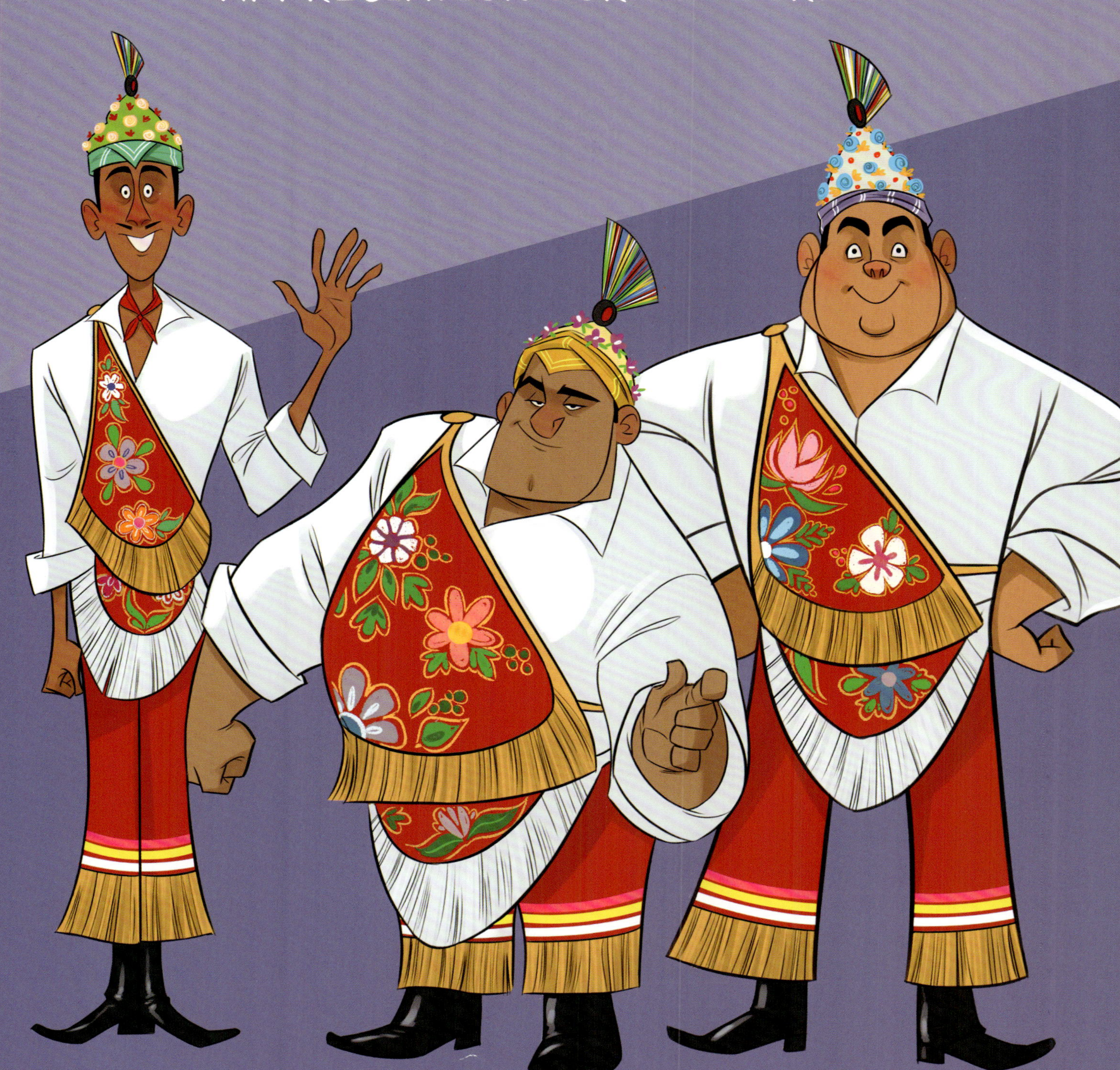

This page:
The Norse
God, Odin

Opposite page:
The military
captain

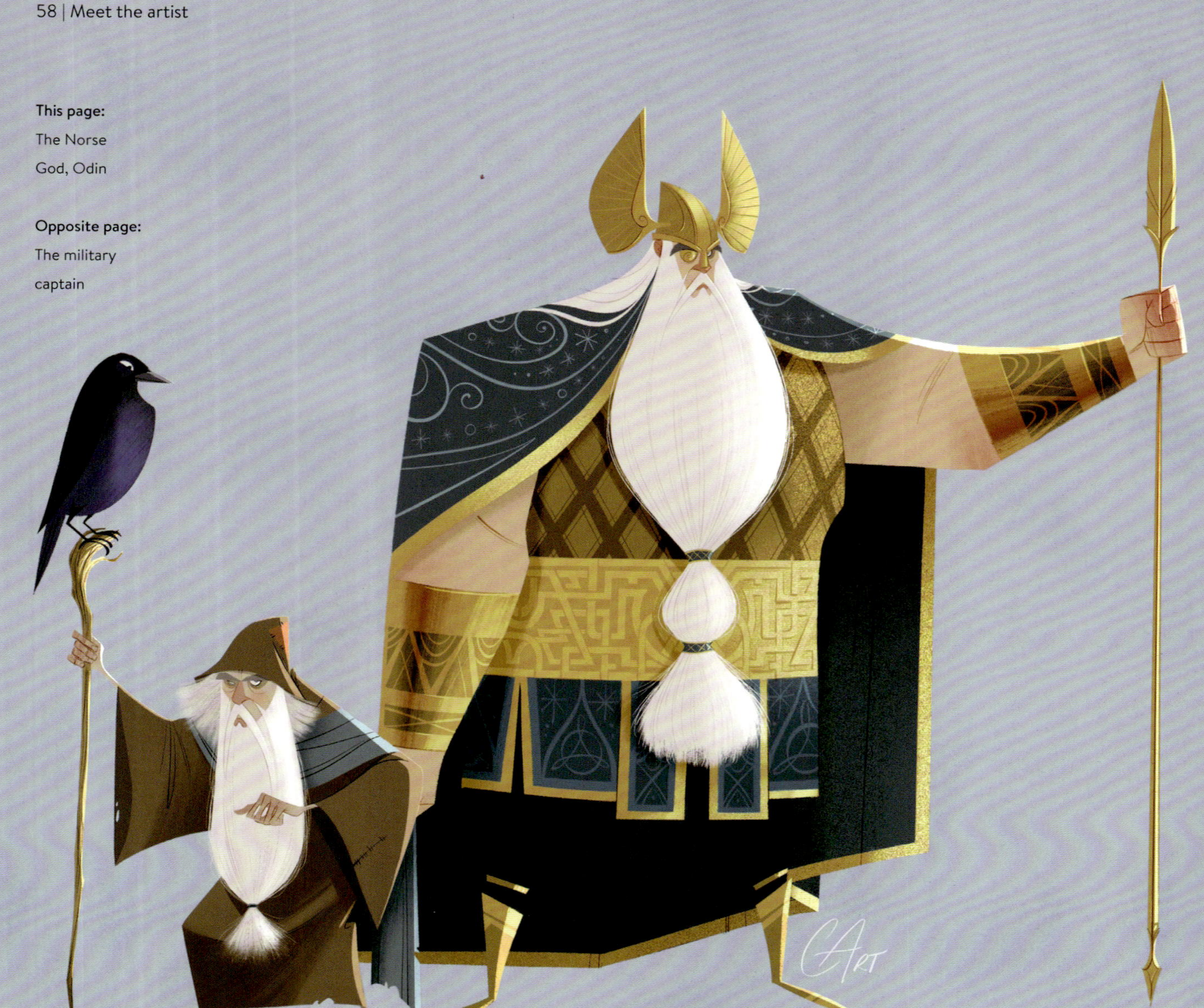

"YOU NEED TO HAVE BOTH IMAGINATION AND THE WILLINGNESS TO EXPERIMENT, AND TAKE CHANCES WITH YOUR DESIGNS"

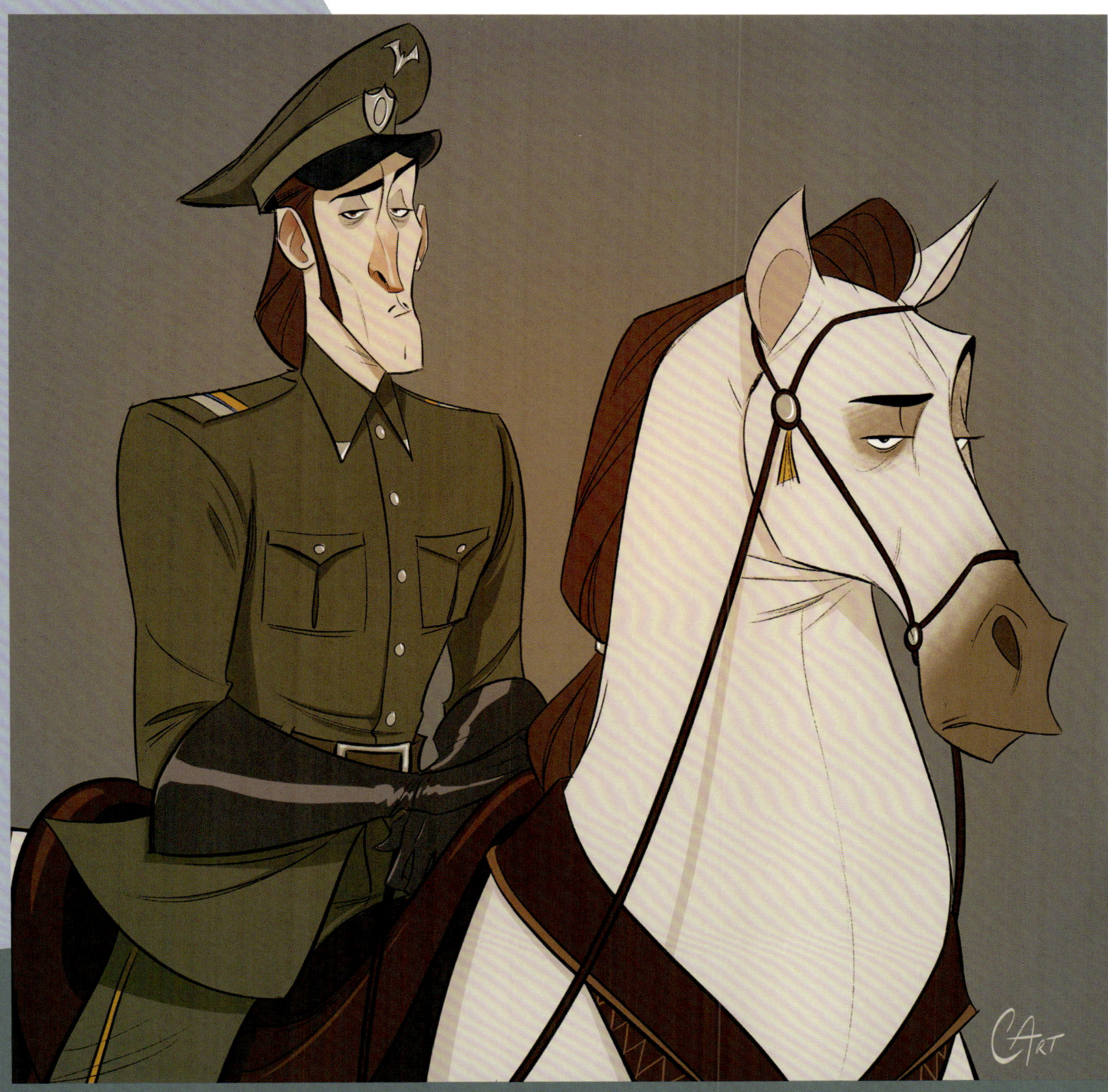

What do you think are the most important qualities to have to be a successful character designer?

I think to be a successful character designer you need to have a grasp of some of the fundamental techniques of drawing, such as figure drawing, gesture drawing, shape language, line of action and so on. But mostly, you need to have both imagination and the willingness to experiment, and take chances with your designs.

What advice would you give to artists just starting out today?

I've been asked this question quite a bit lately, and what I always say is, "Practice, practice, practice!" Always be drawing! I encourage new artists to try using new tools and to play around with unfamiliar art media. Don't be afraid to get loose, experiment, and go big with your designs.

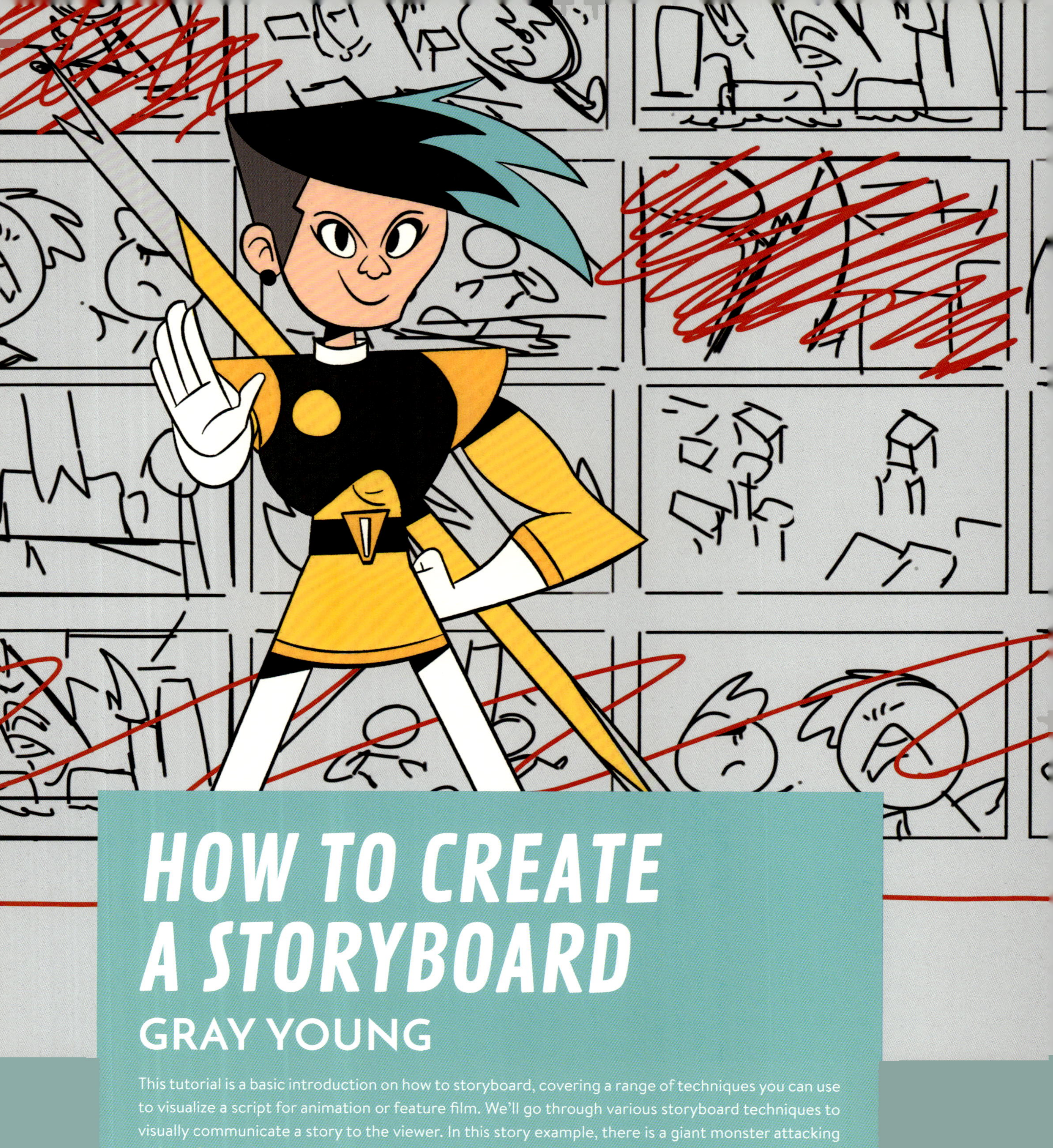

HOW TO CREATE A STORYBOARD

GRAY YOUNG

This tutorial is a basic introduction on how to storyboard, covering a range of techniques you can use to visualize a script for animation or feature film. We'll go through various storyboard techniques to visually communicate a story to the viewer. In this story example, there is a giant monster attacking a Mega City, and it's down to two heroes and their giant robot fighting machine to save the day! The industry standard program for storyboarding is Toon Boom Storyboard Pro, but for this example I've used Adobe Photoshop to illustrate some example boards.

READ THE SCRIPT!

When you get the script it's your job as a storyboard artist to read through it thoroughly, and then read it again until you're familiar with all the scenes and can start to visualize them in your mind. Next, you need to identify the biggest and most complicated scenes and prioritize them when boarding. Remember, you don't have to start on page one and end on the last page. Once you've double-checked everything and decided which scene to prioritize, you can get straight into boarding.

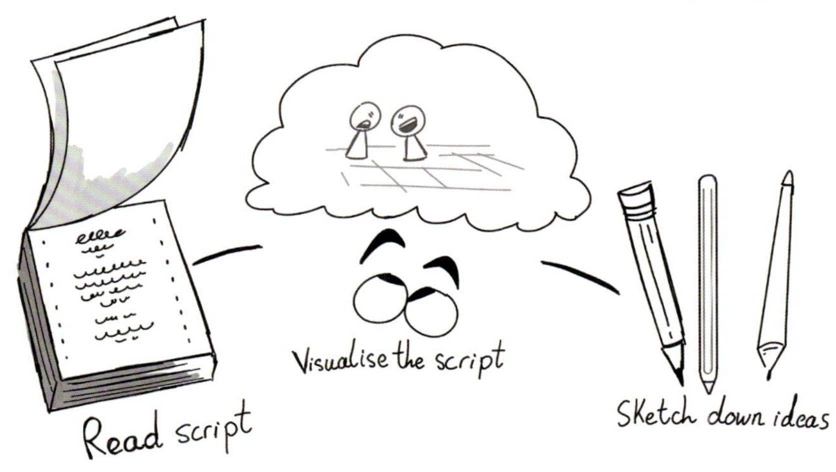

THUMBNAIL SKETCHES

Before you start storyboarding it's important to plan out the scenes through sketching thumbnails. Sketch small, so you are focused on the overall composition of each shot, not focusing on the intricate details such as acting. At this stage, it's about blocking in the most important parts of the scenes. This overall plan will help to prepare your entire storyboard. It doesn't matter what medium you use for thumbnails, analogue or digital – just use whatever you're most comfortable with.

"SKETCH SMALL, SO YOU ARE FOCUSED ON THE OVERALL COMPOSITION OF EACH SHOT, NOT FOCUSING ON THE INTRICATE DETAILS SUCH AS ACTING"

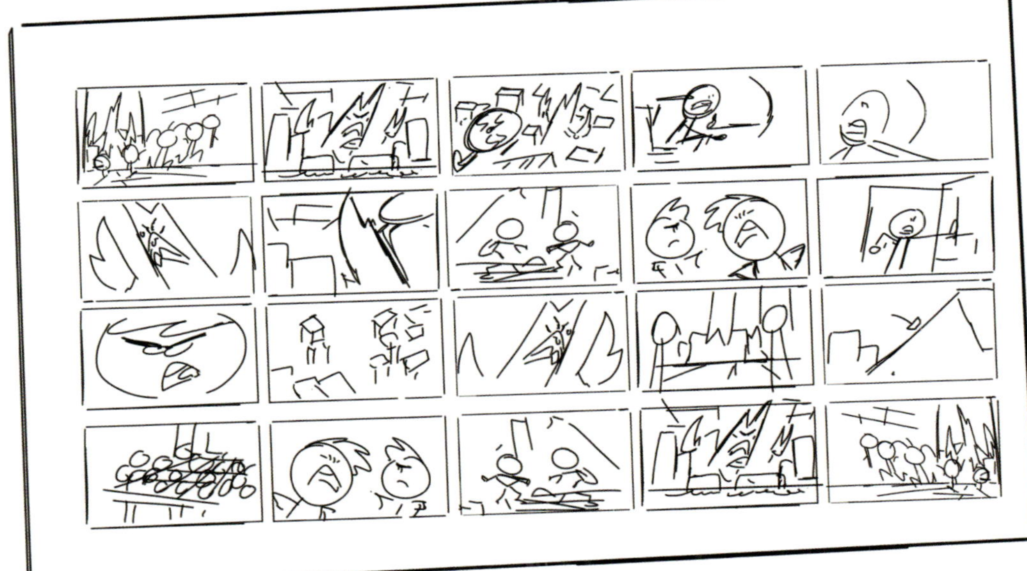

This page (top): Read the script a few times to visualize the scenes in your mind

This page (bottom): Thumbnail your scenes and remember to draw small while sketching

PRIORITIZE YOUR SCENES

Structure your schedule around the most time-consuming scenes – don't leave the biggest scenes until last! For example, pages and pages of dialogue or a highly intense action scene are going to be high priority. Identify the shorter simpler scenes and keep them lower on the priority list. This is so you aren't mentally exhausted when it comes to storyboarding these larger scenes.

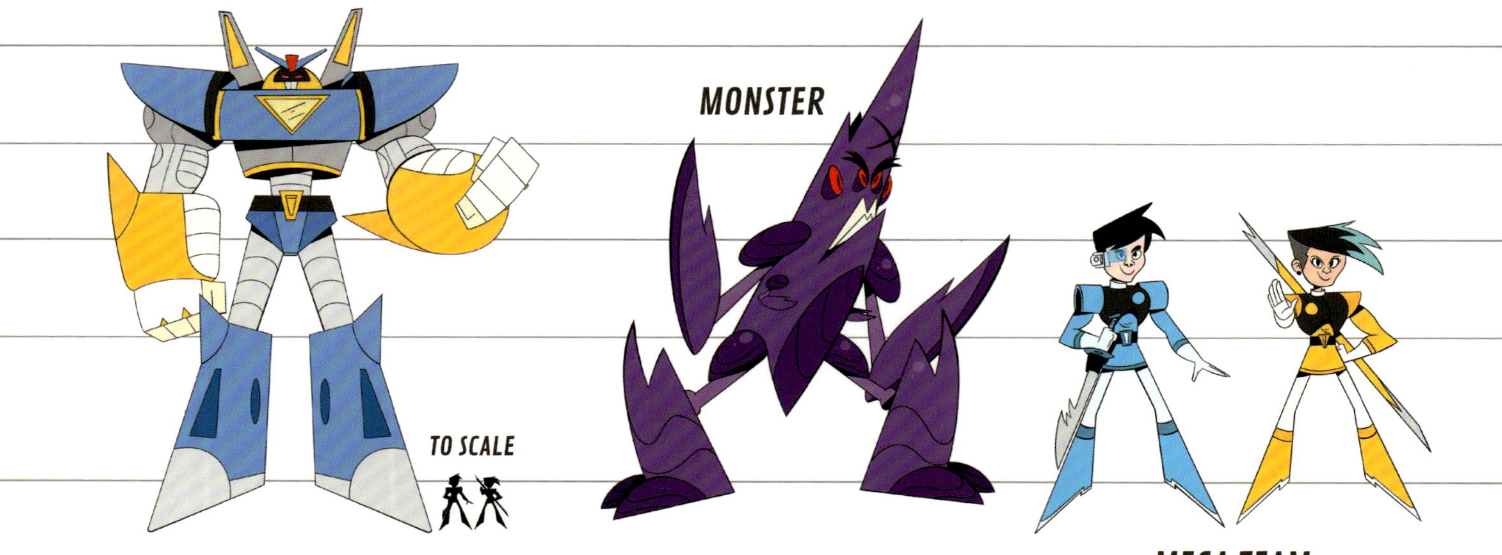

REFERENCES FOR YOUR BOARDS

When storyboarding you will usually be given a folder of assets for the production, including characters, props, backgrounds, models, and anything that's crucial to the story. The line-up here are the characters we will use in these storyboards. It's important to study and familiarize yourself with these characters and assets so that your boards stay "on model." On model means keeping their defining features intact – keeping them recognizable, and the proportions consistent. Other people on the team will be referencing these boards so it's important they can tell who is who and what is what.

THE SHORT ARM TECHNIQUE

For storyboarding, you're going to be drawing literally thousands of images of the characters. With that in mind it's okay (and necessary!) to draw a simplified version of each character. This is called the short arm technique and it's going to save you a lot of time!

When you're learning how to draw a new character for the first time, feel free to trace over the character design reference in order to stay on model. Eventually, you'll know each design by heart. In this example, the image on the left is the detailed version of the character, and alongside is the character drawn in short arm technique. You can miss out minor details such as the nose and armor details, but the key body shapes and proportions should remain intact.

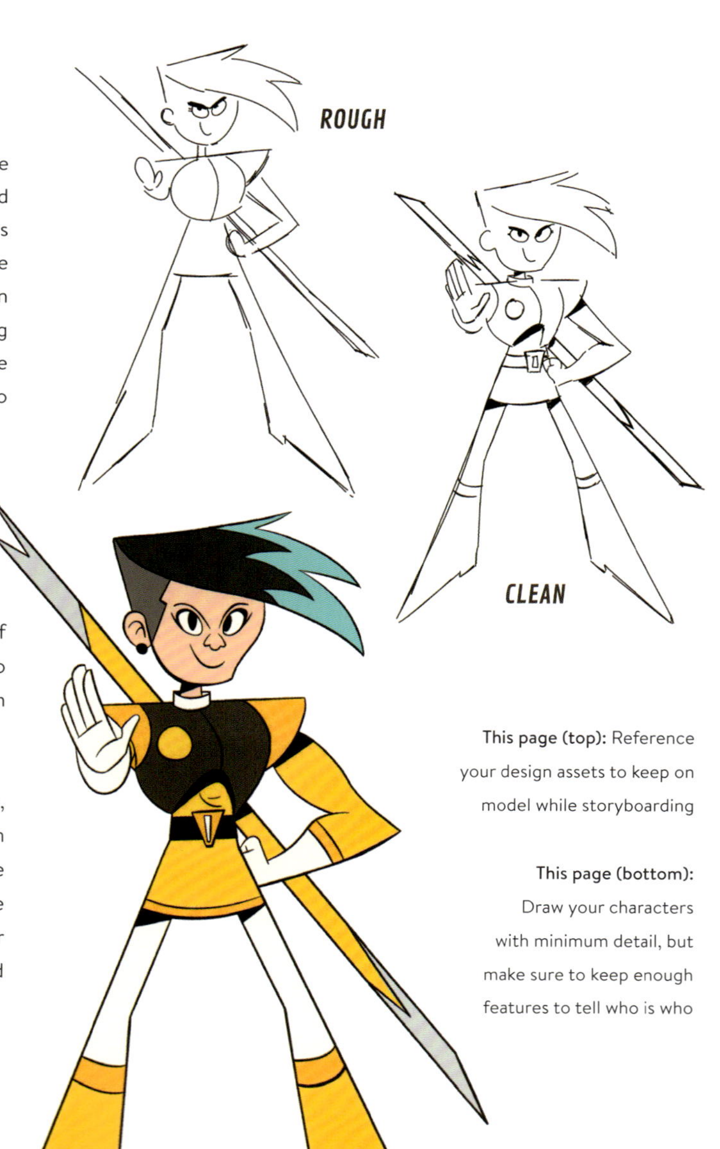

This page (top): Reference your design assets to keep on model while storyboarding

This page (bottom): Draw your characters with minimum detail, but make sure to keep enough features to tell who is who

DRAWING GRIDS AS GUIDES

Grids are an essential tool when storyboarding. They give a guide to perspective and show the camera angle used in the shot. Without grids, it can be difficult to distinguish the camera angle. This is especially important for the designers in animation so they can design the backgrounds appropriately.

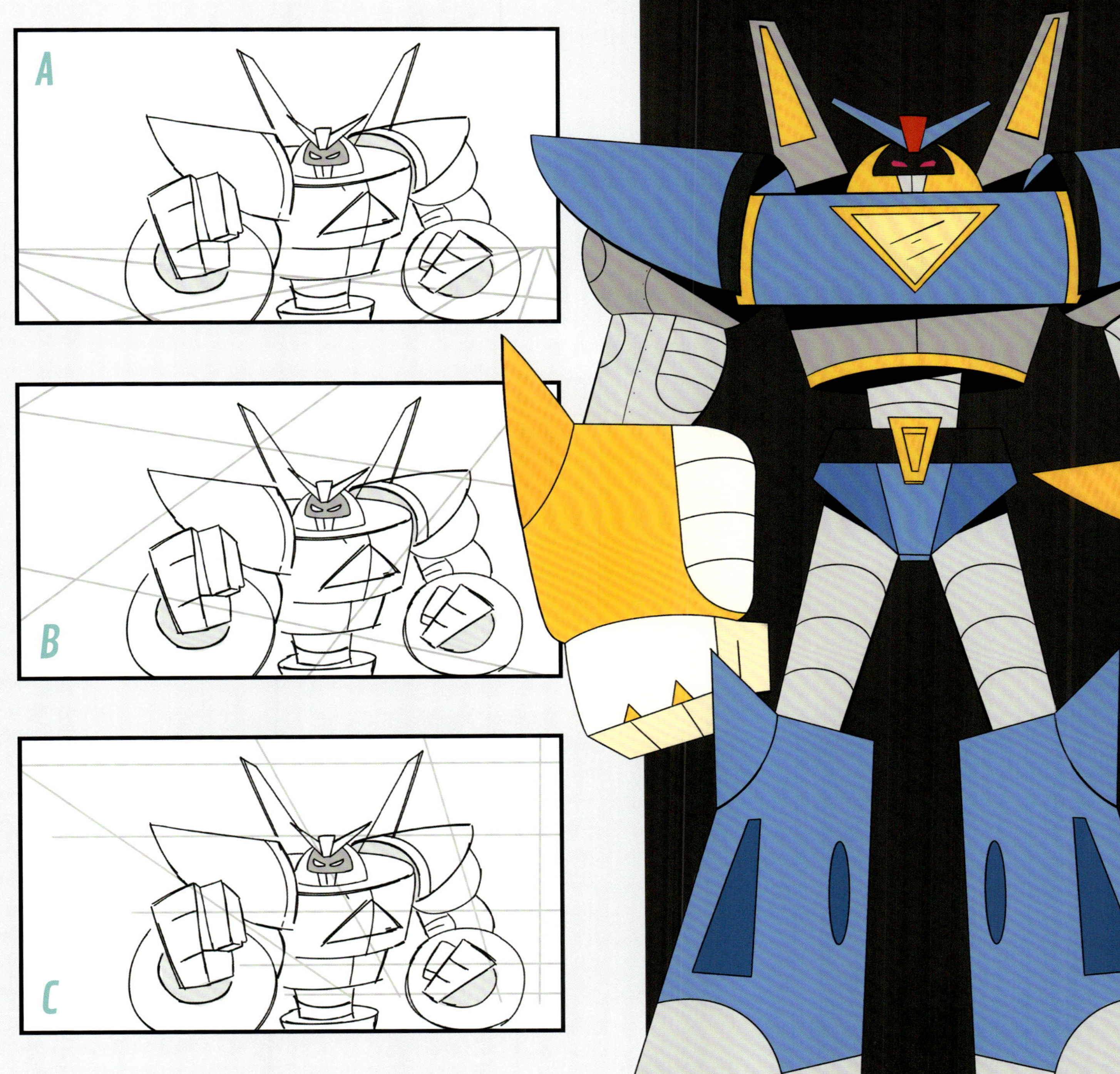

This page: Here are three examples of grids showing different perspectives of the character – **(A)** We are at eye-level with the character **(B)** We are looking down at the character from a high angle **(C)** A low angle shot of the character.

THE RULE OF THIRDS

When you have a busy scene with a lot going on, the rule of thirds is super useful for maintaining a clean composition. It's also a frequently used technique to draw the viewer in to what is most important. Divide the scene both horizontally and vertically into thirds, forming nine sections. Human eyes are drawn to the intersections of these lines, marked here with red circles. By placing the most important aspect of your shot on these intersections, the viewer's attention will be focused here first. In this example, I've drawn a stand-off between the Mega Robot and the opposing monster, positioning both characters on the intersections.

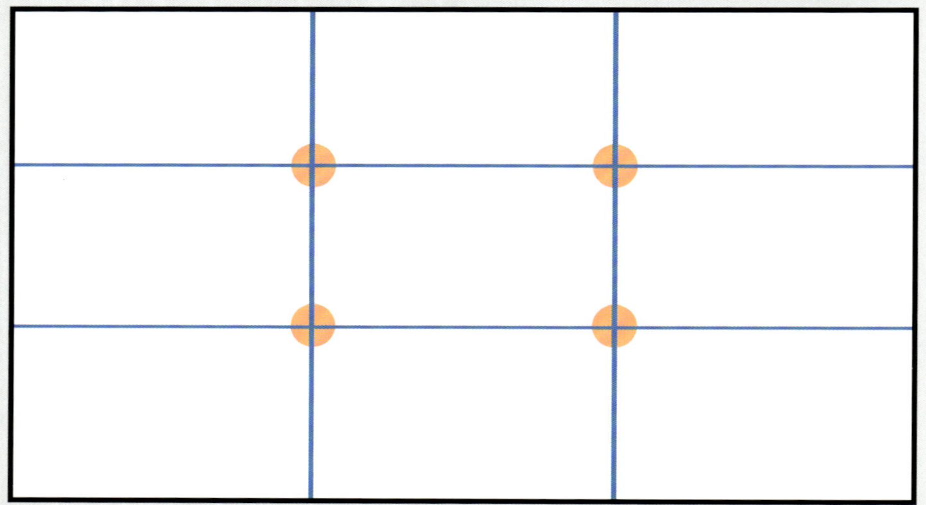

This page: Divide your screen into nine squares and have your point of interest between the intersections

Opposite page (top): Establish your location to contextualize where your scene is taking place at the start of each new scene

Opposite page (bottom): Use a center line to help keep your shots consistent when cutting between characters

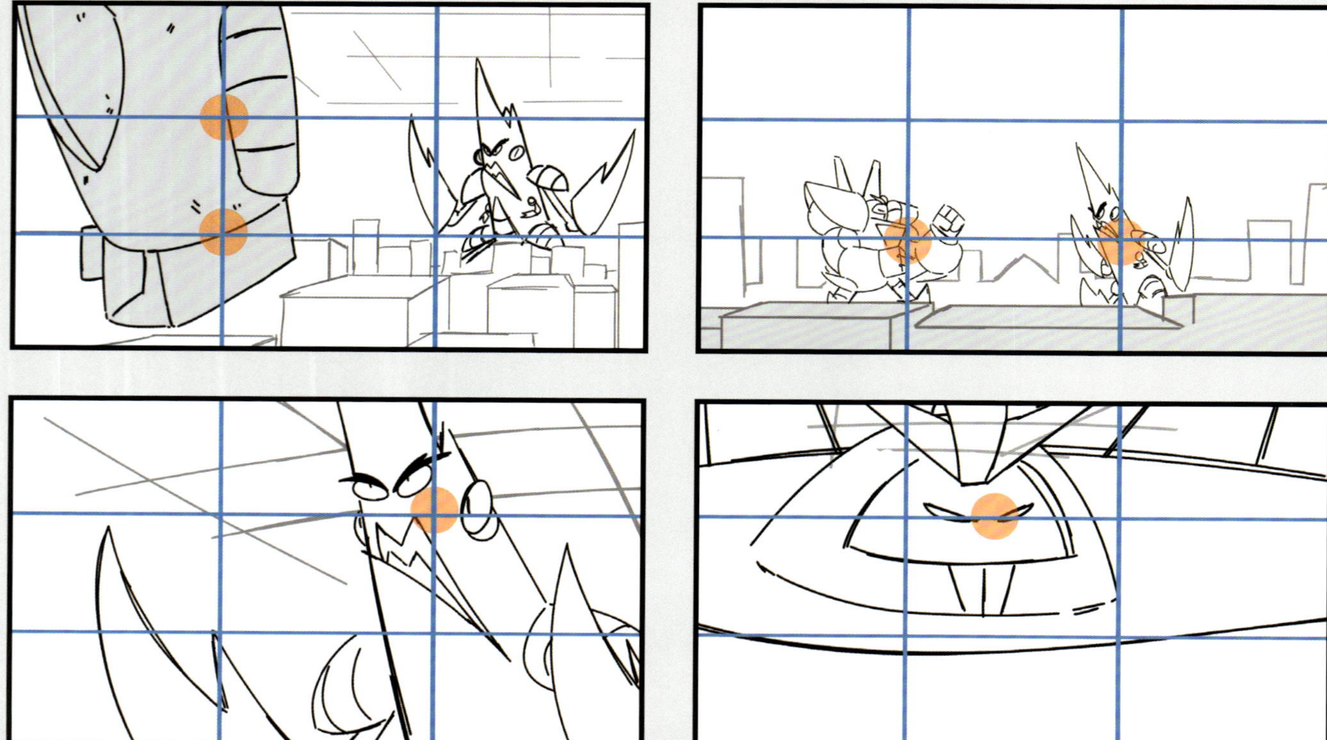

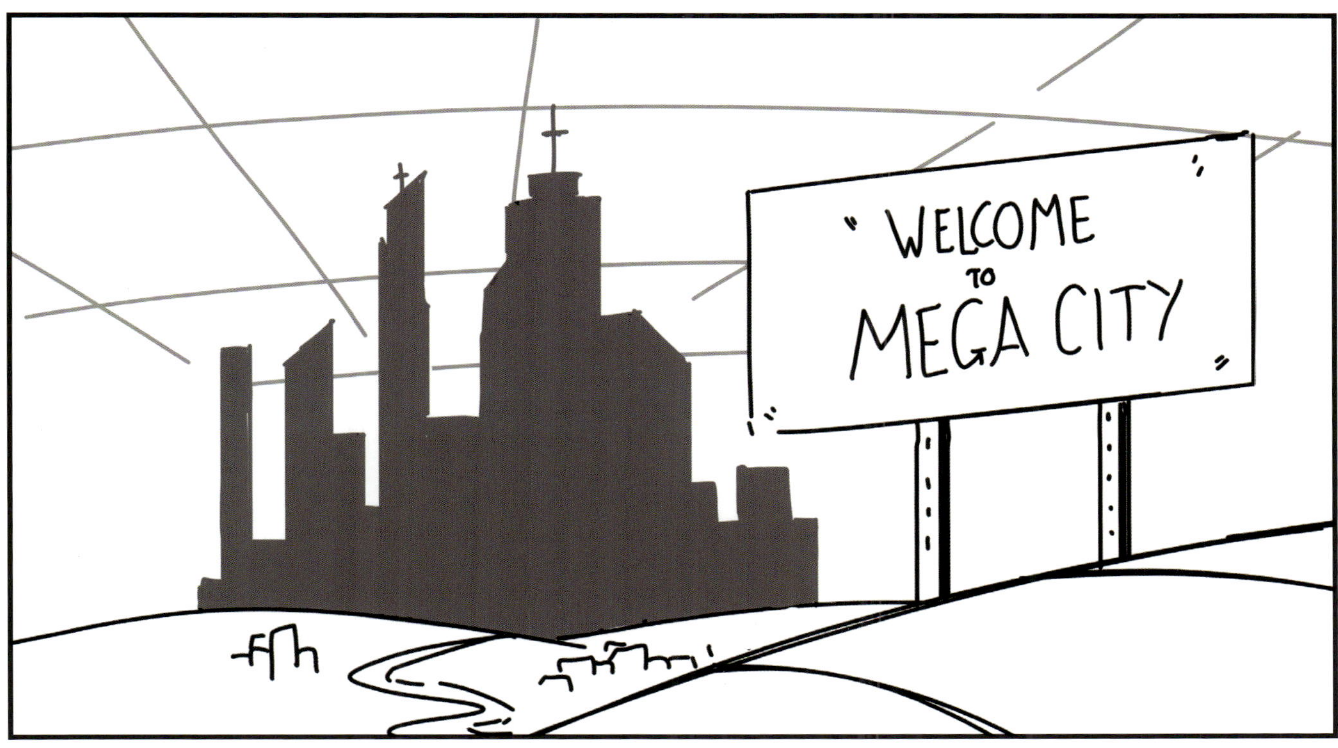

ESTABLISHING SHOTS

An establishing shot contextualizes the scene by showing the location. In animation for TV, establishing shots are mostly used for opening an episode – for example a living room setting or an outdoor environment. When we go from scene to scene, it's vital that we establish where we are each time the location changes so that the viewer knows where the action is taking place. This example is an establishing shot of Mega City, indicating that the following scenes take place at this location.

THE CENTER LINE

Imagine there is a vertical line down the middle of the shot and there are two characters on either side of this line, one on the left and one on the right. When you next cut to one of the characters in this scene, make sure to keep them off center, to the left or right, as they were in the previous shot. This technique is especially useful in a conversation back and forth between two characters. If you suddenly have the character jumping to another part of the screen, you're confusing the viewer and taking their attention away from the story. The center line helps with rhythm and consistency between shots.

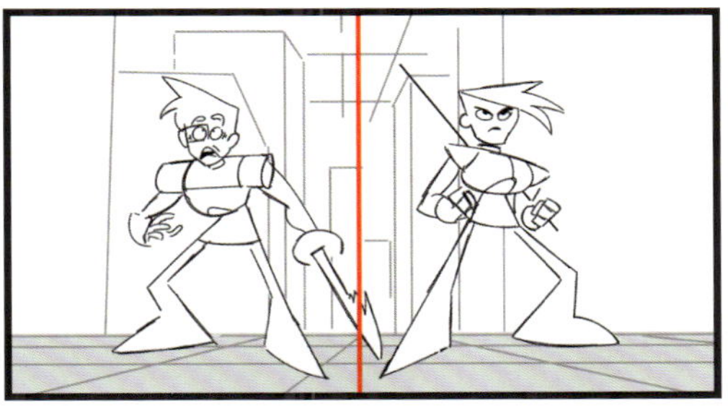

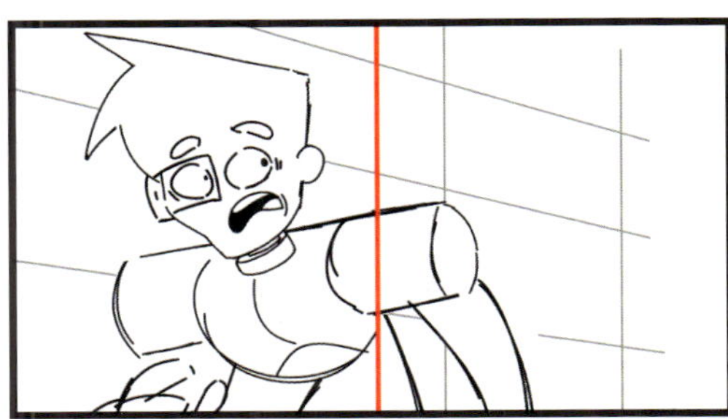

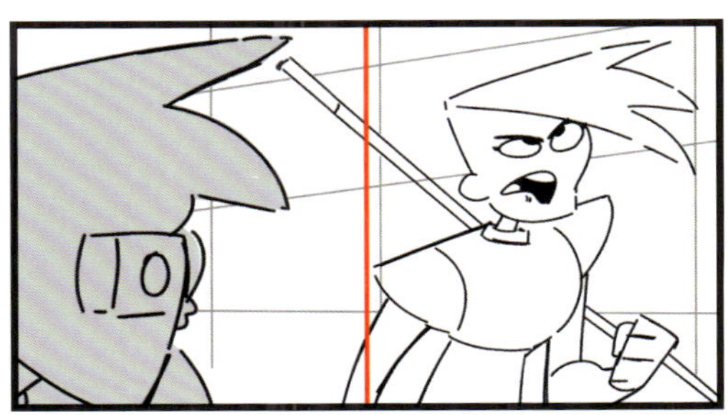

THE 180° CAMERA RULE

Following the principle of the center line, the 180° camera rule is a semi-circle area originating from the camera which allows your image to cut to a different shot within this area. As with the center line, it is used for consistency and to not break the rhythm of the shots. It helps to avoid random angles that don't connect to one another and grounds the viewer, making it clear which direction we are viewing the action from. It's okay to step outside of the 180° area, but only when showing a particular point of interest – for example, a close up of someone placing something in their pocket.

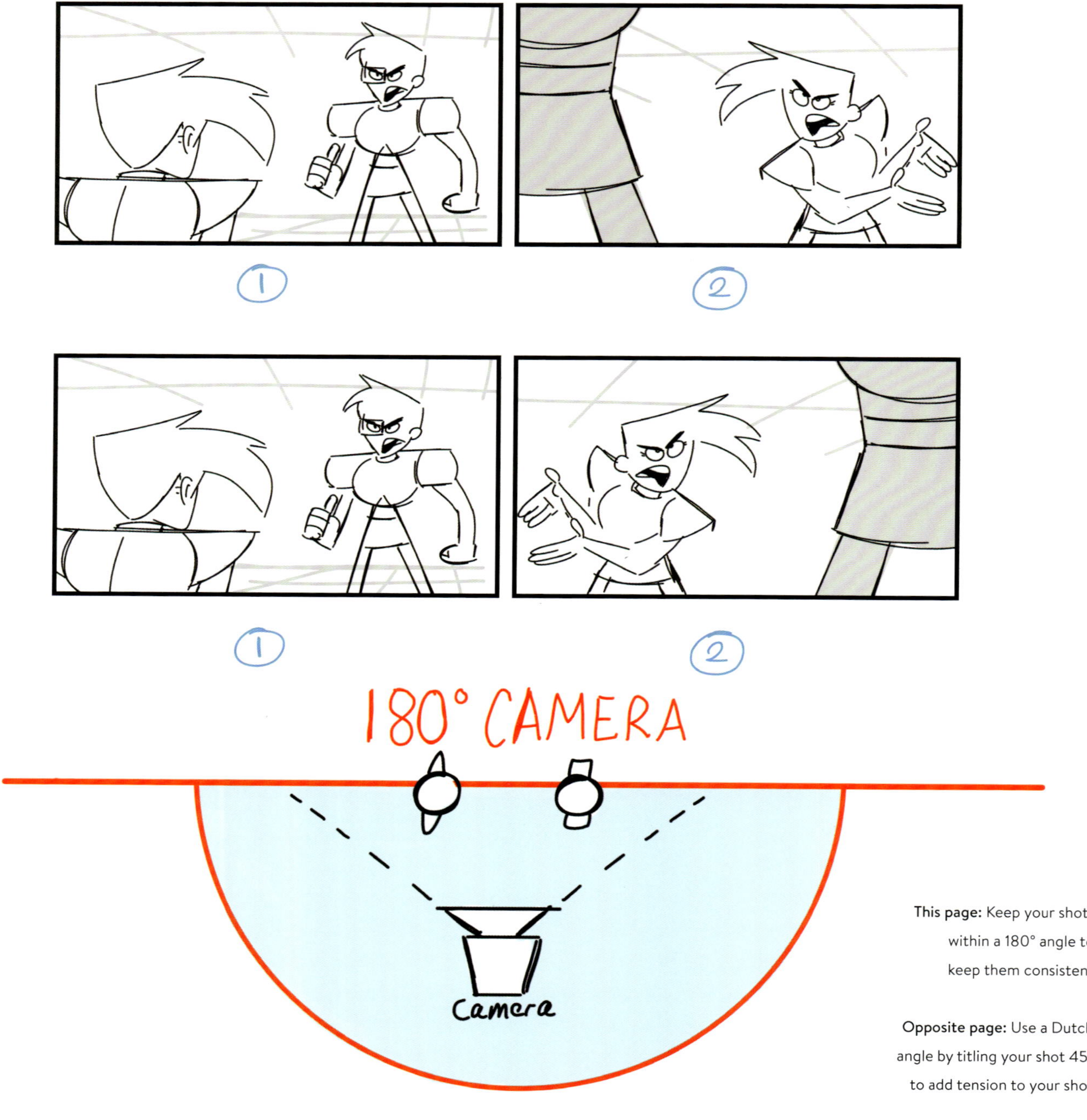

This page: Keep your shots within a 180° angle to keep them consistent

Opposite page: Use a Dutch angle by titling your shot 45° to add tension to your shot

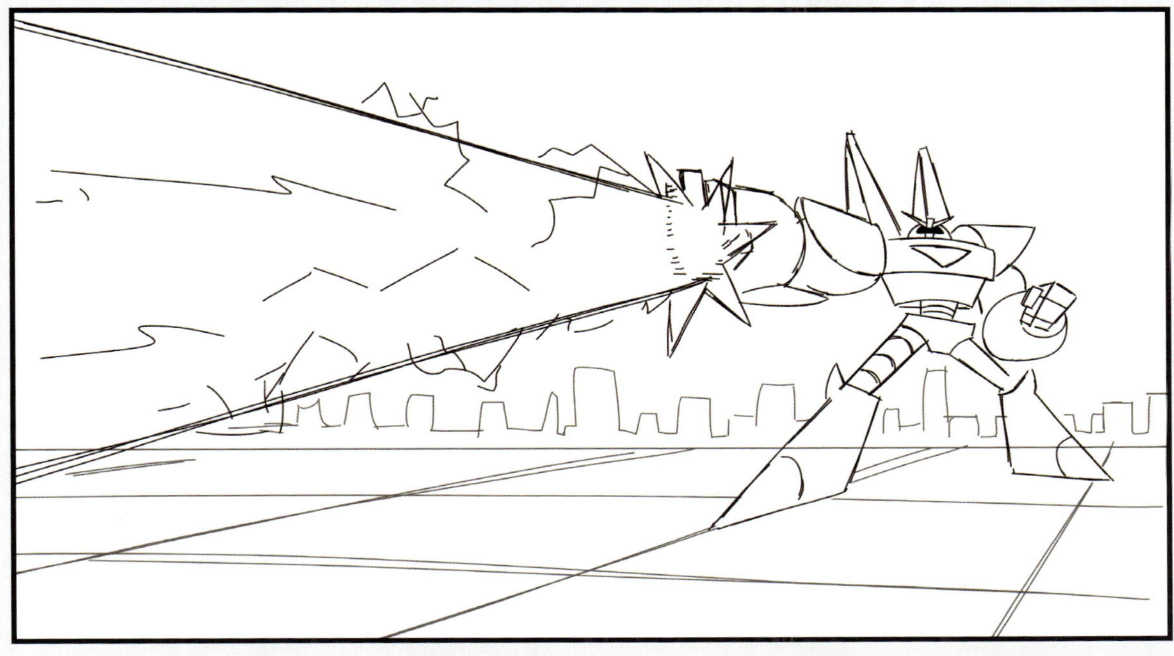

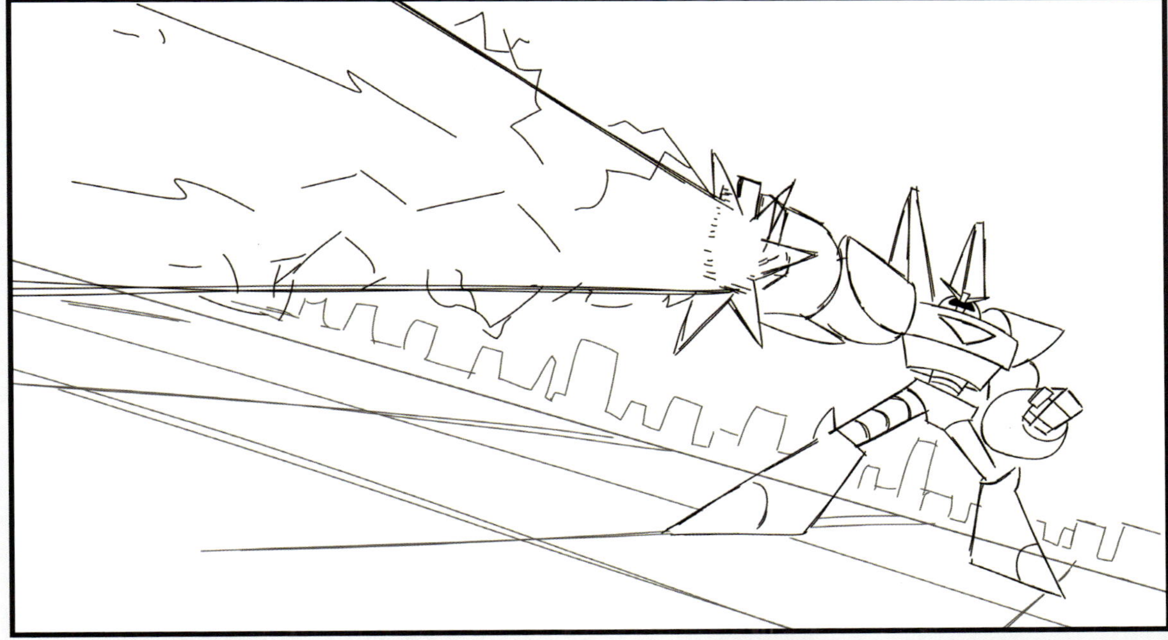

THE DUTCH ANGLE

The Dutch angle is a very useful tool that can help intensify your scenes. This is mostly used in action sequences, but it can also be utilized in scenes which show tension, stress, or excitement. A classic example is a high-speed car chase. In this storyboard, our Mega Robot is firing a Mega Beam from his hand – notice how tilting the camera at a 45°angle intensifies the action shot, thus making the Mega Beam more impactful on screen.

DEEP SPACE AND FLAT SPACE

Deep space and flat space are essentially methods for adding or eliminating depth in your shot. Deep space gives a contextual visualization to the viewer and shows scale, depth, and establishes the location in detail. In this example, I've shown the mass devastation of a part of the city caused by the monster. By adding depth to the scene, we've contextually described the intensity and destruction happening. In contrast to this, flat space eliminates a sense of depth, allowing the viewer to focus their attention on the foreground. Flat space is often used in dialogue sequences between characters and for scenes featuring fight or action sequences.

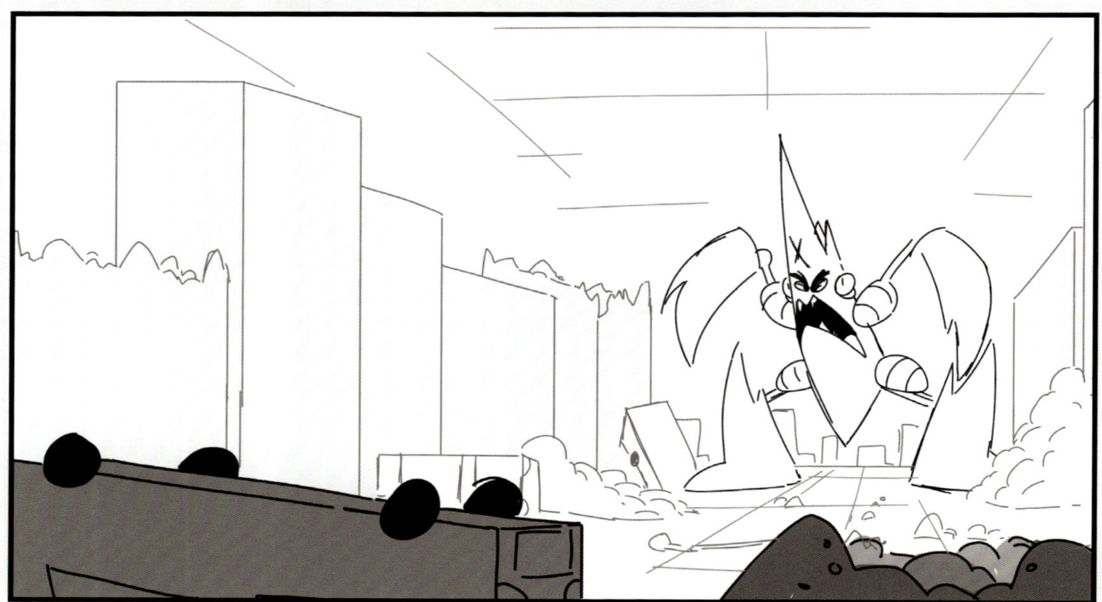

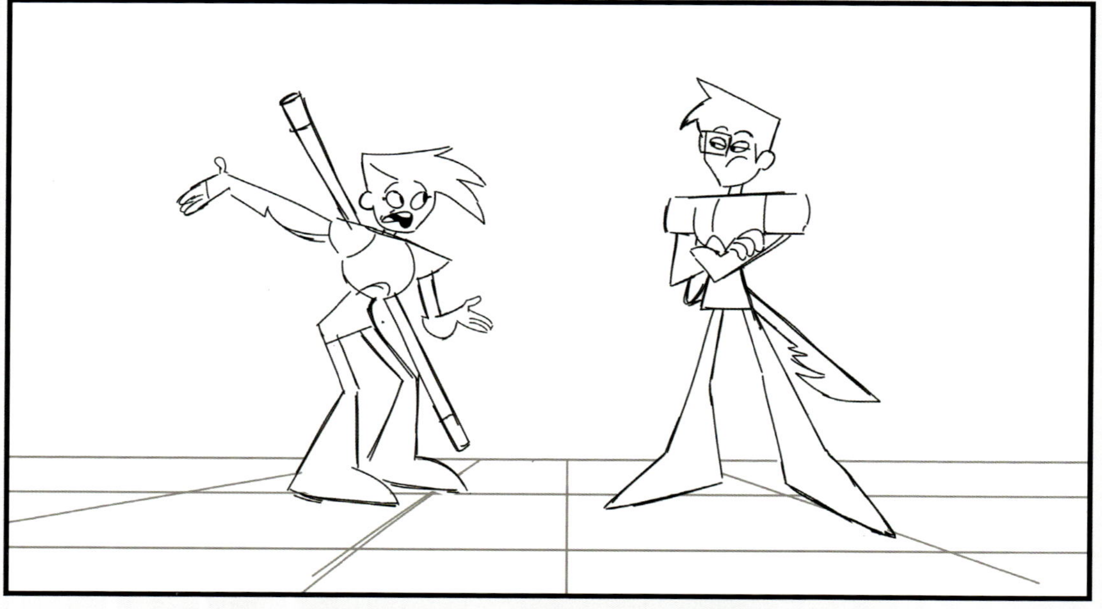

PUSHING THE ACTING

It's important to not only draw the action, but also to show the character's expressions. Try and push the acting in scenes with heightened emotions, to give life and personality to the characters. In my examples, I have two versions of the same exchange happening between the two characters.

In the first example, they are very static in their poses and as a result the conversation looks very boring. In the second sketch I've pushed the acting much further to accentuate their performances and brought the scene to life.

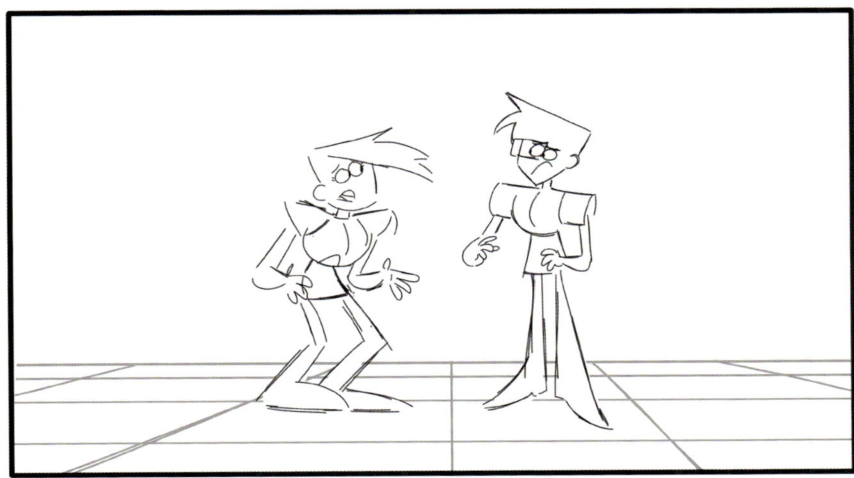

Opposite page: Use deep and flat space to add more depth to your shots

This page: Push the acting in your characters to give them life

"TRY AND PUSH THE ACTING IN SCENES WITH HEIGHTENED EMOTIONS, TO GIVE LIFE AND PERSONALITY TO THE CHARACTERS"

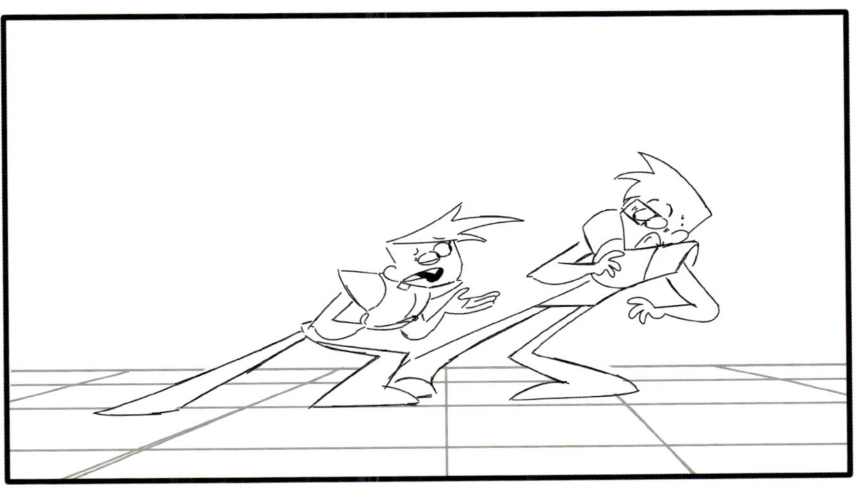

INTERACTING AND REACTING

In addition to individual actions, try to show characters interacting with one another – for example a simple hand on the shoulder can make a character seem more alive, and not as robotic and stiff. If your character is an animal, make the most of expressing their personality through their ears and tails – ears pricked up or flattened can emphasize emotions. Don't forget your characters can interact with props and the environment too!

REVISING YOUR BOARDS

Once you submit the first version of your completed boards, your director will give you notes of things that need to be changed, such as the acting, and any revised shots. I wanted to highlight this because I don't want you to be discouraged that a scene you worked really hard on might come back with lots of changes. A director may even have you re-board an entirely new scene! It's important not to be too precious about your boards. As a storyboard artist, you are an extension of the director's arm – your job is to realize their vision for the project.

This page: Add extra storyboard shots, but not too many – a storyboard artist is not an animator

Opposite page: Be prepared to revise your storyboards after receiving feedback from the director

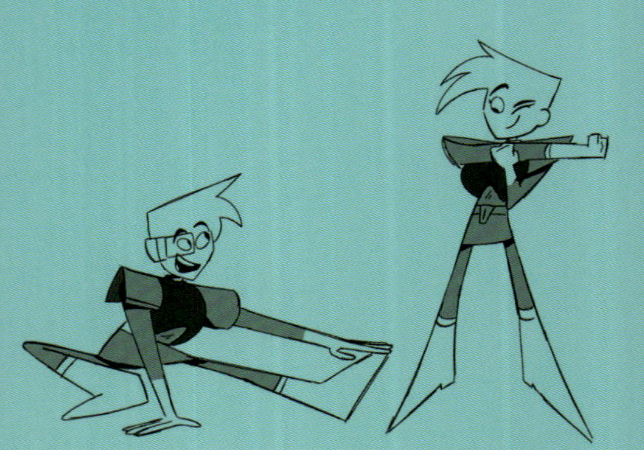

"STORYBOARDING IS A VERY DEMANDING JOB, BOTH PHYSICALLY AND MENTALLY, THAT REQUIRES HOURS OF FOCUS AND A WHOLE LOT OF DRAWING"

KEEPING PANELS TO A MINIMUM

It's vital to remember that you're not an animator, you're a storyboard artist! On social media you'll often see storyboard animatics shared by studios that look almost like finished animation sequences – these are very misleading, and calling them "storyboards" creates unrealistic expectations, especially for people new to the industry. You are not expected to draw every single frame, so make sure you don't add lots of unnecessary panels. In these two examples, we see the heroes running up a corridor. The first example takes place across six panels, which is unnecessary – we only need three panels to describe the action adequately. The only time to add more panels is when the moment is incredibly descriptive, such as for a dance sequence.

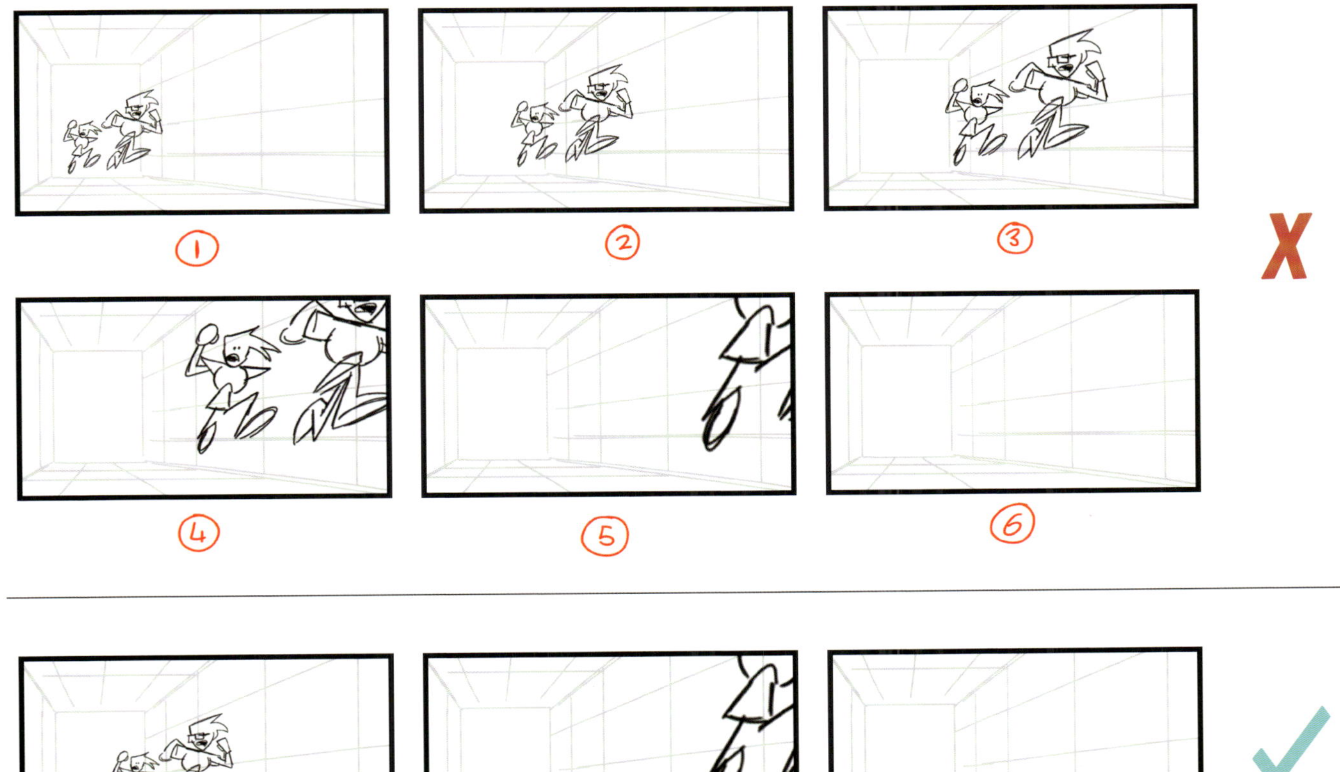

SELF-CARE FOR STORYBOARDERS

Remember to look after yourself! Storyboarding is a very demanding job, both physically and mentally, that requires hours of focus and a whole lot of drawing. Always remember to take regular breaks, and to stretch. Storyboarding is an incredibly rewarding job where you get the chance to work closely with the director and make the story your own.

One of the best things about storyboarding is that you don't have to worry about being super neat and precise – it's just about expressing the story, and there is a freedom in that. Storyboarding gives you a chance to add in jokes, tell a compelling story, and bring your own personality to the boards.

POSING CHARACTERS

MALI BENEDICTO VASANEREKUL

One of the best ways to show off a characters' personality is through the use of body language in your designs. In this article I will show you how to approach this subject, using two of my beloved original characters, Tangerine and Gin, who have opposite personalities and designs. Hopefully, you will find these tips useful to complement your workflow and help bring your characters to life.

KNOW YOUR CHARACTERS

The first step for easily drawing your characters is to know their personalities, and how these translate to the design of their bodies. Design should always complement the story. Tangerine is soft and radiates joy, and Gin is very savage with a sharp tongue.

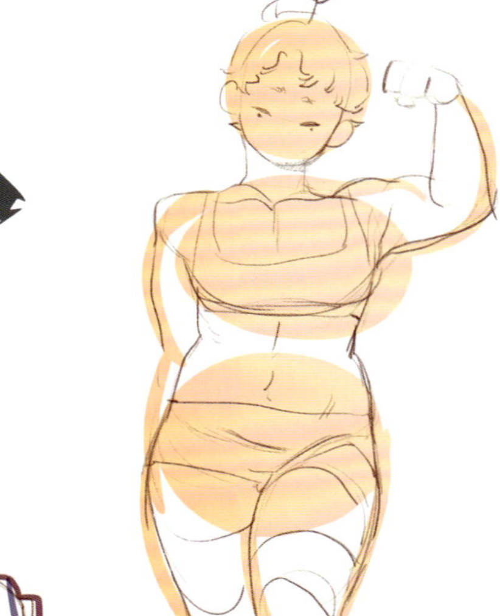
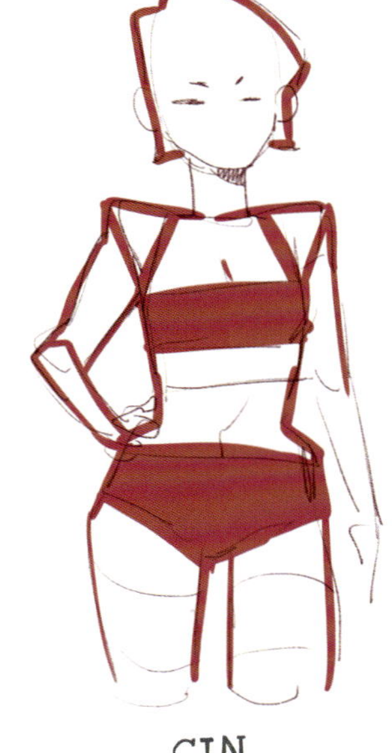

BODY TYPE

TANGERINE

GIN

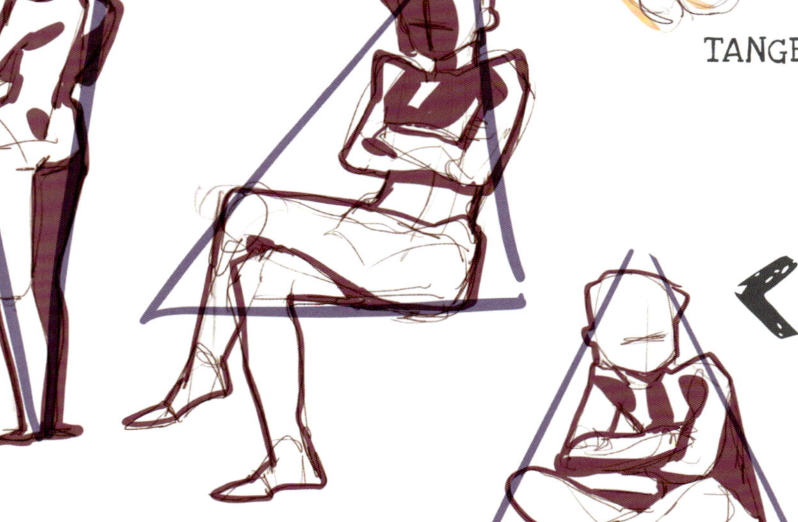

DRAWING ANGRY

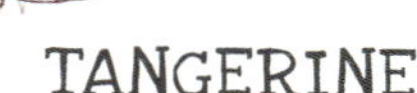

Gin is very expressive, she's not afraid to show her anger. Her shape is aggressive and angular. She shows her anger by behaving like an upset kid, very self-centred. I draw her with arms and legs drawn into the body to reflect this attitude in the design.

APPLYING THE ANATOMY

A complex silhouette will show what fits the character and the situation. You can show more intensity by deforming a character's anatomy – in this case, Gin's shoulders are exaggerated to show her discomfort and frustration.

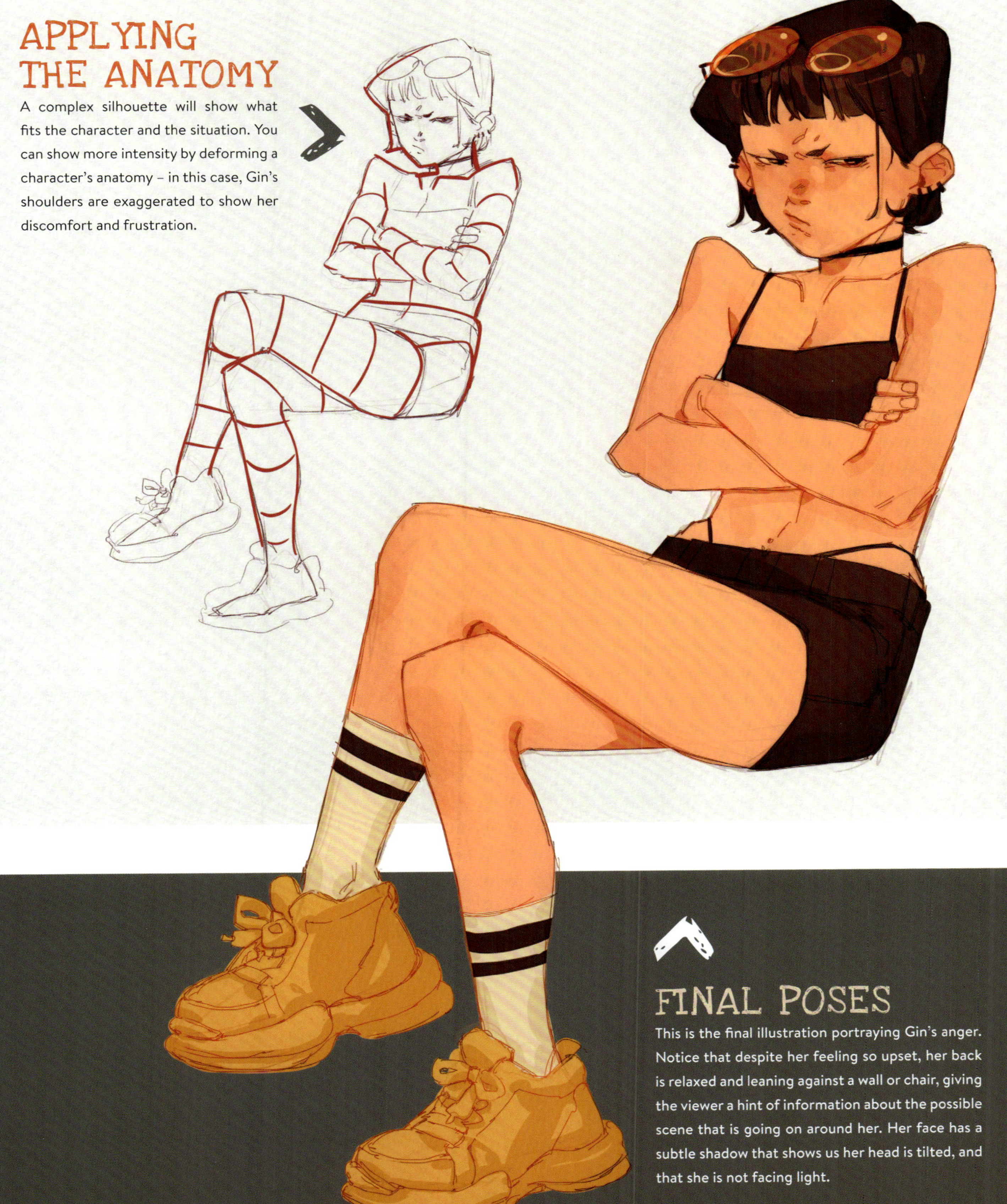

FINAL POSES

This is the final illustration portraying Gin's anger. Notice that despite her feeling so upset, her back is relaxed and leaning against a wall or chair, giving the viewer a hint of information about the possible scene that is going on around her. Her face has a subtle shadow that shows us her head is tilted, and that she is not facing light.

MEET TANGERINE

And now, Tangerine! She is the opposite of Gin – very optimistic, bright, and easy going. As you can see here, her lines are based on round forms and lines, to match her personality and body type.

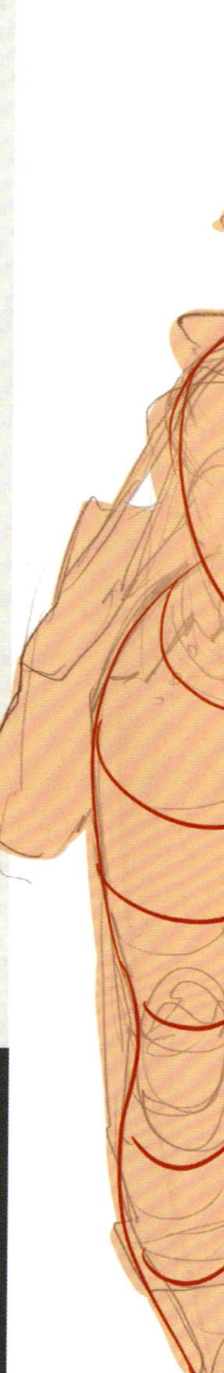

AN ANATOMY TRICK

Are you wondering what all the lines are on the sketches of Gin and Tangerine? I call these the "sock lines!" They are good for visualizing the directions of arms and legs, and how the volume works on those areas and body parts. Drawing imaginary socks is all it takes!

ON THE MOVE

Tangerine is always moving – she can't stand still for long because her energy keeps her going. Drawing her with one foot off the ground helps portray this dynamism. Her warm personality is what inspires me to always draw her hugging other characters or objects.

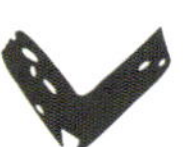

"THE COLOR OF THIS CHARACTER IS VERY IMPORTANT AS IT SHOWS THE TEMPERATURE AND VIBE OF THE SITUATION"

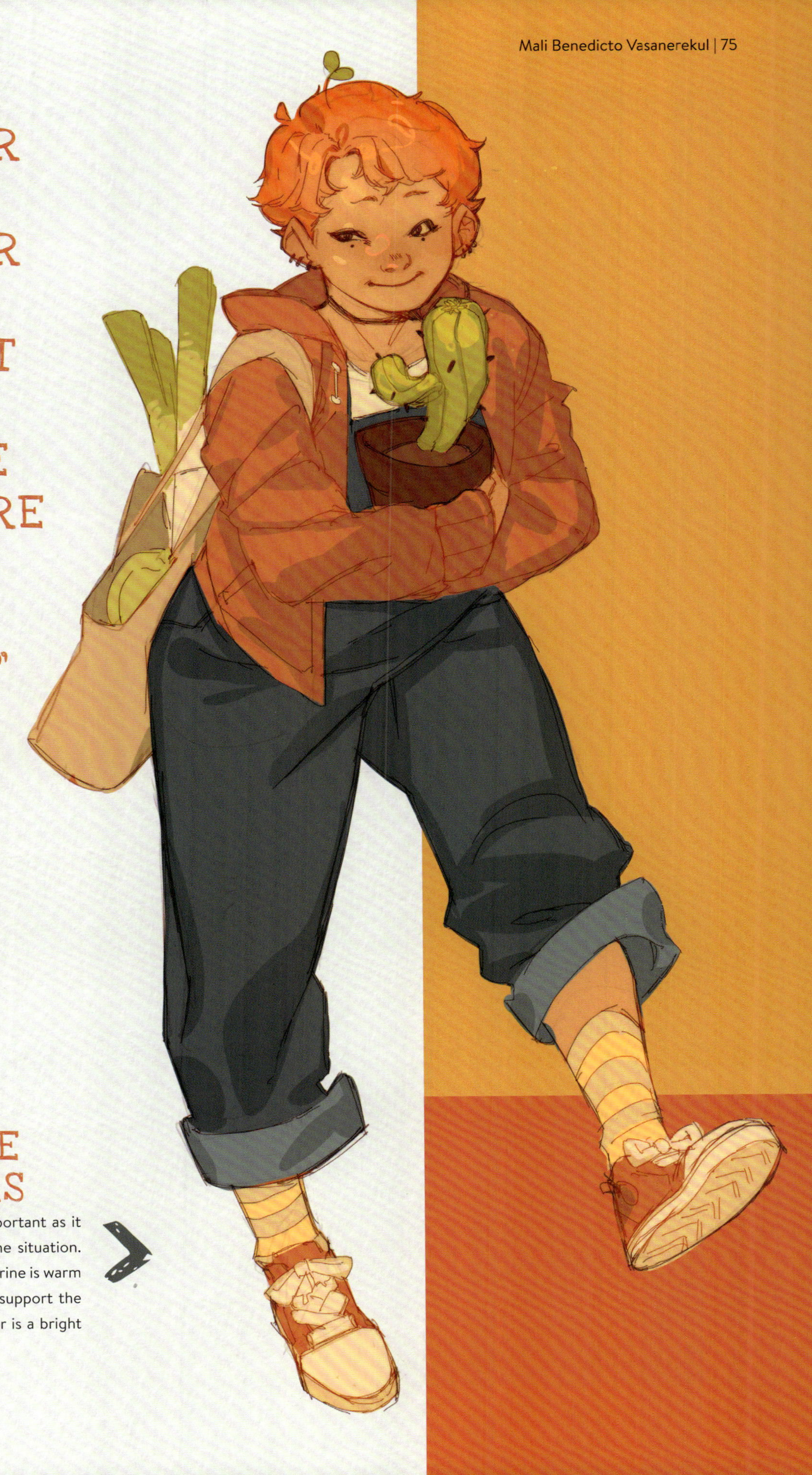

CHOOSING THE RIGHT COLORS

The color of this character is very important as it shows the temperature and vibe of the situation. The feeling I want to show is that Tangerine is warm enough to give the best cuddles and support the whole world! That's why her base color is a bright pinkish-orange.

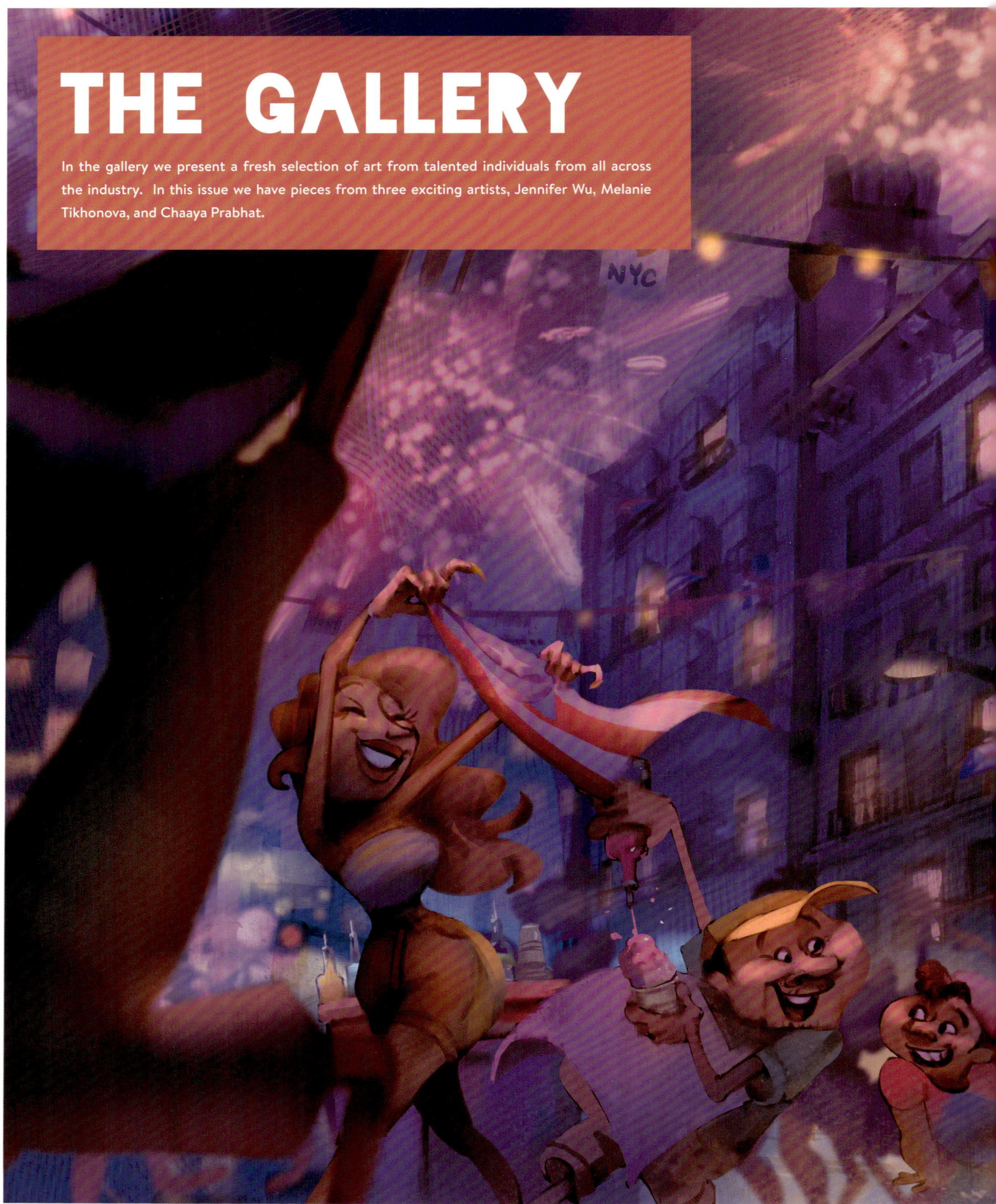

THE GALLERY

In the gallery we present a fresh selection of art from talented individuals from all across the industry. In this issue we have pieces from three exciting artists, Jennifer Wu, Melanie Tikhonova, and Chaaya Prabhat.

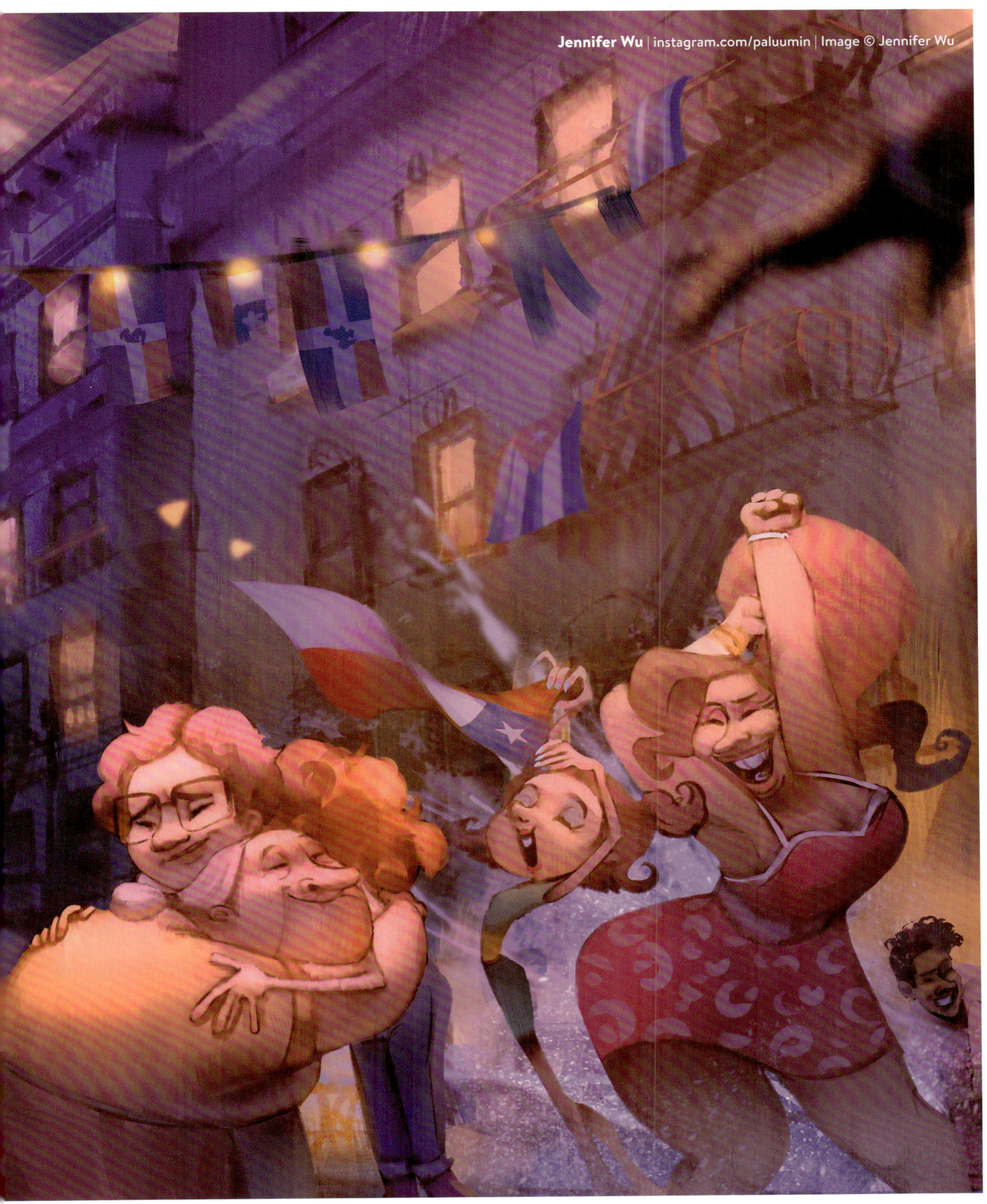
Jennifer Wu | instagram.com/paluumin | Image © Jennifer Wu

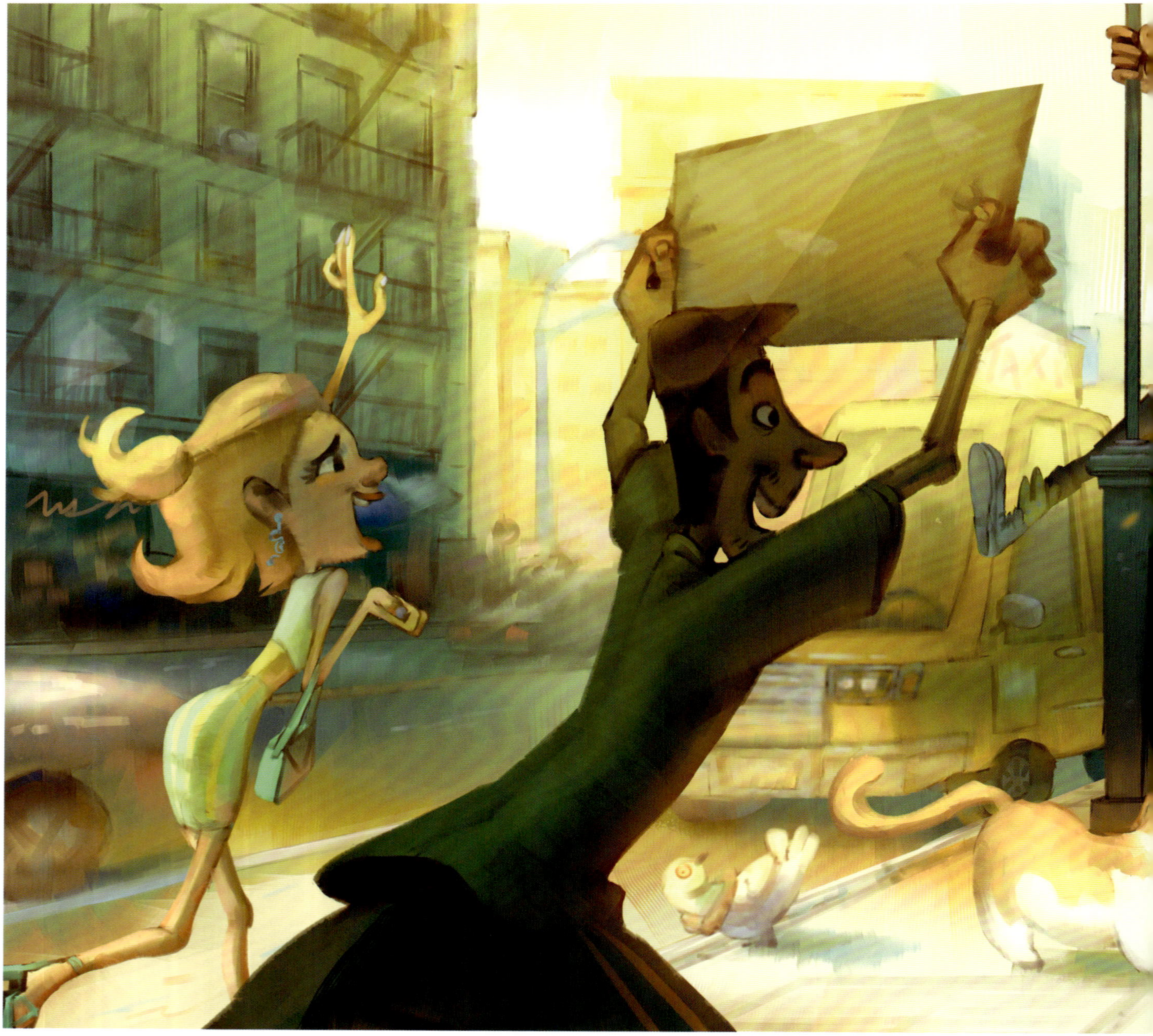

JENNIFER IS A CHARACTER DESIGNER AND VISUAL DEVELOPMENT ARTIST WHO HAS ALWAYS HAD A PASSION FOR STORYTELLING THROUGH PAINTINGS AND CHARACTERS. ONE OF HER FAVORITE PARTS OF THE JOB IS USING EVERY STORY OPPORTUNITY TO LEARN SOMETHING NEW ABOUT THE WORLD.

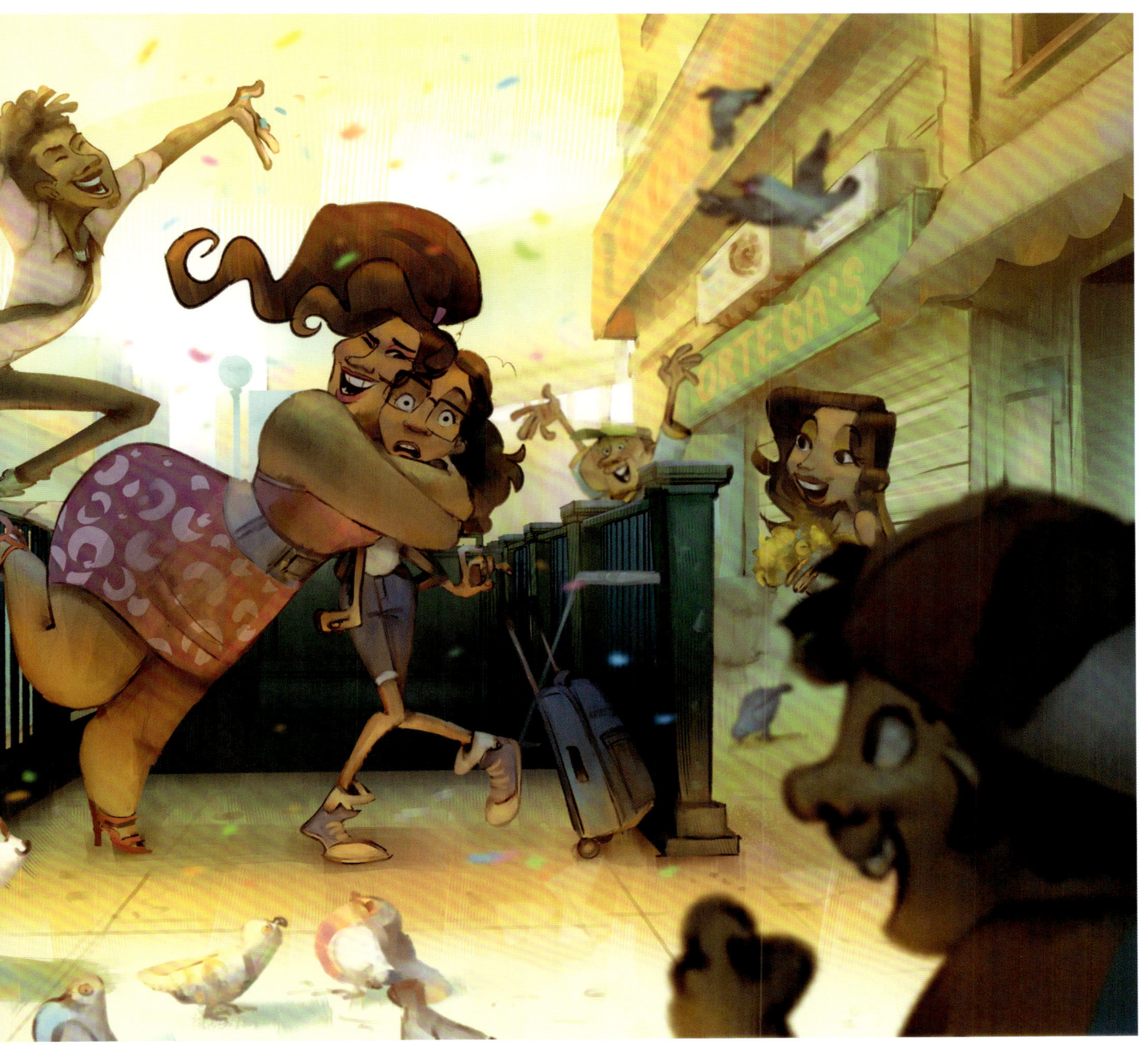
ORTEGA'S

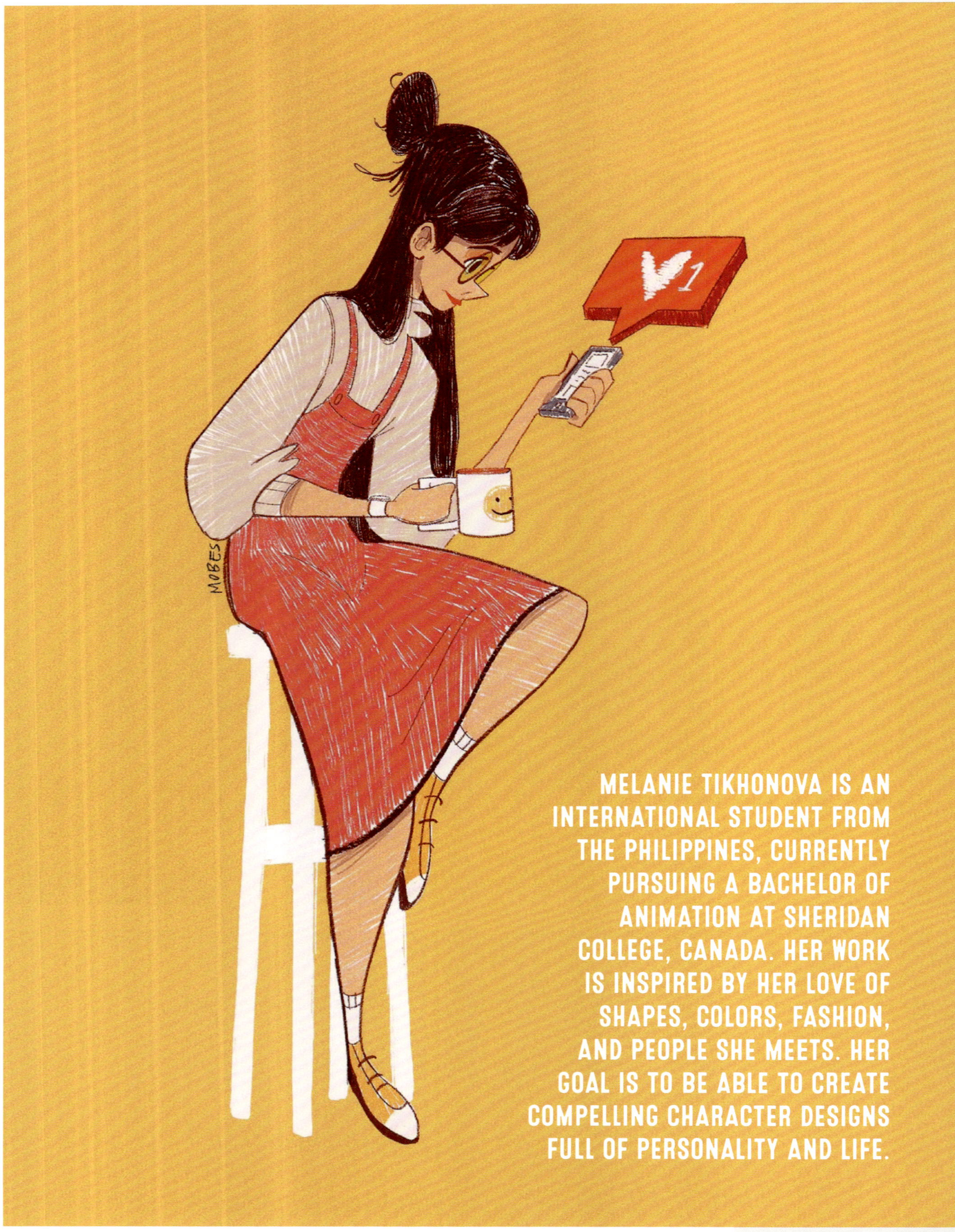

MELANIE TIKHONOVA IS AN INTERNATIONAL STUDENT FROM THE PHILIPPINES, CURRENTLY PURSUING A BACHELOR OF ANIMATION AT SHERIDAN COLLEGE, CANADA. HER WORK IS INSPIRED BY HER LOVE OF SHAPES, COLORS, FASHION, AND PEOPLE SHE MEETS. HER GOAL IS TO BE ABLE TO CREATE COMPELLING CHARACTER DESIGNS FULL OF PERSONALITY AND LIFE.

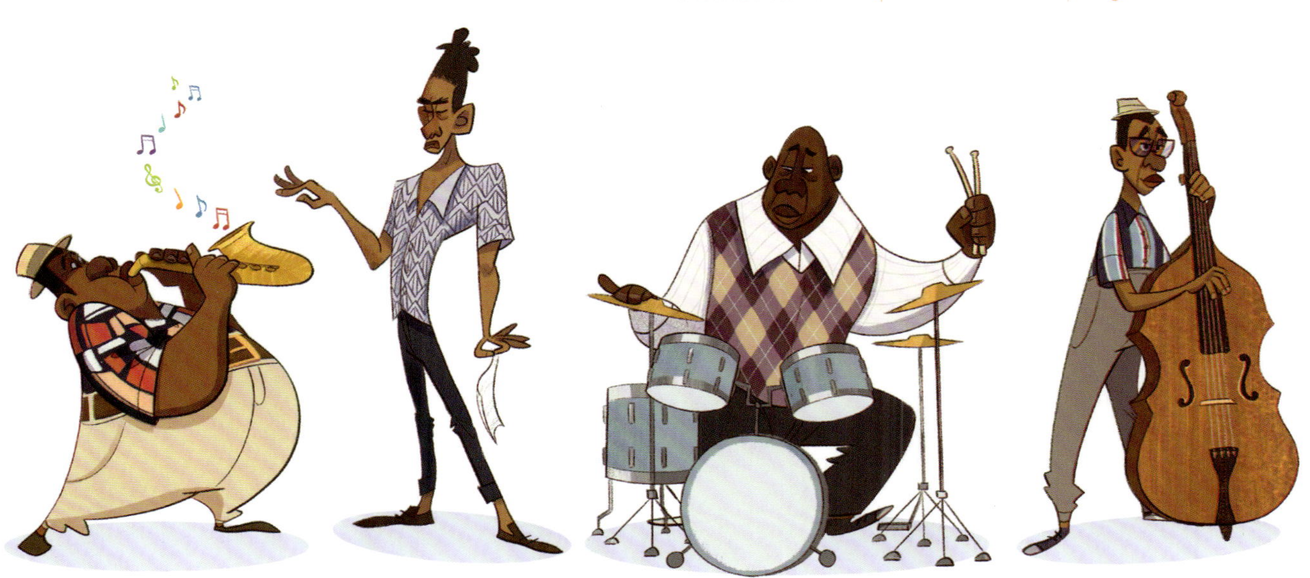

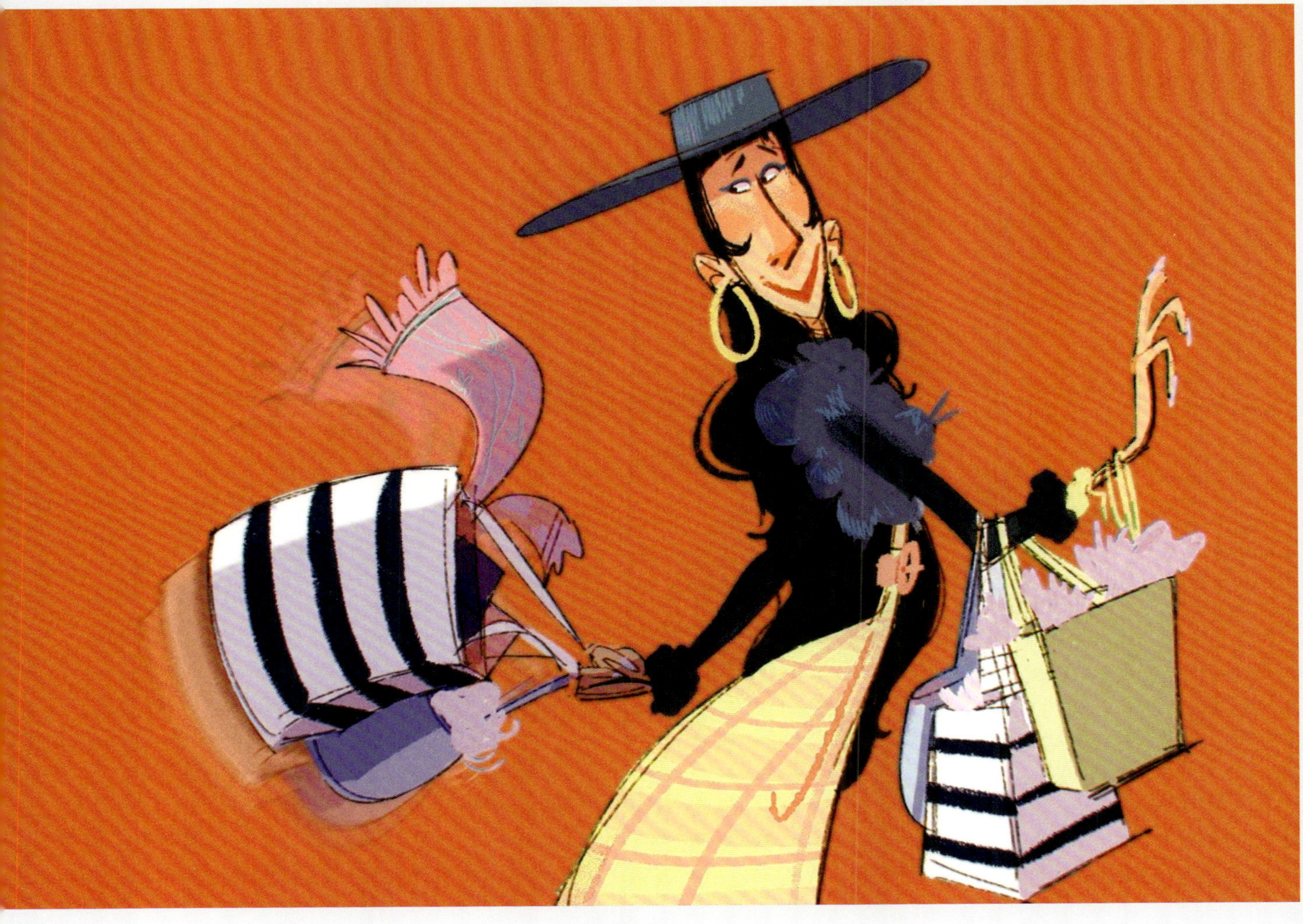

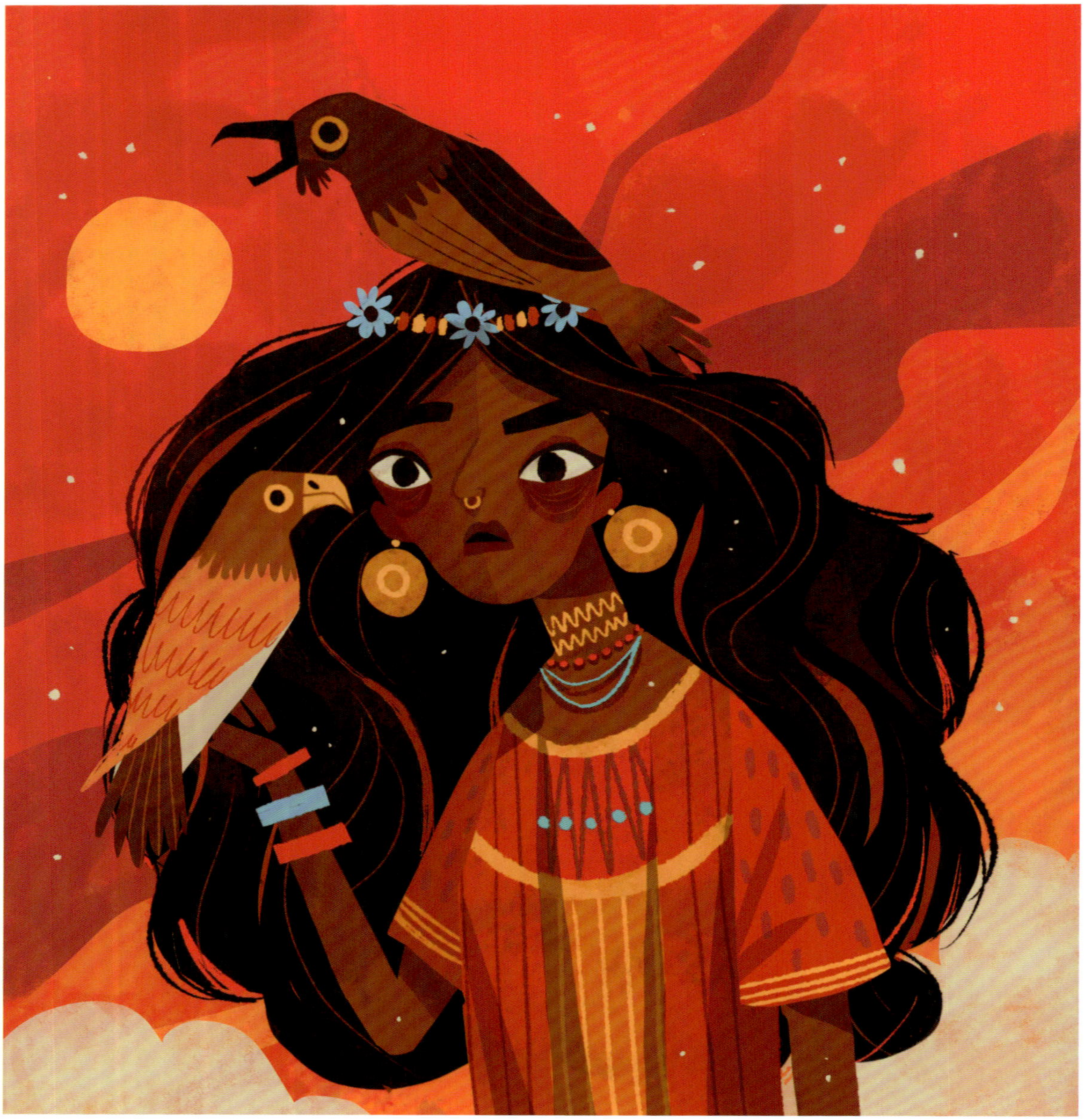

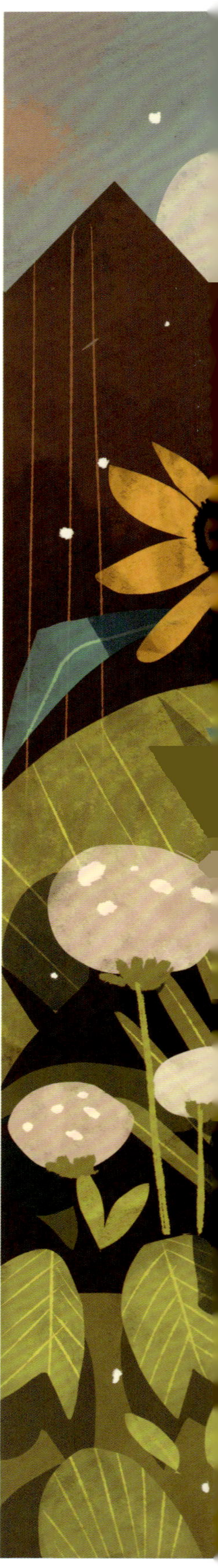

CHAAYA PRABHAT IS A GRAPHIC DESIGNER, ILLUSTRATOR, AND LETTERING ARTIST. AFTER COMPLETING HER M.A IN GRAPHIC DESIGN FROM SAVANNAH COLLEGE OF ART AND DESIGN, SHE IS NOW WORKING INDEPENDENTLY IN CHENNAI, INDIA. SHE HAS WORKED WITH SEVERAL CLIENTS SUCH AS PENGUIN UK, HACHETTE, FACEBOOK, AND GOOGLE ON PICTURE-BOOK AND DIGITAL ILLUSTRATION PROJECTS. SHE HAS PREVIOUSLY RECEIVED AWARDS FOR HER PORTFOLIO AND PROJECTS FROM BEHANCE AND ADOBE.

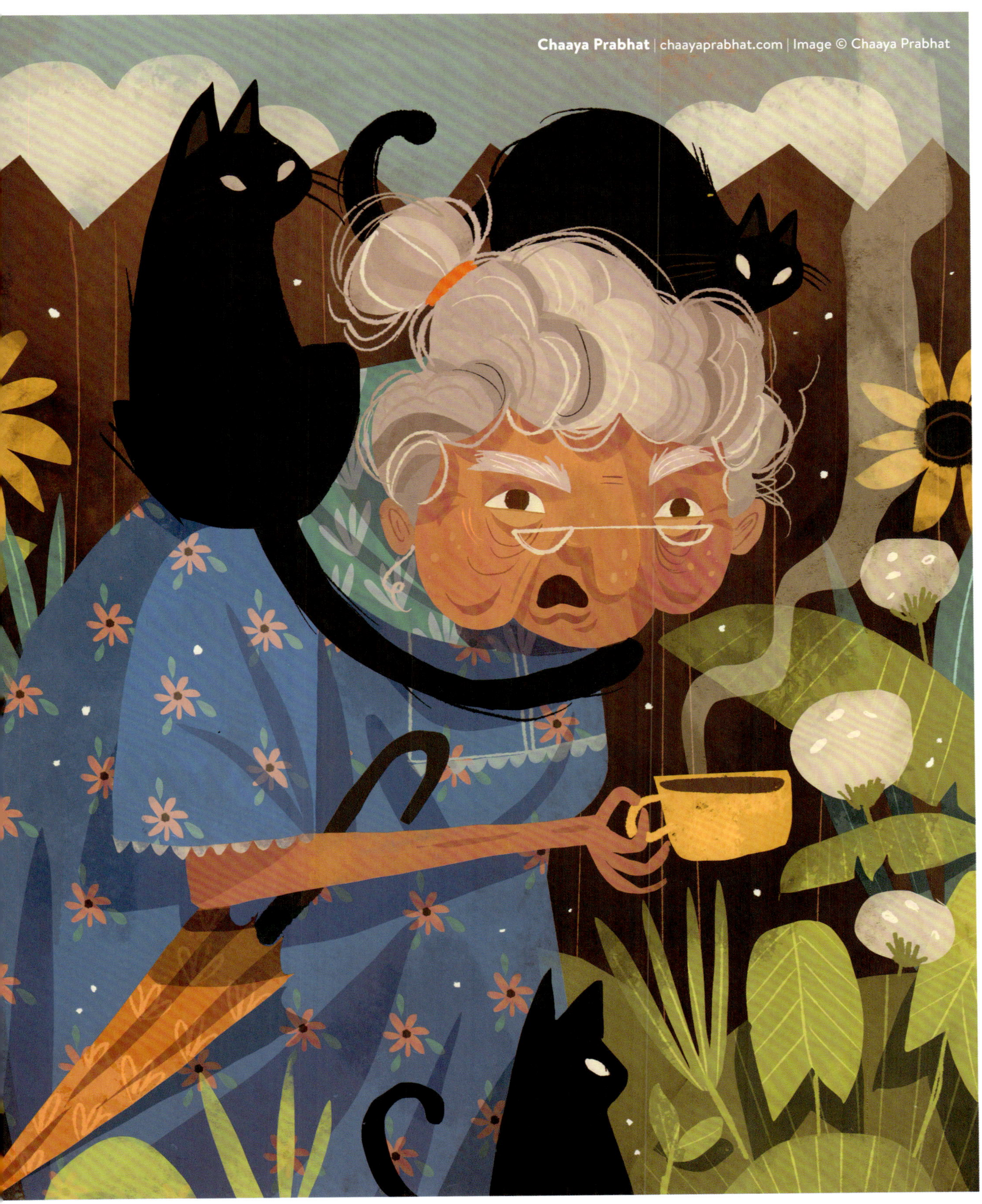
Chaaya Prabhat | chaayaprabhat.com | Image © Chaaya Prabhat

CHARACTERIZE THIS:

MOON, HAIR

ISAAC JADRAQUE

In this article I will explain the process I have followed designing a character from the following prompts: hair and moon. From the start, I looked for inspiration from classic characters, such as the werewolf, and in stories associated with the mysticism of the moon. All the work was completed digitally, specifically in Photoshop and Procreate. Join me on this short, but intense, journey.

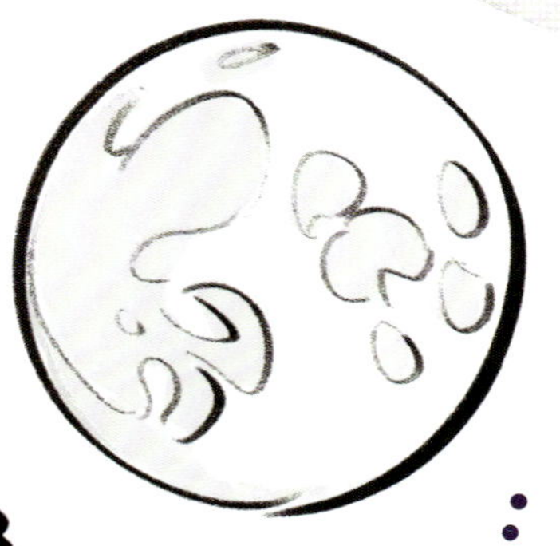
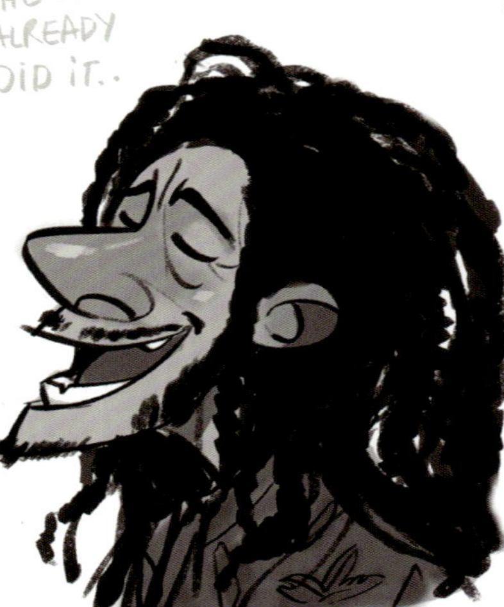

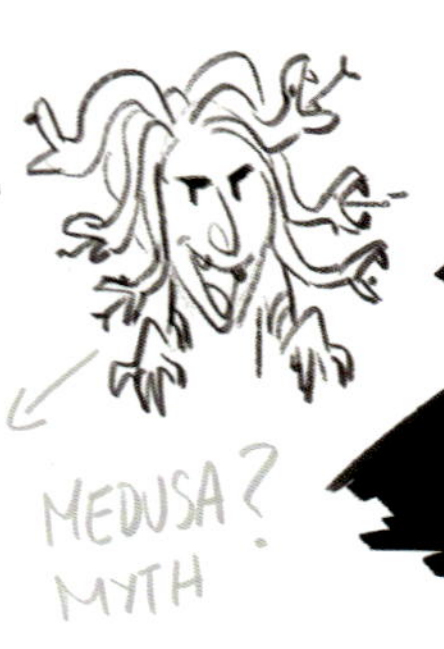

IDEAS, COME TO ME!

To start it's good to draw or write what ideas, concepts, and associations come to mind. I liked the idea of a beard "coming to life," so I needed to draw a character with a very long beard, to give me room to play with this concept.

LET IT BREATHE

When you get stuck with an idea or design, stop looking at it for a while. Get up, go for a walk, have a drink, or even save it for the next day if you have time!

WHAT DO YOU WANT TO SAY?

Look for the pose that best tells the story or situation of the character at a particular moment. Pay attention to making sure the silhouette is clear and readable.

FIND YOUR WORKFLOW

Not all designers follow the same steps, or in the same order. Find a workflow that combines creativity and efficiency, and suits you.

CHOOSE A PATH AND WALK IT

Once you have a rough idea of the type of character you want to draw, try making a few different versions. The more varied in shape, size, and proportions, the better!

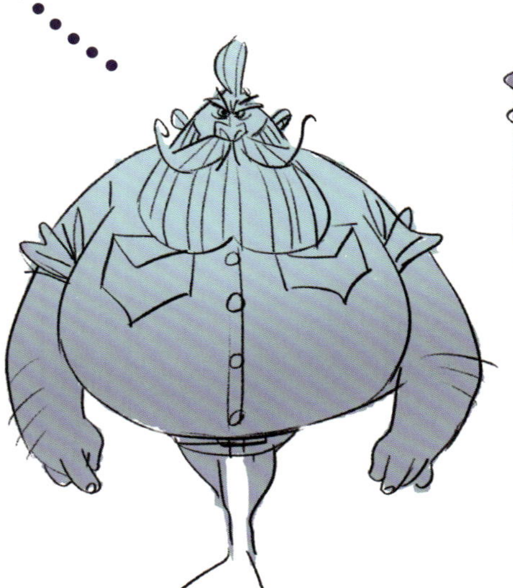

All images © Isaac Jadraque

GETTING TO KNOW YOU

Even if you aren't going to animate your character, I recommend you draw a front and profile view, to get a general idea of the volume. You don't need to do a full turnaround, these two angles should suffice.

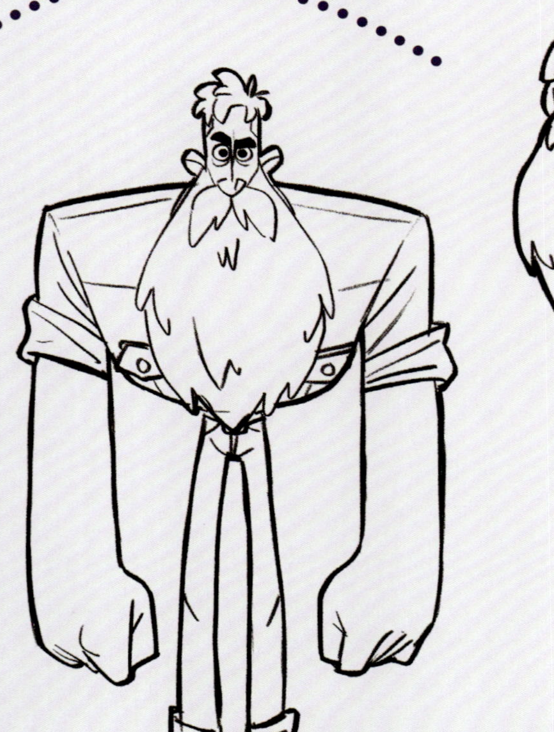

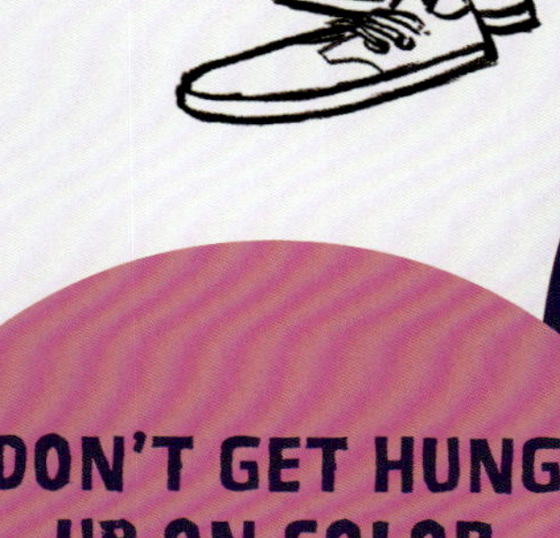

DON'T GET HUNG UP ON COLOR

There are great designers who rarely put color in their designs (e.g. Carter Goodrich). In character design, although color can sometimes be key to a brief, it is more important to focus on the rhythm, silhouette, and emotions of the character.

WHAT'S YOUR STORY?

Whenever you can, try to add more detail to the character's backstory. I wanted to do some scenes and expressions that would show what it would be like to fight with your own beard. I think this could lead to some funny situations!

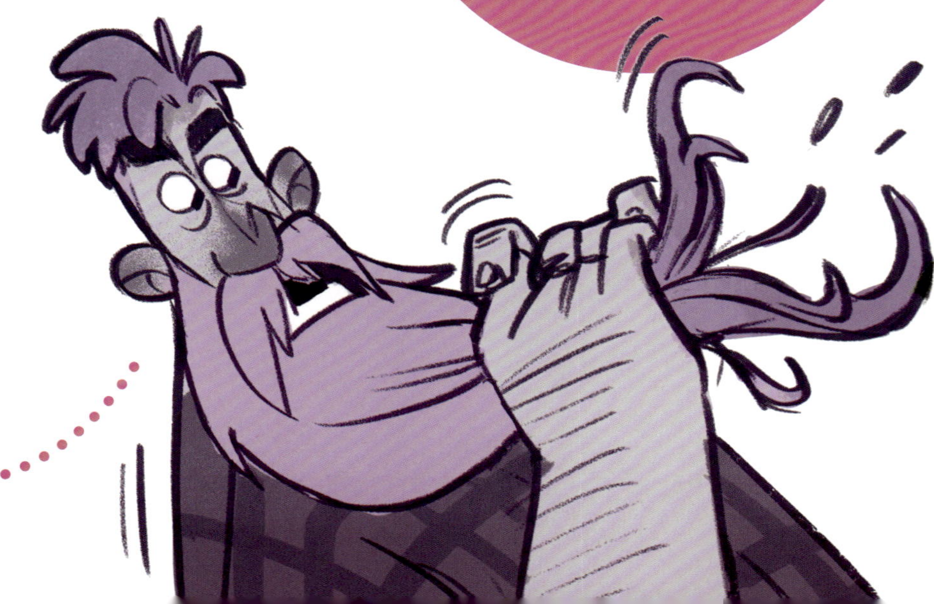

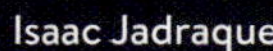

A HAIR-RAISING FINALE

For the final design I usually try for a fairly organic look, half
between sketch and a highly polished finish. I add some textu
and backlighting, and the Hipster Monster takes flight!

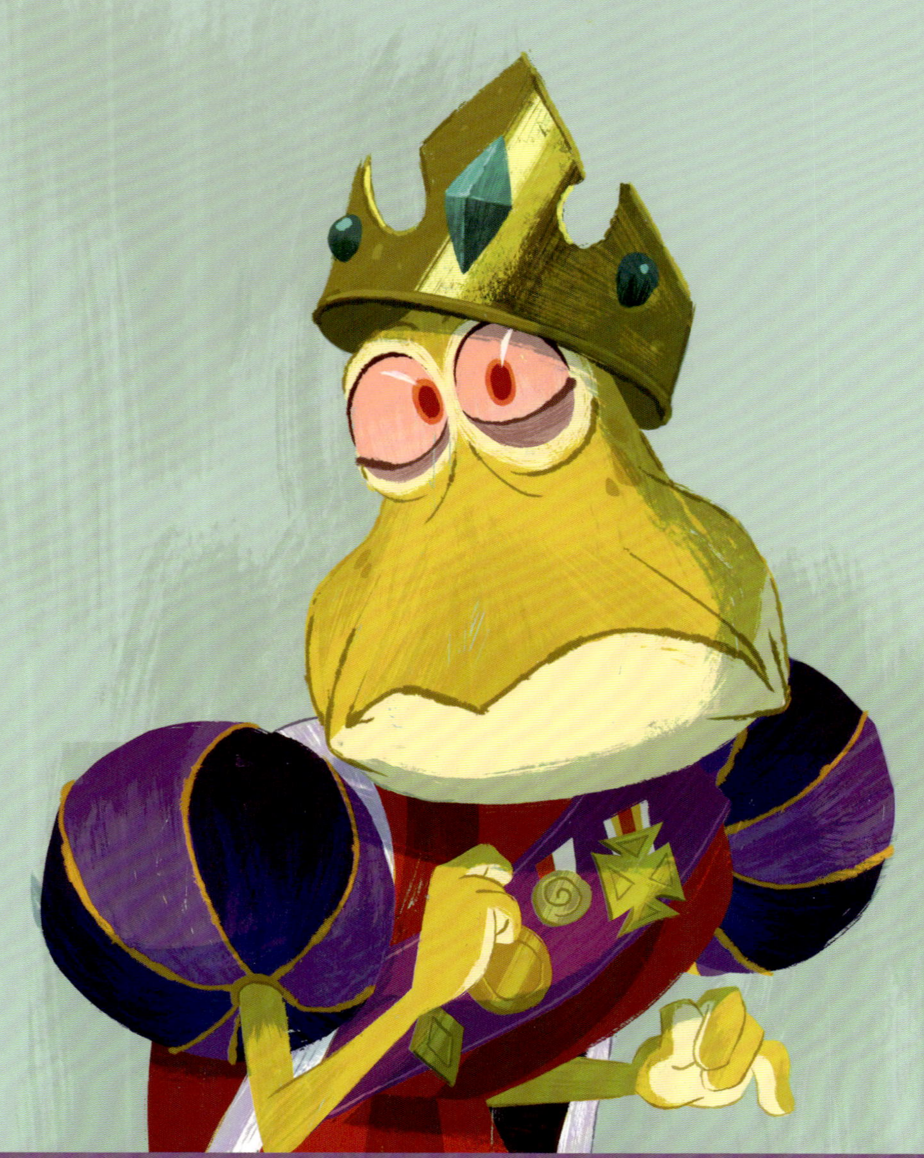

HOPPING OFF THE PAGE

JUSTIN RUNFOLA

I love character design and I love a challenge, so when the opportunity came along to tackle a *CDQ* tutorial I jumped at the chance. I will be leading you through my process of creating an interesting and engaging design from the prompt "jumpy, yellow, leader." Although there are many ways to arrive at a final design, I'll share my specific thought process, sketch habits, and problem-solving ideas. Along the way I will be address some key processes I use when creating a unique, engaging, and successful design. I will encourage the freedom to use your imagination, and to develop ideas and references we discover throughout.

Final image © Justin Runfola

AN IDEA SPAWNS!

I play the three words over in my mind and think about what I might want to do. The most prominent idea that comes to mind is some kind of frog royalty. With any initial thought that comes to mind I first ask myself, "Will I get bored of this?" to make sure I end up working on something that is a fun challenge for me. The whimsy and playfulness I can imagine, associated with a royal frog with a "yellow" streak, peaks my interest enough to move forward and sketch out my first thoughts.

This page: In my initial sketches the image that starts to form resembles a frog prince

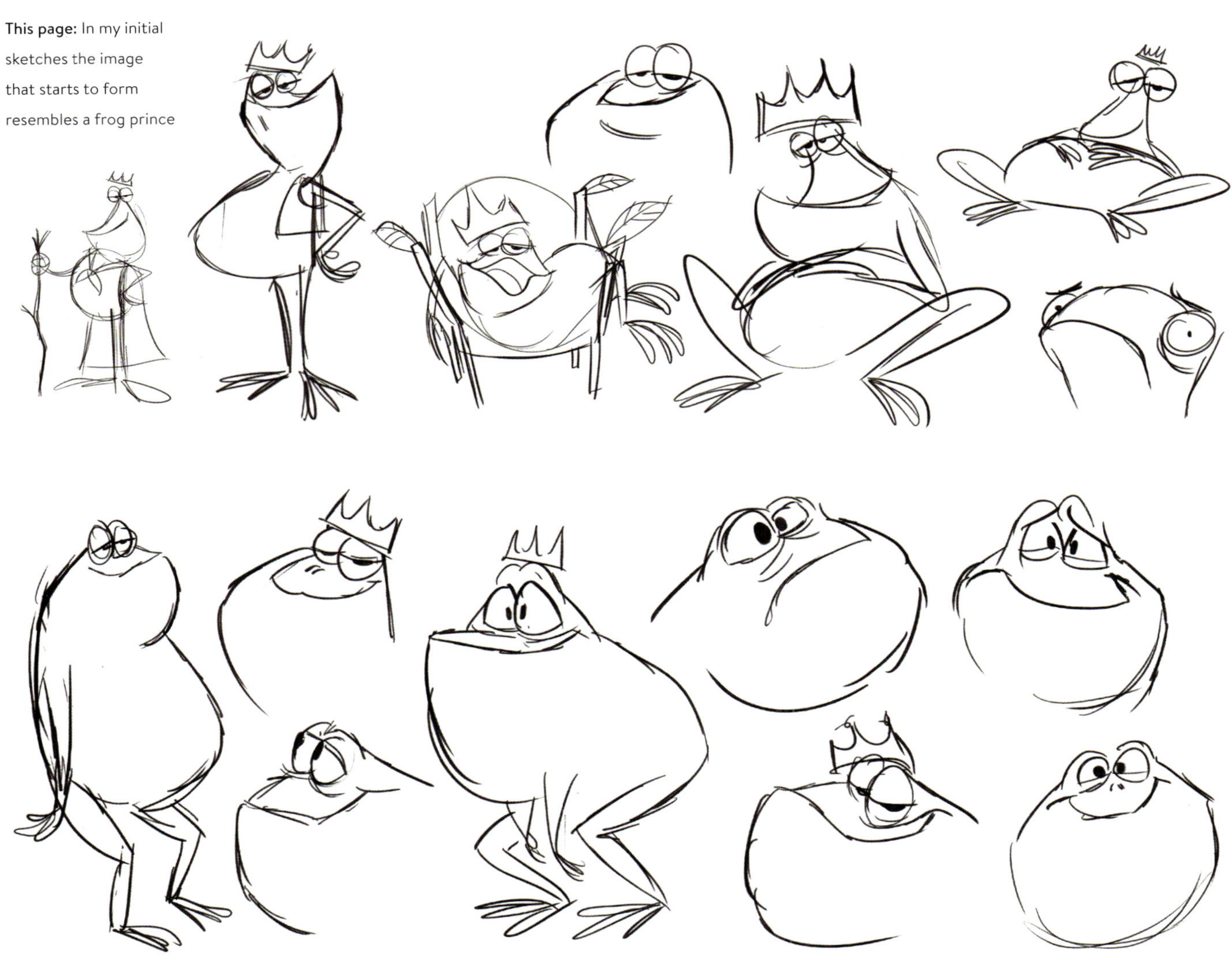

FROM SMALL BEGINNINGS

I've settled on a subject to draw so now it's time to let my imagination run wild, putting any and all ideas onto the page. These ideas are coming straight from my imagination, I don't yet have any rules or constraints to apply and so I'm free to experiment and see what shapes, styles, and lines may or may not work, through trial and error. As I work through various expressions and poses, a story about the character starts to emerge.

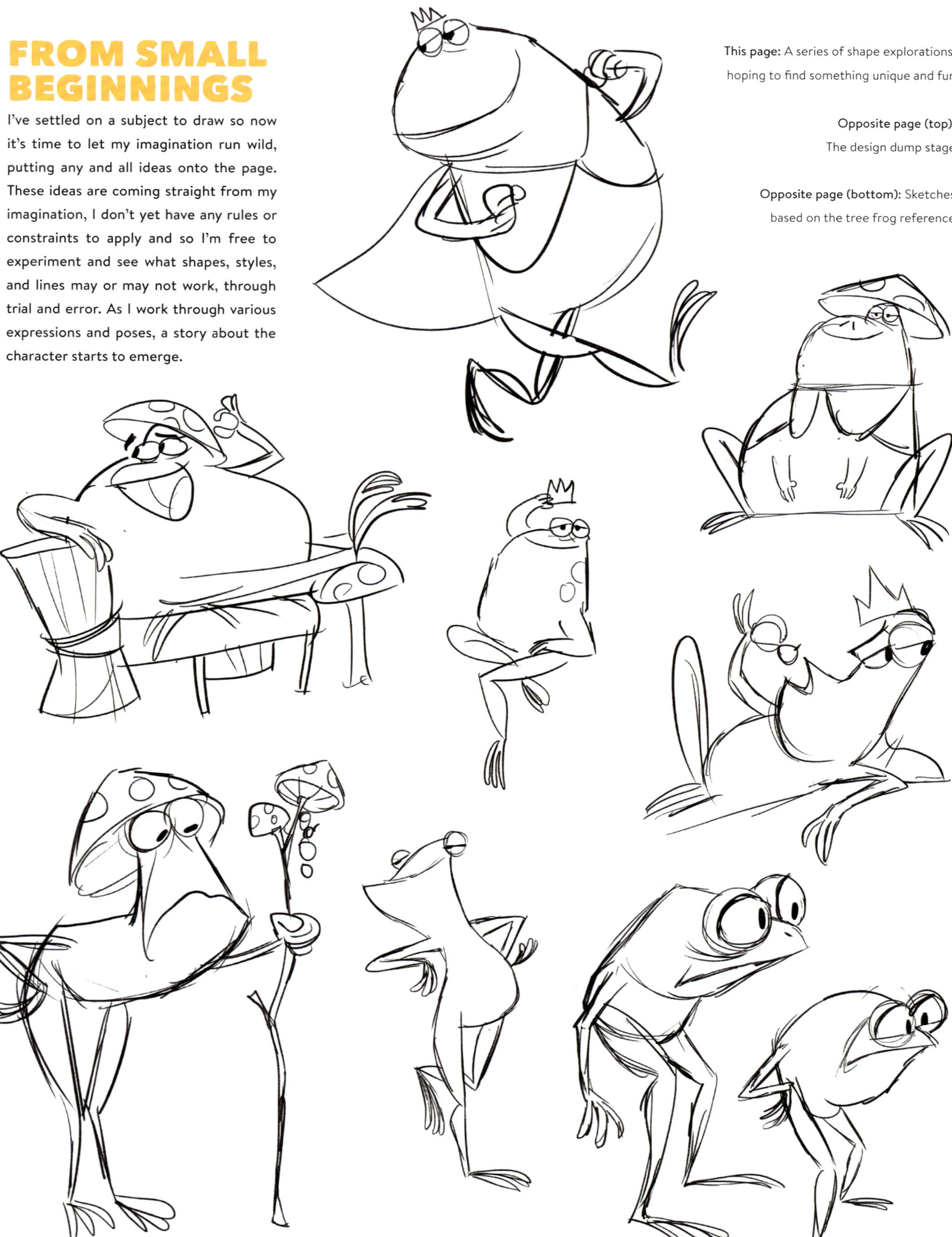

This page: A series of shape explorations, hoping to find something unique and fun

Opposite page (top): The design dump stage

Opposite page (bottom): Sketches based on the tree frog reference

THE DESIGN DUMP

Once I'm given a direction, I pick up my pencil and get started on what I call the design dump! I start with very basic, crude doodles of what I think the character could look like. While the final design may vary wildly from these original ideas, having them down on paper can be really useful and sometimes I will end up circling back around to an early, discarded design.

Getting this design dump out at the start of the process is key, as at this point my designs are raw and uninfluenced by any outside references or more developed ideas. The raw stage in a character's lifespan can reveal some gems that I can pull out later on if things get tricky. I like to complete the design dump with papers, pens, crayons, pencils, markers, and highlighters — anything I can just grab and go wild with while trying to wrangle my ideas!

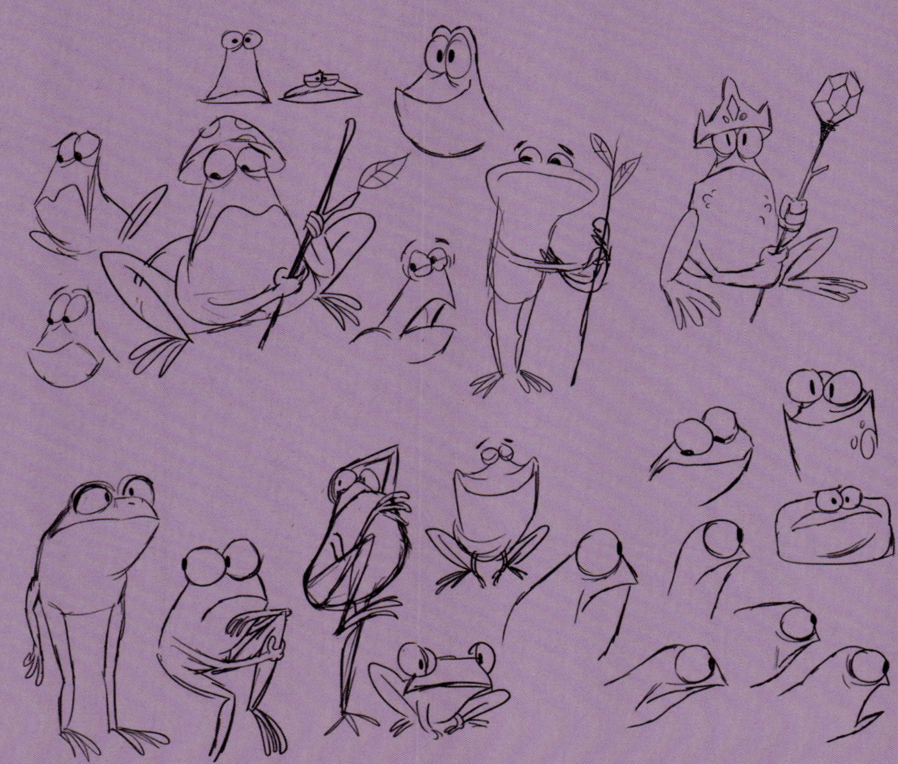

ONE GIANT LEAP

After my initial exploration, I now want to see which of the shapes and expressions I discovered in the last step will work best with the original prompt. I pull references for different kinds of frogs and settle on drawing a tree frog, as they are small, jumpy, frail, and come in all different colors. I start sketching and asking myself questions about the character: How old is he? How did he become a royalty? Is he a good leader? Does he have a crown or a sceptre, and what are they made of?

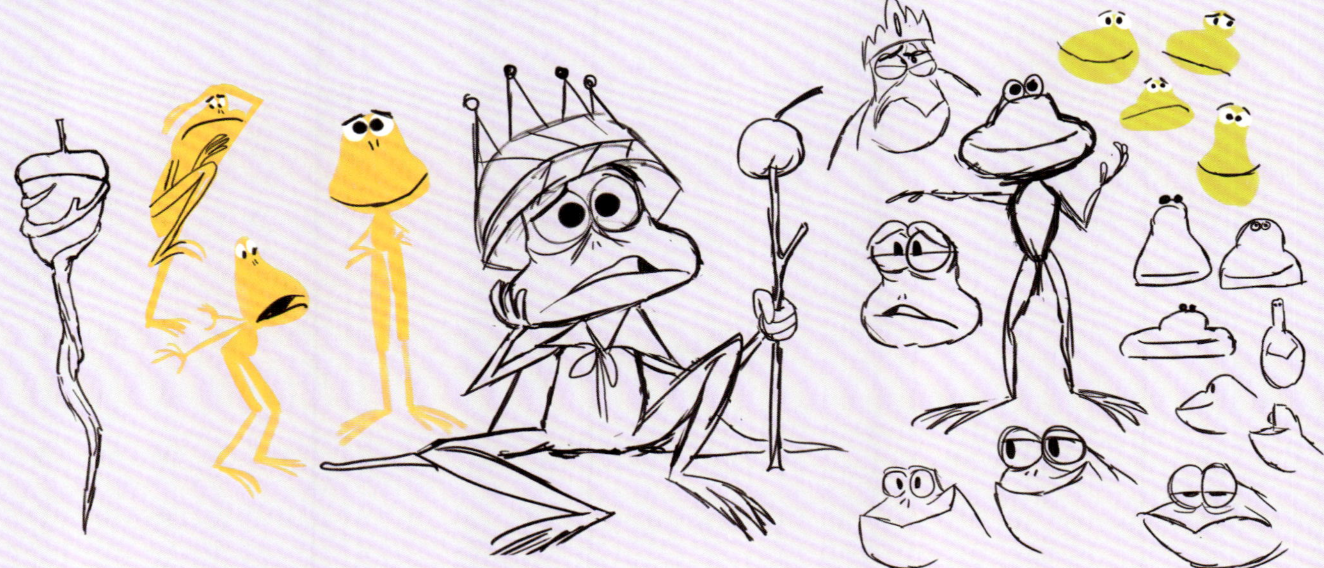

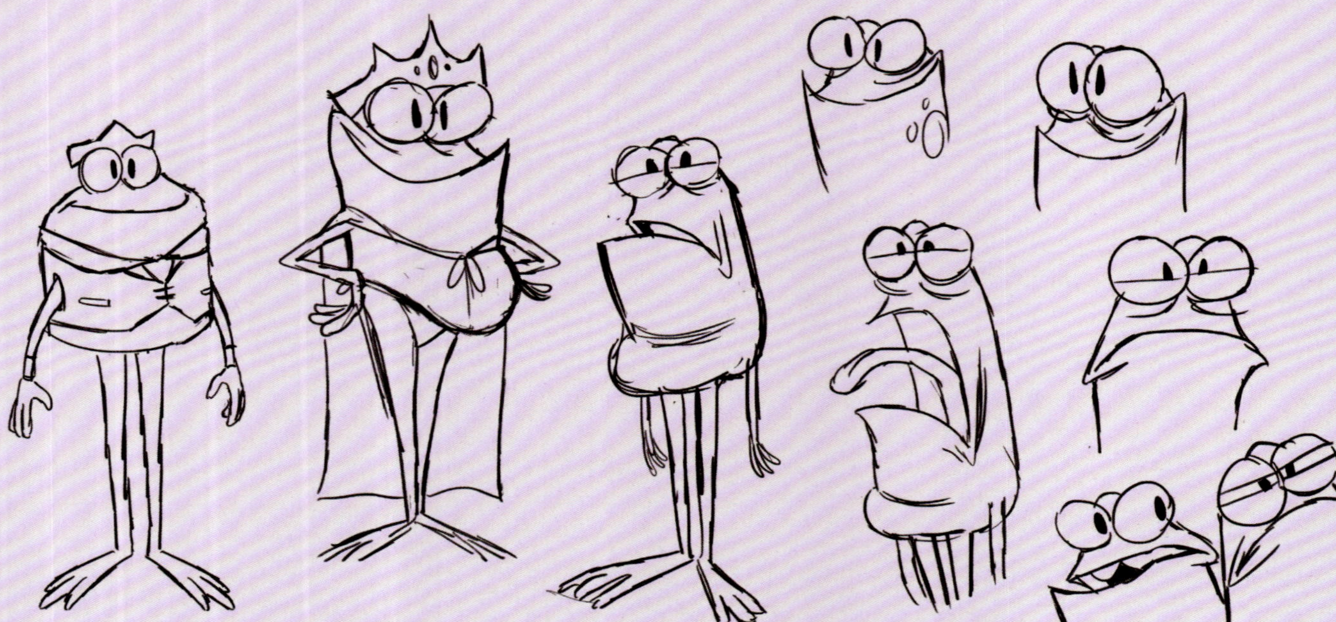

A FROGGY FAIRY TALE

The most important questions for me at this stage are: what is my character thinking, and why does he feel that way? If I can answer these questions at this early stage, then I find the physical characteristics of my design will come naturally. For most projects I would usually get a script and the answer to these questions would be found in the text, but when developing a character on my own it's helpful (and fun!) to create a back-story.

Here's what I come up with: Once upon a time there was a frog king beloved by all who had a son, our character, the young frog prince.

Unfortunately, the king dies tragically at the hands of vicious intruders. While fleeing from these attackers, the young prince accidentally vanquishes his foes, but the tribe only see his actions as deliberate and heroic, and crown him as their new king. Too afraid to let his subjects down, the young prince accepts his new title, but privately worries one day he may be forced to prove himself and be exposed as the coward he believes himself to be.

This page: Early sketches, now that my story is in place, of the young frog prince

Opposite page: Early costume explorations from my interests and research

IMAGINATION BEFORE REFERENCES!

As a character designer, reference material is a key part of the creative process, but I also make sure to spend a day or so drawing from my own imagination before I look at any references. To me, this is important because sometimes references can influence my creative flow. I don't want to get hung up on trying to copy specific anatomy from reference material — that can come later once I have the basic shapes and an idea of what direction I want the design to take.

THE PRINCE'S NEW CLOTHES

It's up to me what sort of world I'm going to create — is it going to be realistic or fun and cartoony? I opt for the latter and run with the idea. I try an obvious costume idea first, a fisherman's outfit, just to get it out of my system. I want my character to look more fun, even ridiculous and silly. I gather references for 15-17th Century European royalty, and explore using puffy sleeves, feathers, capes, and jewels to make the frog prince look over-dressed and uncomfortable. I get to a point where the look matches the way I want the character to be portrayed.

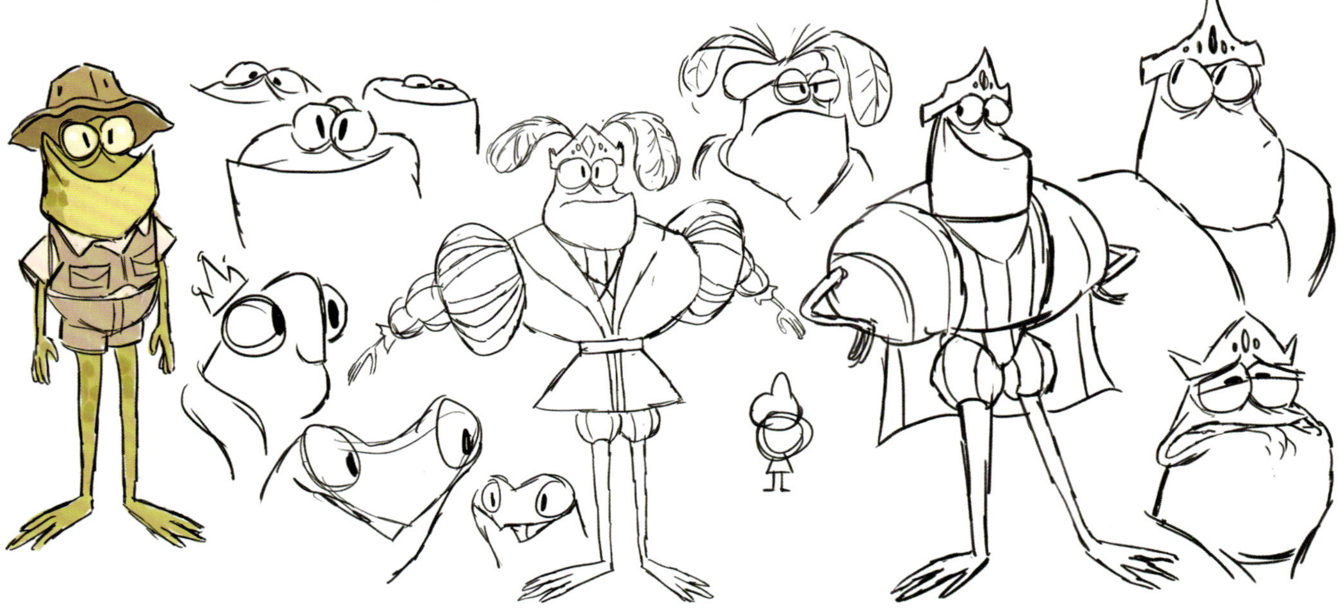

> ## "I GET TO A POINT WHERE THE LOOK MATCHES THE WAY I WANT THE CHARACTER TO BE PORTRAYED"

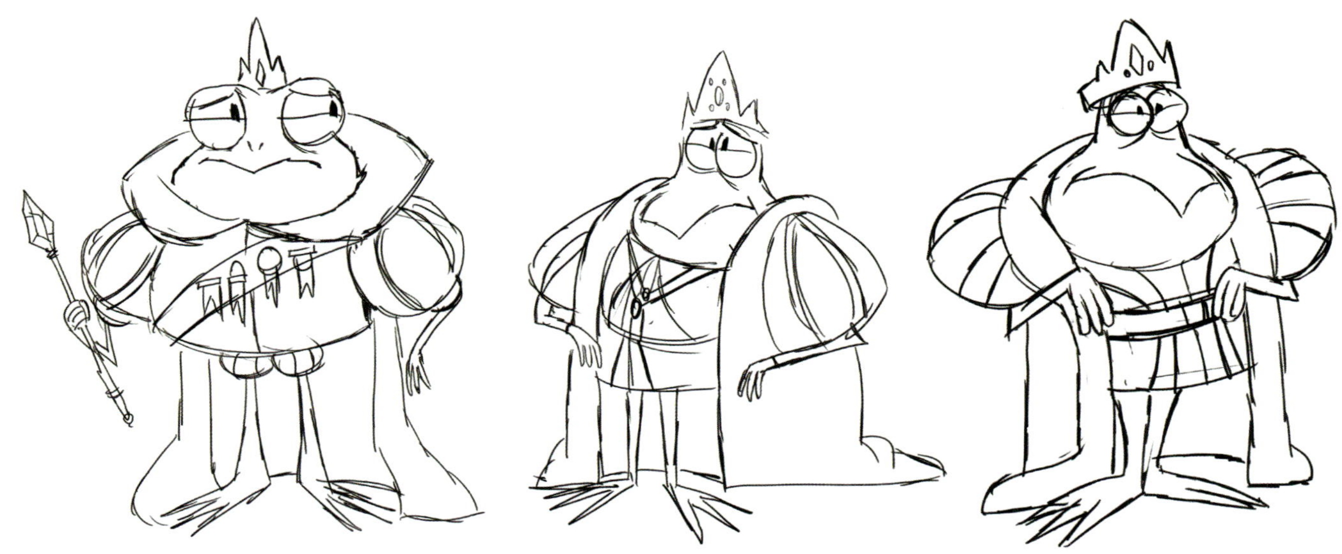

HOW TALL IS TOO TALL?

At this point I have some costumes and shapes that I like, but as I am drawing the prince he keeps getting taller and taller! I want to stay faithful to the character as inspired by the words "jumpy" and "yellow," and although frogs have long legs I feel a character like this shouldn't be portrayed as tall. I choose to prioritize personality over the "correct" anatomy of a frog. In the same way a deleted scene in a film might be great in isolation but doesn't help the overall flow of the story, certain aspects of design might look cool but detract from the overall concept.

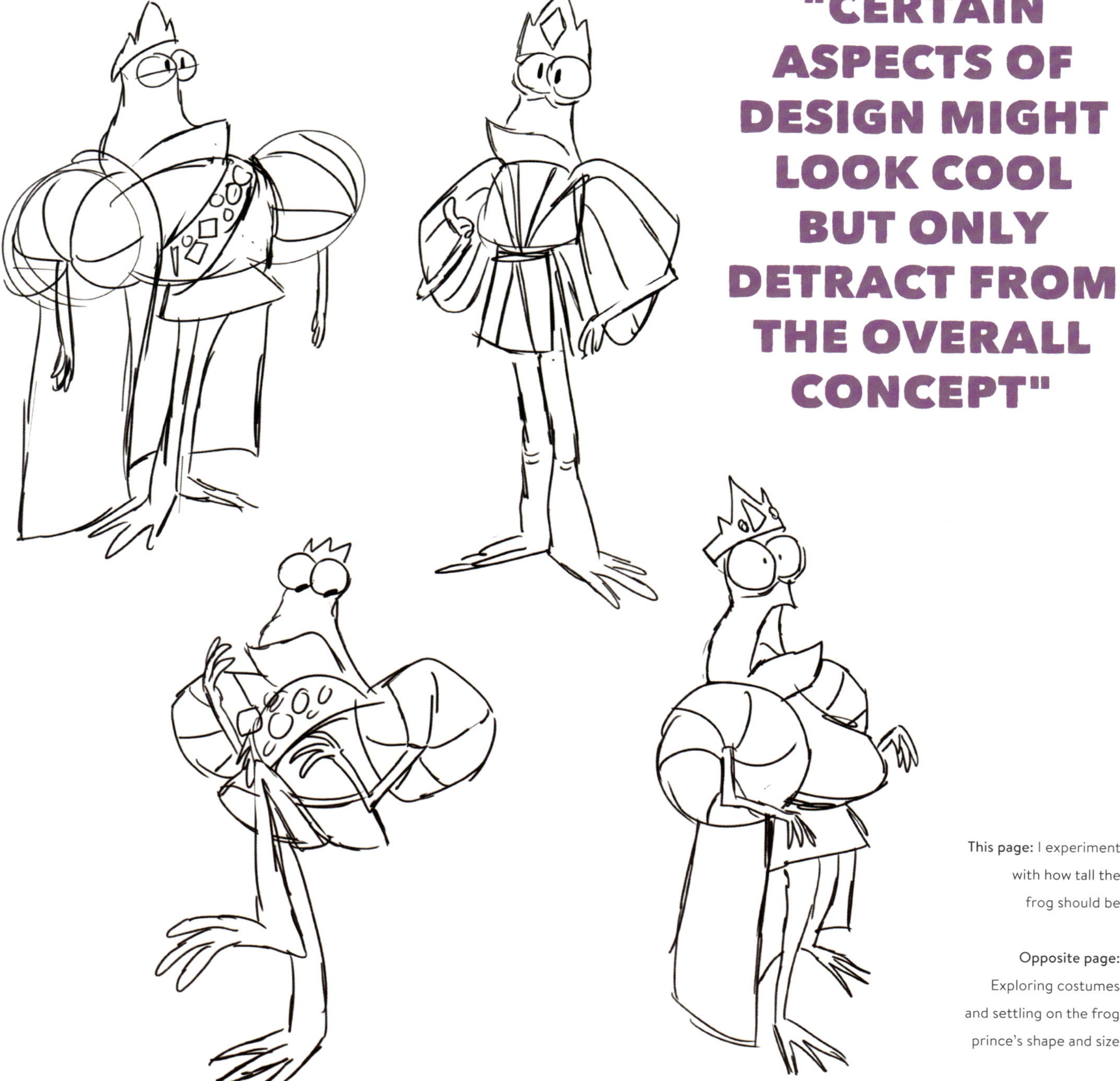

"CERTAIN ASPECTS OF DESIGN MIGHT LOOK COOL BUT ONLY DETRACT FROM THE OVERALL CONCEPT"

This page: I experiment with how tall the frog should be

Opposite page: Exploring costumes and settling on the frog prince's shape and size

FINAL FITTING FOR PRINCE FROG

Up until this point I've been working on the general development of my idea — now it's time to get into specifics and answer the final questions that come naturally from the push and pull of ideas. I'm asking myself how I can keep my character looking like a frog while also clothing him as an overdressed prince. I nail down the details in his crown and his outfit, and refine the shape and size of his body. This is the last step in creating his overall look — from here on I will be exploring how his final form will move and act within an environment.

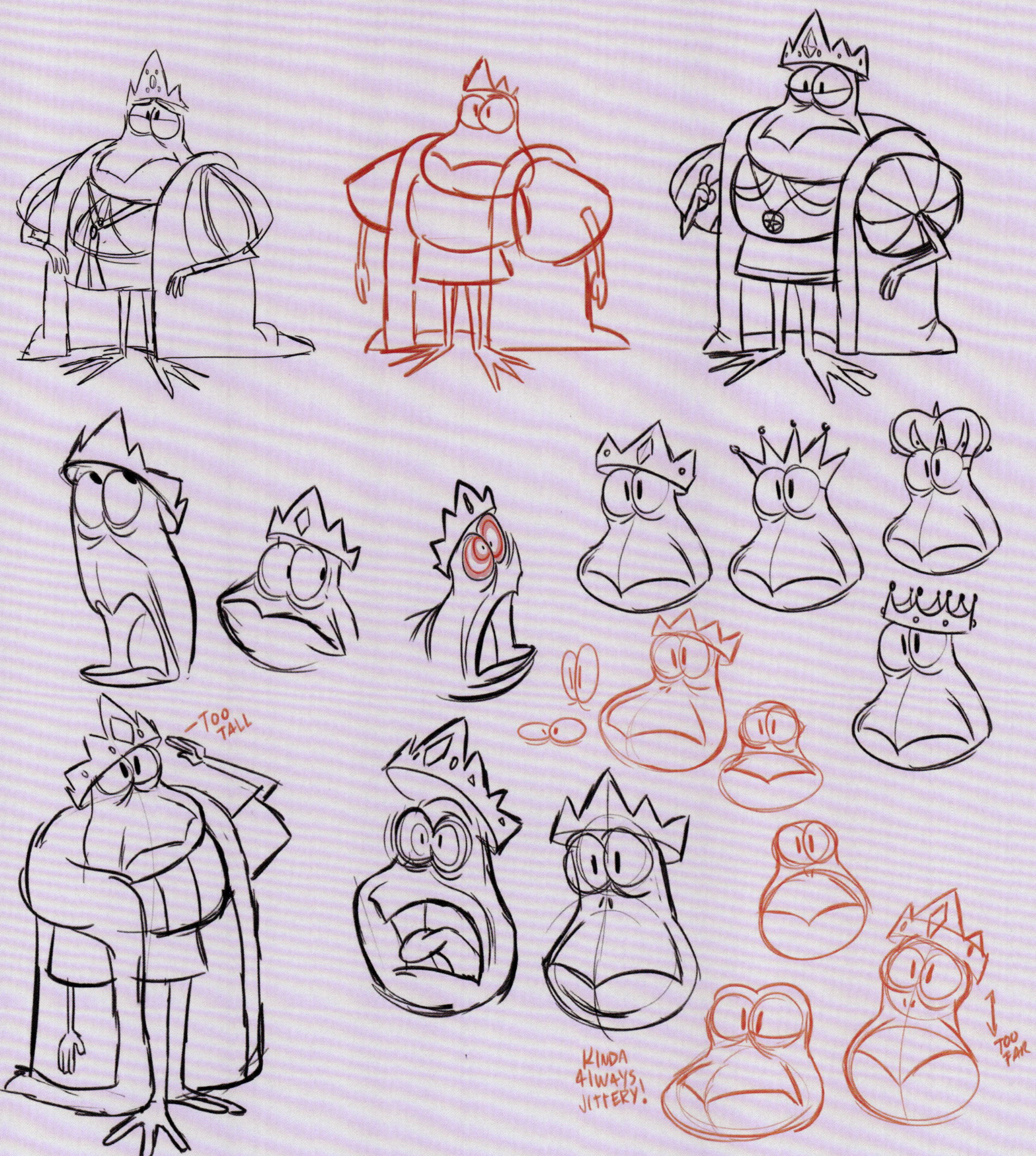

PURPLE REIGN

This step in my process is usually optional, but sometimes I want to do a few more sketches, squashing and stretching the design to see what works best. I start to explore color based on the costume and frog references that I had previously pulled. Purple symbolizes royalty and luckily for me it's also my favorite color! I also need to find a shade of yellow that suits the prince aesthetically but also conveys the "yellow" personality trait.

"PURPLE SYMBOLIZES ROYALTY AND LUCKILY FOR ME IT'S ALSO MY FAVORITE COLOR!"

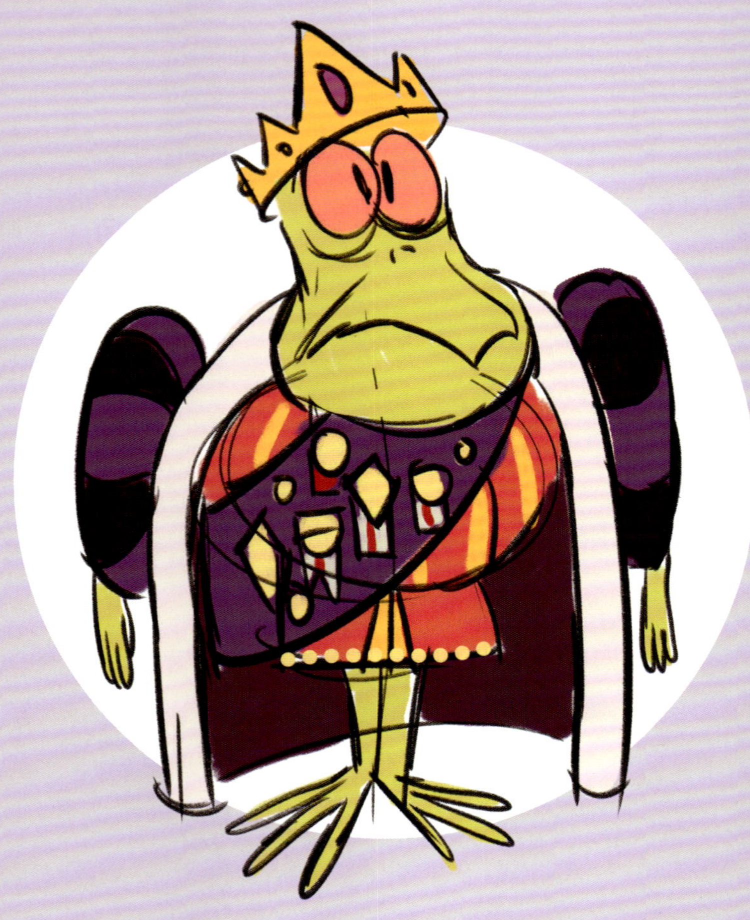

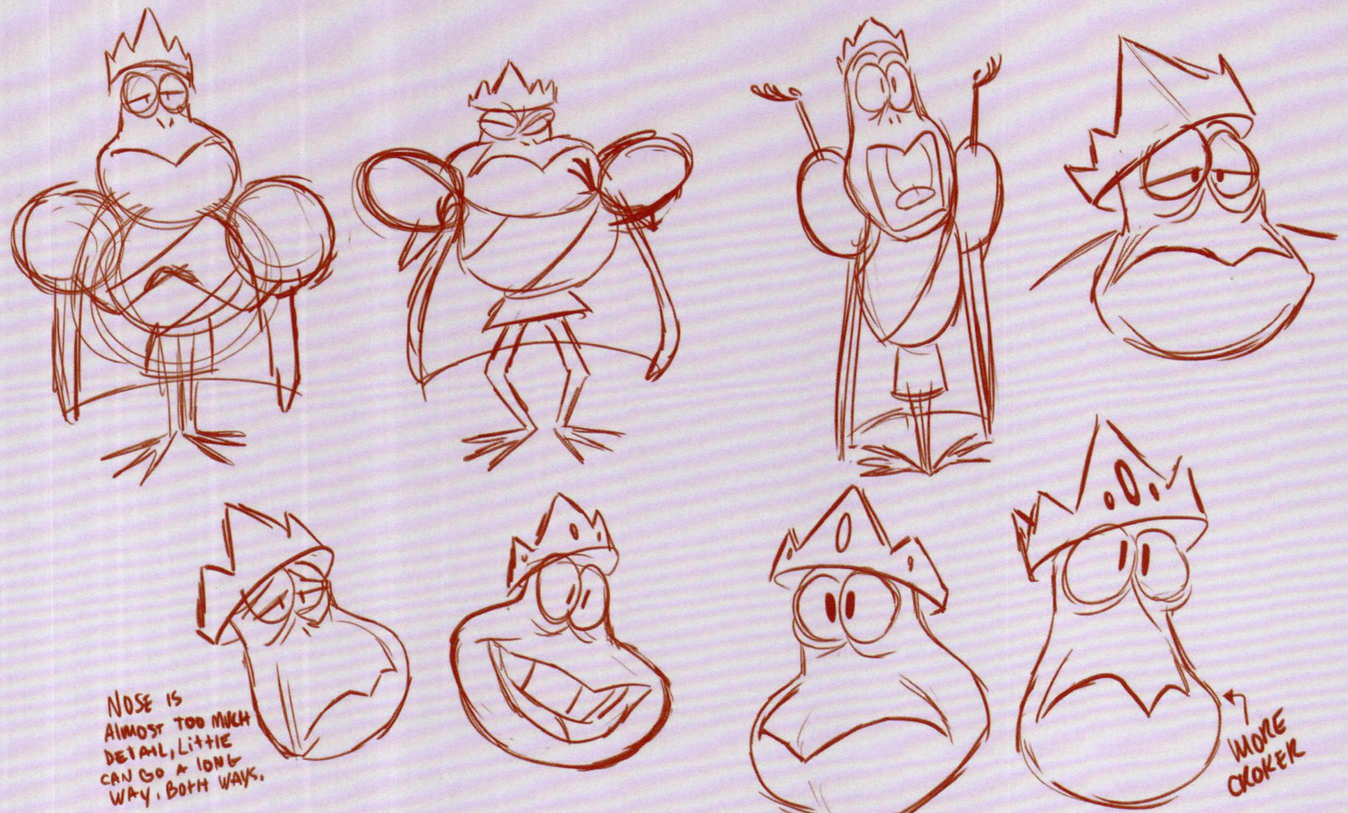

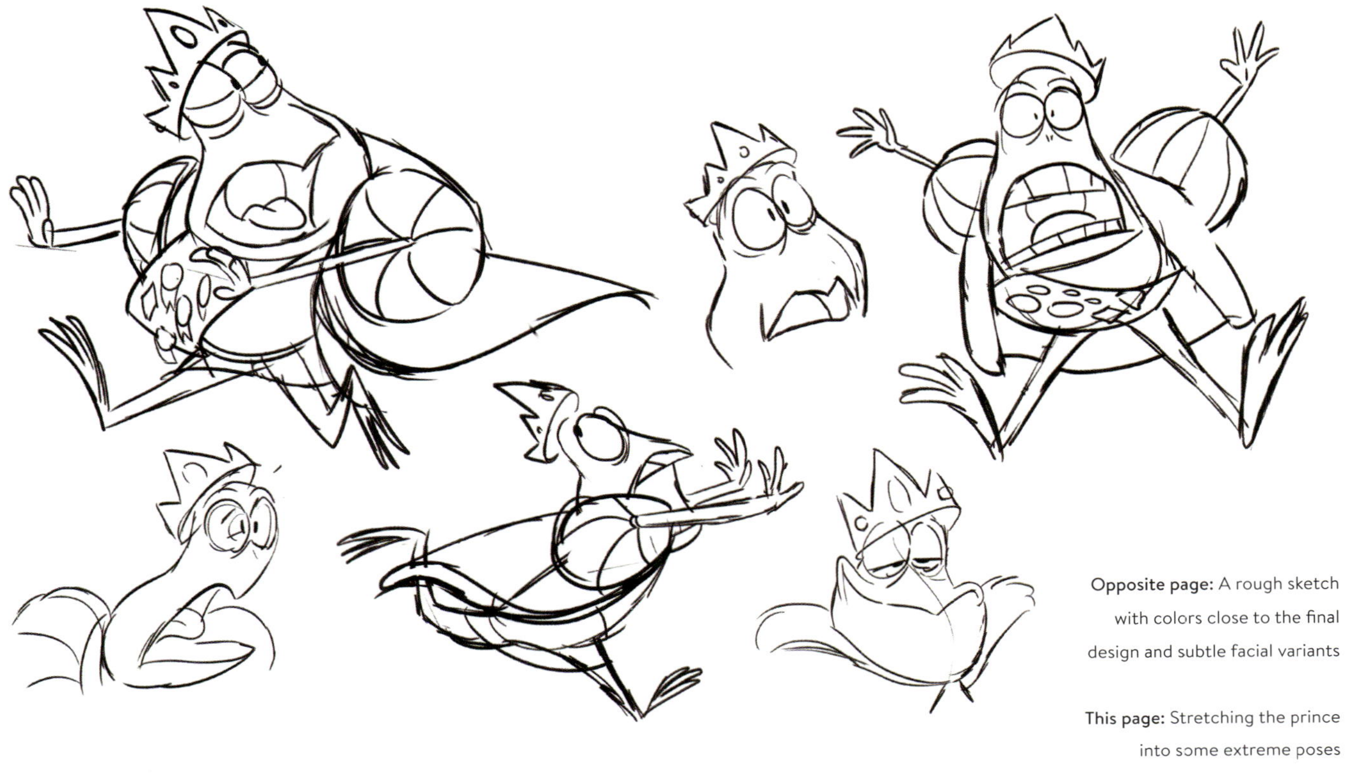

Opposite page: A rough sketch with colors close to the final design and subtle facial variants

This page: Stretching the prince into some extreme poses

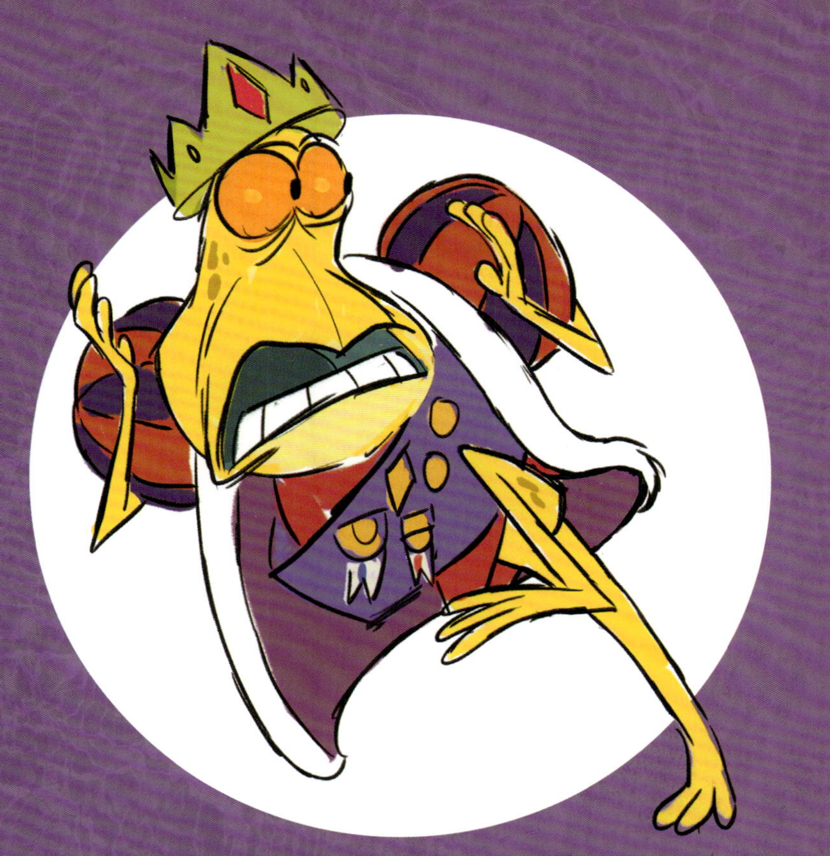

IF THE CROWN FITS...

Now that I'm getting close to a final design I start working my frog into some extreme poses, pushing the limits of the character's look. While drawing these wilder designs I'm looking for tangents and if the anatomy remains correct, discovering how my frog prince can and can't move. — even though I've created a cartoony character it still needs a solid structure that is built to be active. I decide that the puffy sleeves suit the frog's personality more than the flatter alternative and lock those in, and then play with the design of the crown. I find that if it sits uneven and oversized on the prince's head it helps convey to the audience his jumpy nature.

TO WEAR PANTS OR NOT TO WEAR PANTS?

I think I've settled on the design at this point, but I'm still playing with whether or not I want to make my frog more humanlike or accentuate the animal in him. It all boils down to one question — pants or no pants? I also experiment with drawing him in more animalistic poses, sitting squat as a frog would. I'm trying to find a pose that shows he's been a king for so long he's become bored and jaded. I'm also still trying to find a yellow that feels like just the right shade.

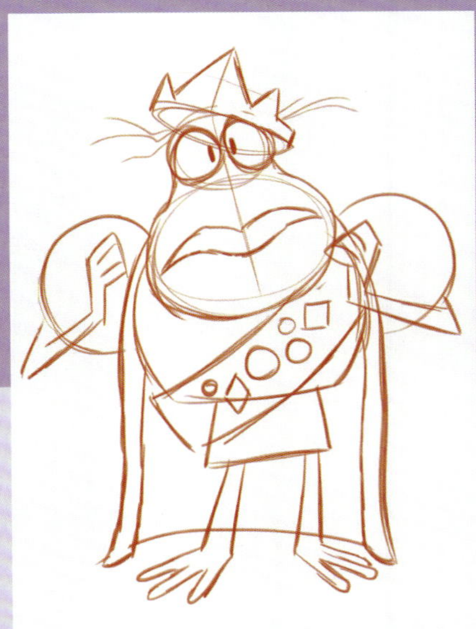
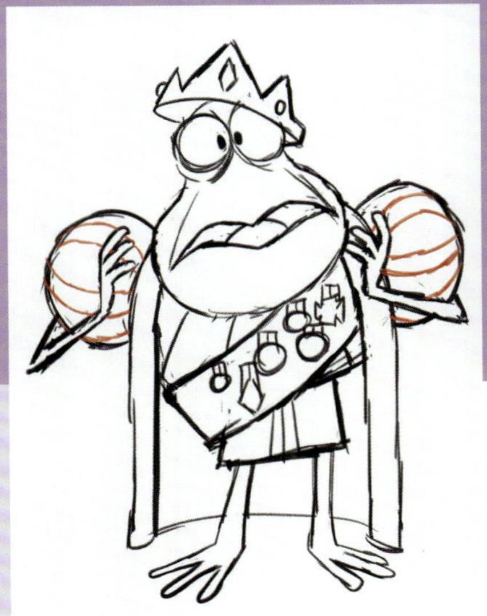
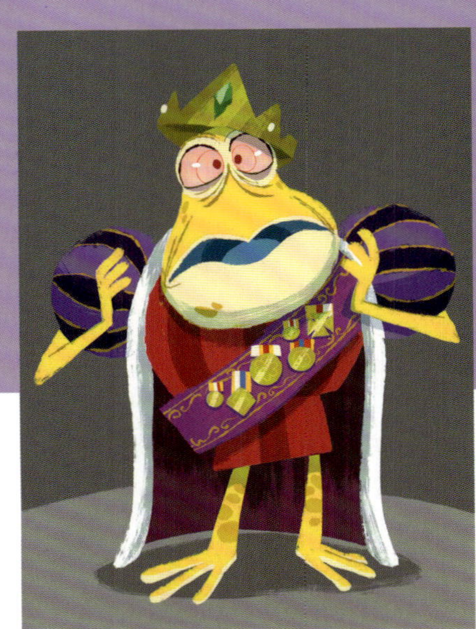

HOP THIS WAY

Finally, I have experimented and explored enough and commit to a design. First, I do a rough construction drawing of what the frog's arms will look like inside his clothing, forming basic shapes to build the character on top of. From that drawing I begin to block in the character, starting with the yellow color and then taking the elements I liked best from the color roughs, and applying them to the painting. These early drawings are where I will try detail that may end up being too much for the final design — for example, the metals on his royal sash, the embroidery on his puffy sleeves, and the spots on his skin. These are the sorts of things I will experiment with when doing a color rough and ask myself "How much is too much?" It's good to see how far you can push a design, but know when to pull back for the sake of clarity.

A FROG'S LIFE

With the design finished, it's time to move on to acting class! I'm pleased with how my frog prince is looking — I love the puffy sleeves and the oversized crown! Now, I need to actively portray the brief, "jumpy, yellow, leader." By creating poses that act like freeze frames from different moments in the character's story, I can see how all the elements are coming together. Usually, I will do a handful of these drawings and do my best to provide the directors and animators with as much information as they will need to bring the character to life.

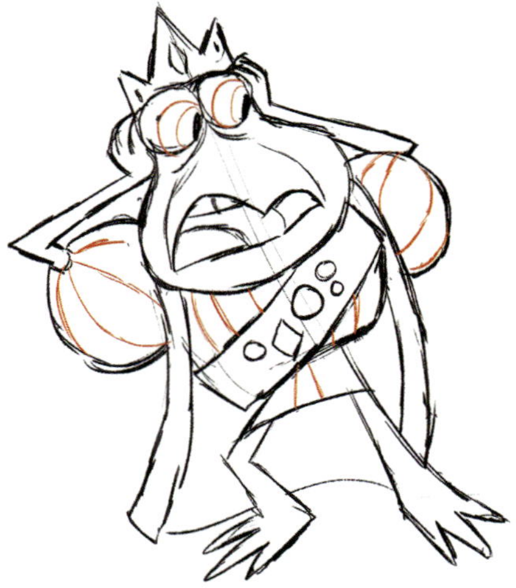

Opposite page:
Positioning the frog as sleepy and bored says lots about his character

This page (top):
Adding finer detail to the frog prince

This page (bottom):
Capturing the frog prince in motion

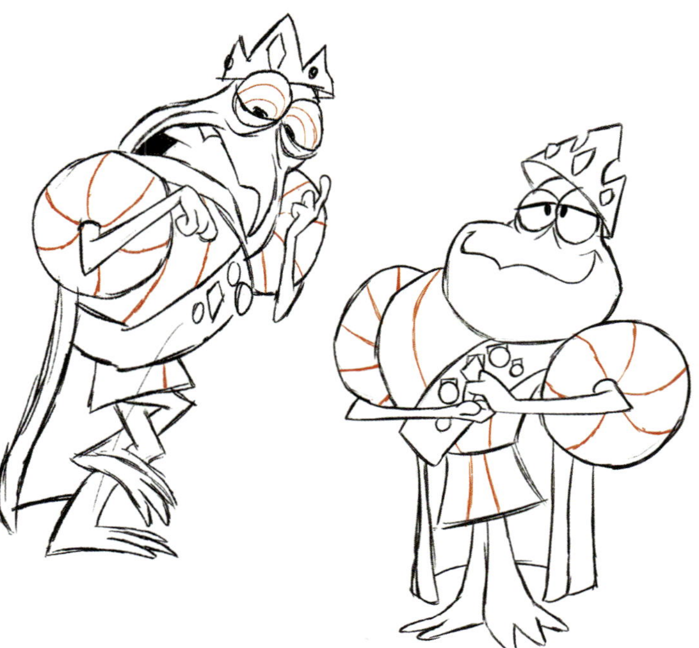

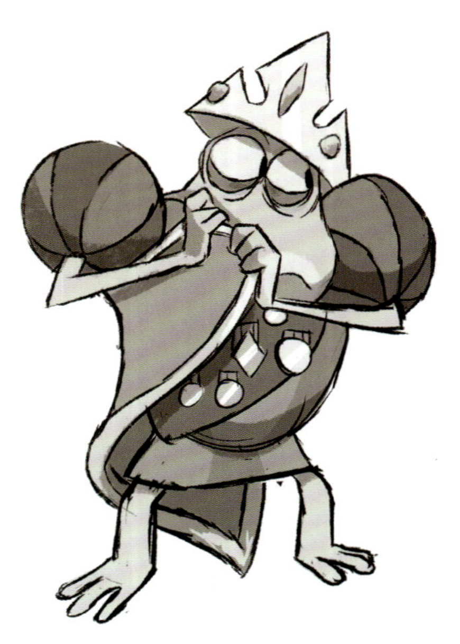

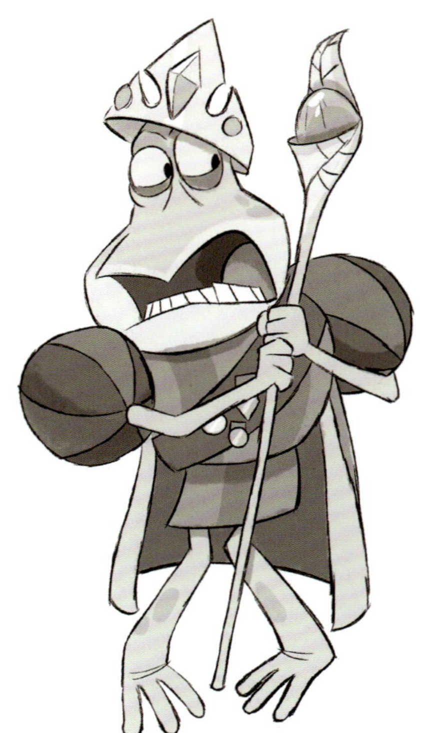

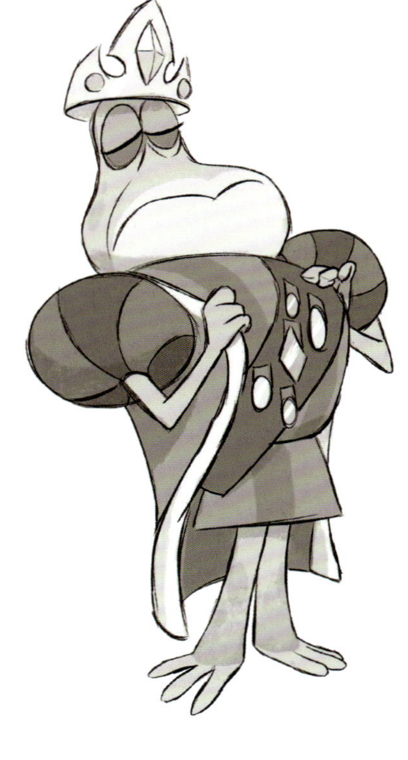

This page (top): Experimenting with the frog prince's personality

This page (bottom): Choosing the final pose

Opposite page: Final image © Justin Runfola

THE PRINCE BECOMES A KING

I continue to dive a little deeper into the frog's story with some more poses. I want to show him gradually assuming the role as king, but still feeling a bit like a fraud! Having this particular trait of his personality come through in the drawings is important to me and an important part of communicating how the design works in the context of the story. Continuing to iterate like this can feel redundant and excessive, but I find the more I draw, the more I discover.

UNCOMFORTABLE IN HIS OWN SKIN

Now I take everything that I've explored and considered throughout the process, and combine them to create a final design. I draw my frog with a staff to illustrate his royal position, but as I want to make sure his uncomfortable nature comes across, I decide his body language in this pose feels a bit too open. In the second sketch, I try a version of the frog that feels a bit more nervous and closed off, jumpy and scared. Here, he is actively protecting himself, flinching away from whatever is coming his way.

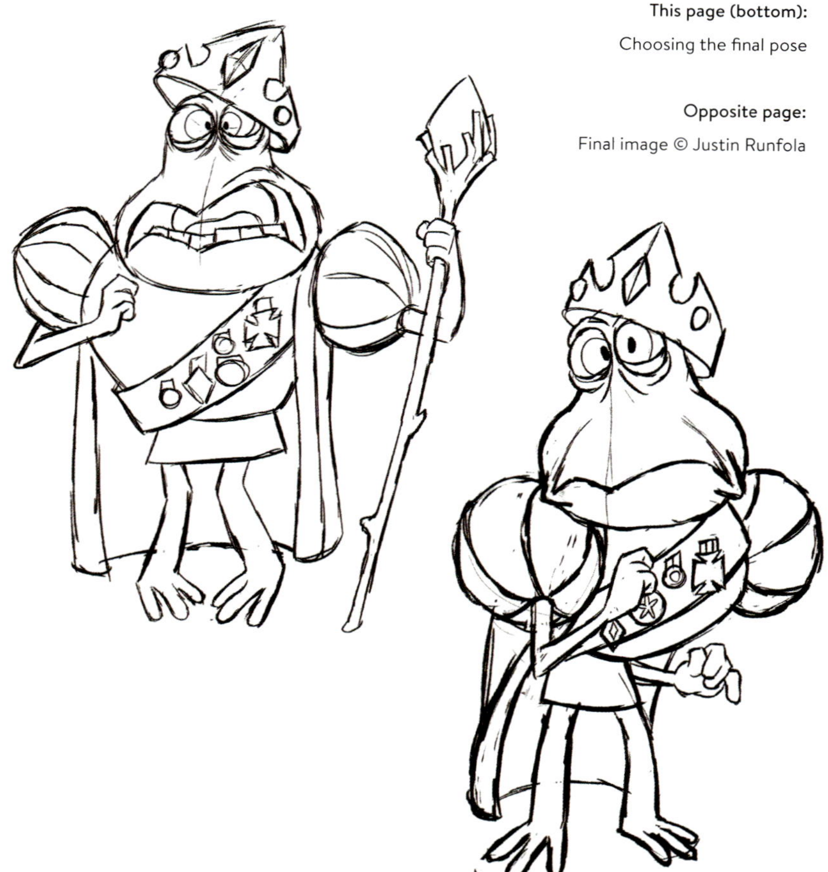

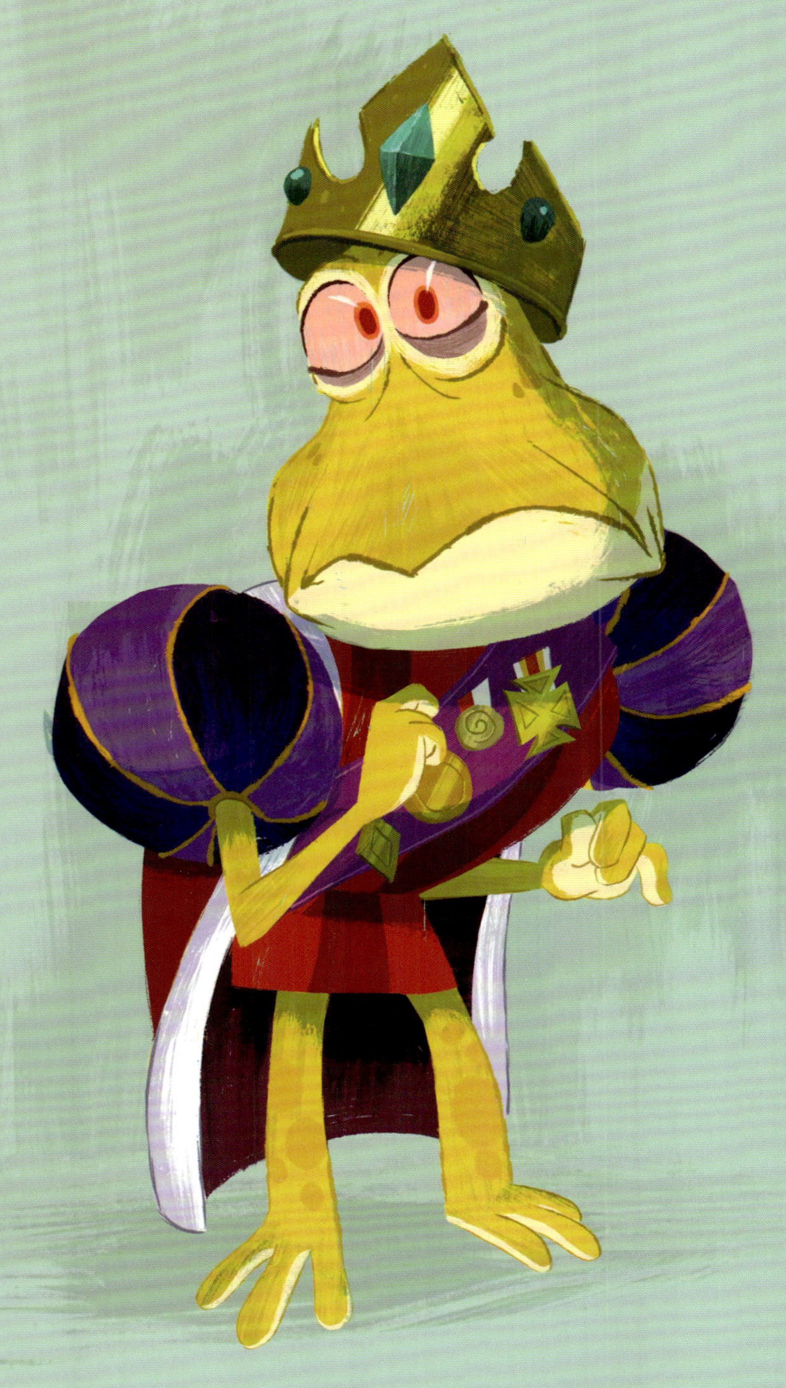

THE YELLOW-BELLIED FROG PRINCE

Of these final two sketches I decide that the nervous expression and hunched posture of the second design fits the jumpy character I have in mind. The yellow that I settled on does a good job of representing the frog prince's timid personality, while still showing his regal side and status as a leader. It was fun to work out the details of this character and design something that fit the original brief. In the end, I have a yellow-bellied frog prince who is ready to hop out of trouble's way!

CONTRIBUTORS

CHRIS ABLES

Freelance Illustrator & Visual
Development Artist

chrisablesart.com

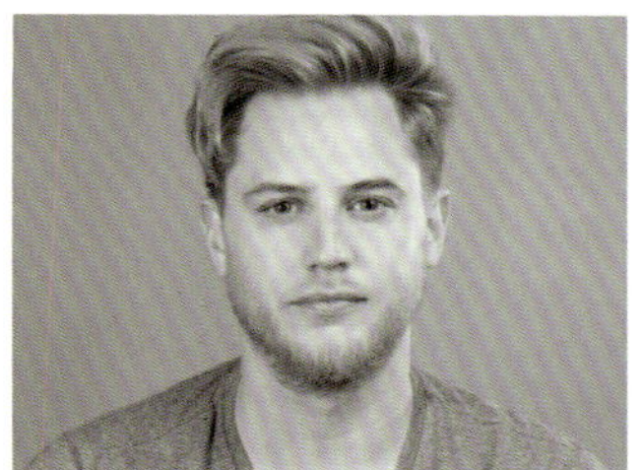

Chris is a professional illustrator and
artist with over 10 years experience
working in animation, film, television,
and publishing.

MELANY ALTUNA

Character Designer at Disney TVA

melanyaltuna.net

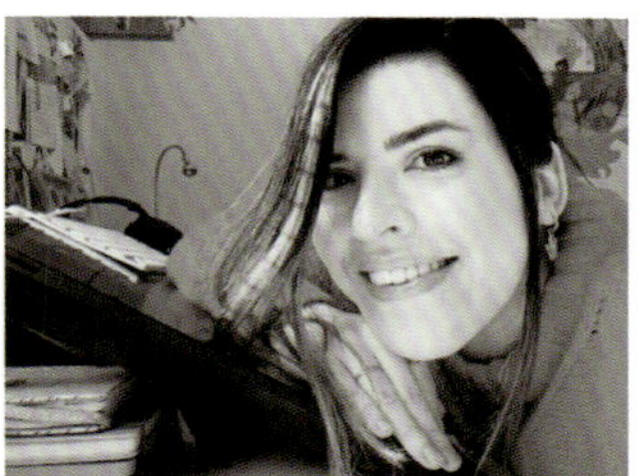

Melany is a Character Designer and
Illustrator from Caracas, Venezuela,
currently living in Los Angeles with her
cat, Boss, and her handsome husband.

MALI BENEDICTO
VASANSEREKUL

Concept Artist at Petoon Studio

artstation.com/minemikomali

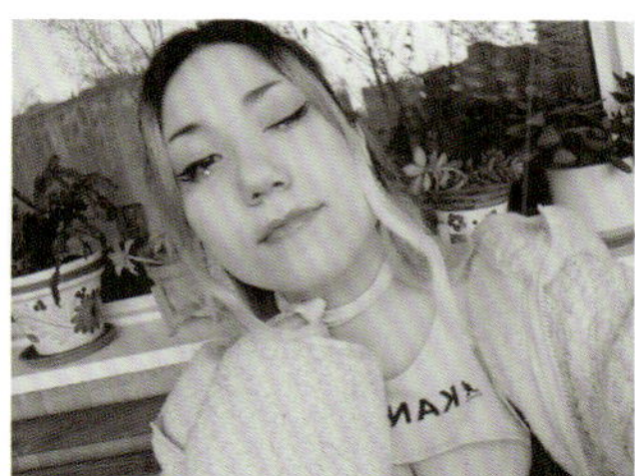

Mali is an illustrator from Spain. She
has worked as a comic artist, concept
artist, and illustrator since she was
fifteen years old.

FEDERICO ETCHEGARAY

Character Designer &
Storyboard Artist

fedetch.com

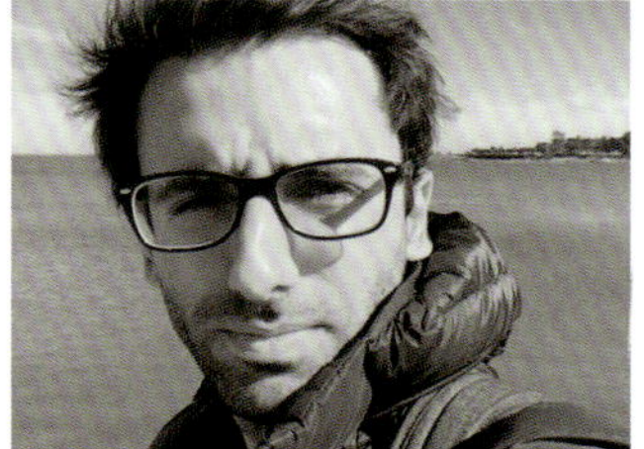

Born in Uruguay, Federico now lives
in Los Angeles and works with studios
such as Disney TV, DreamEast, Warner
Bros, and Wild Canary.

ISAAC JADRAQUE

Character Designer & Visual
Development Artist

isaacjadraque.com

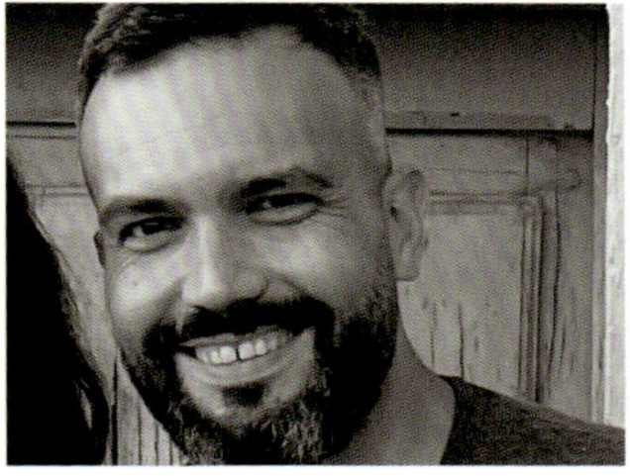

Isaac works as a freelance character
designer for animation, video games,
and advertising, and teaches character
development at university.

TARANEH KARIMI

Principal Artist at GameHouse

taraneh.me

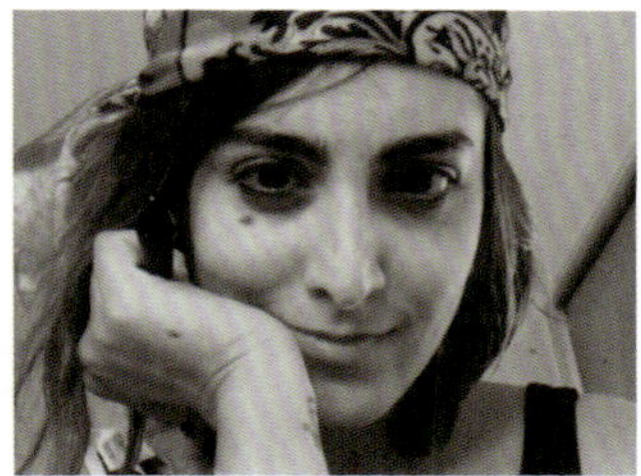

Taraneh is a 2D concept artist based
in the Netherlands who has worked
in motion graphics, advertising, and
games for almost a decade.

HYUNA LEE

Freelance Artist, clients include
DisneyTV, Netflix, and others.

leepixx.portfoliobox.net

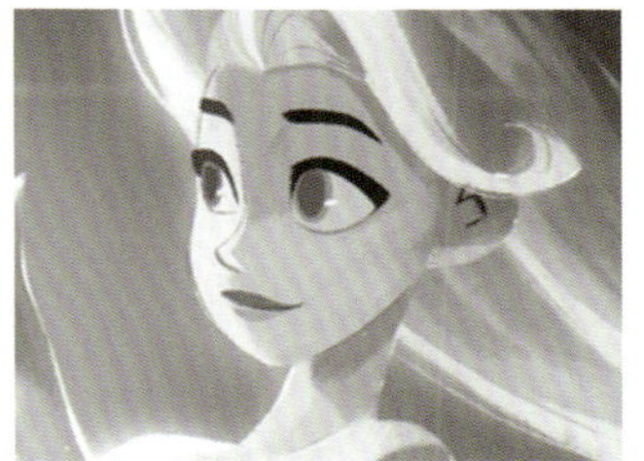

Hyuna Lee lives in Korea and is an
illustrator in the animation and
game industries. She tries to capture
atmosphere, color, and cute moments!

FELIPE RODRIGUEZ

Freelance Character Designer

feliperodriguezart.com

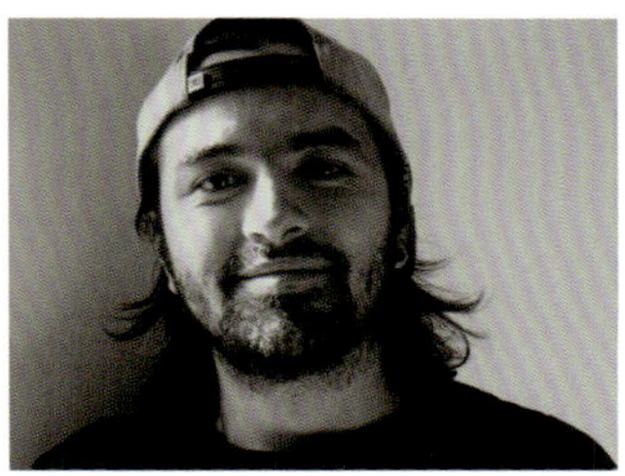

Felipe is a Colombian illustrator and
character designer. He has worked as
a freelance artist for Latin American
series and animated films.

JUSTIN RUNFOLA

Visual Development Artist
& Character Designer

justinrunfola.com

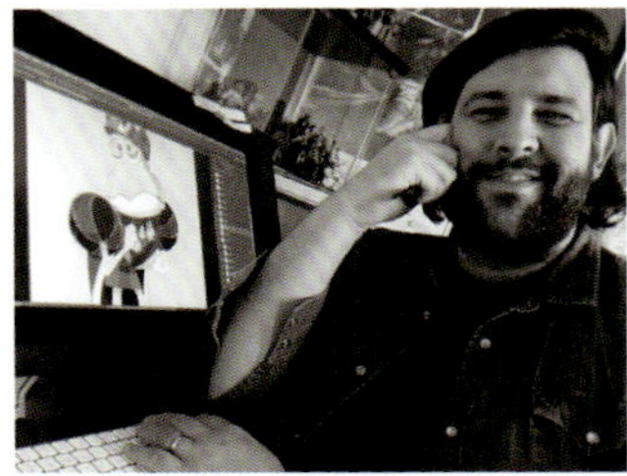

Justin has been an artist all his life,
working as an editorial illustrator
before moving into animation. He is
currently based in Burbank, California.

GRAY YOUNG

Storyboard Artist – Blue
Zoo Animation Studio

grayyoungdesign.com

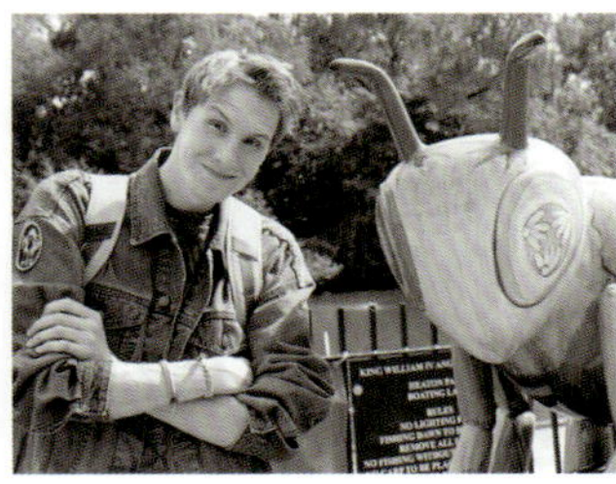

Gray is a character designer and
storyboard artist from the UK. He
has worked on animated TV shows for
Nickelodeon and Disney Junior.

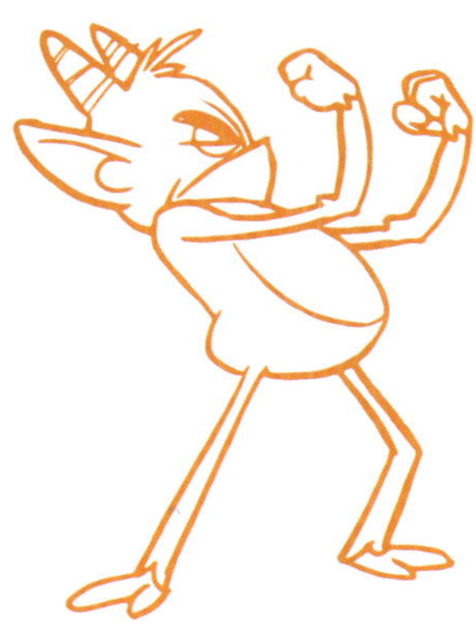

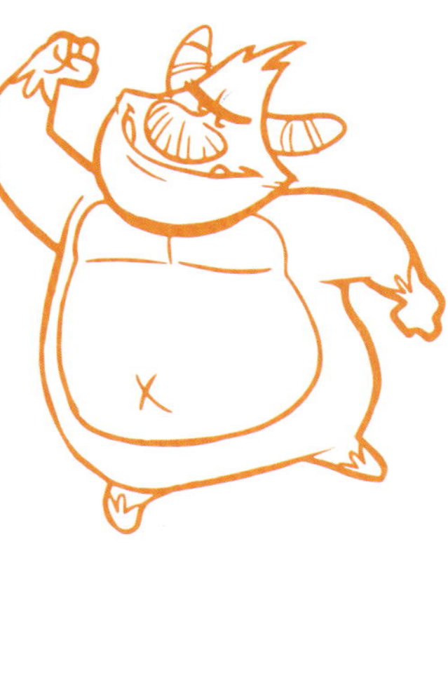

CLOAKS & CAPES

BY LORENZO ETHERINGTON

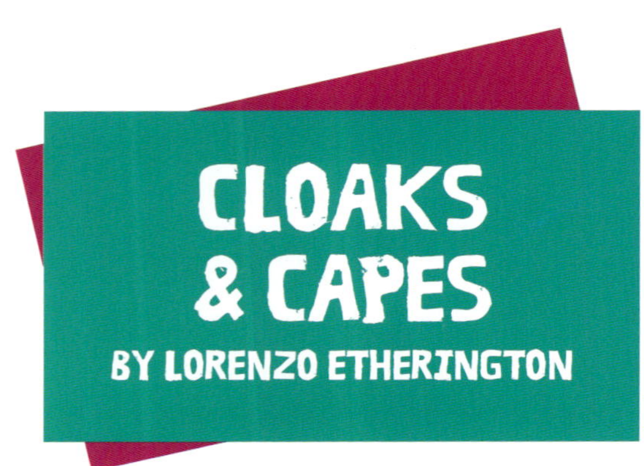

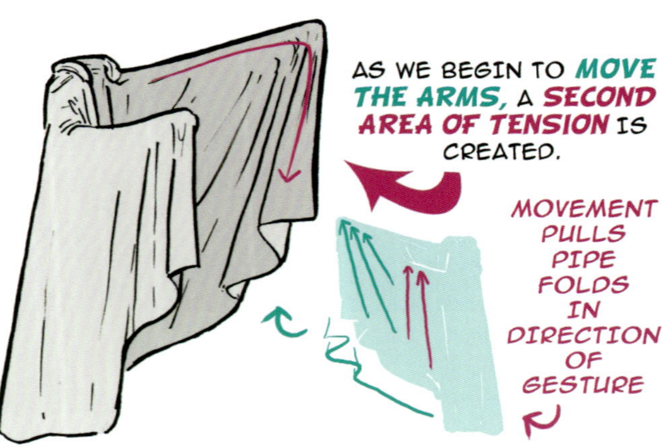

AS WE BEGIN TO **MOVE THE ARMS**, A **SECOND AREA OF TENSION** IS CREATED.

MOVEMENT PULLS PIPE FOLDS IN DIRECTION OF GESTURE

USE **CHANGES IN DIRECTION** OF THE FABRIC TO **CONTRAST ROUND** AND **HARD ANGLES.**

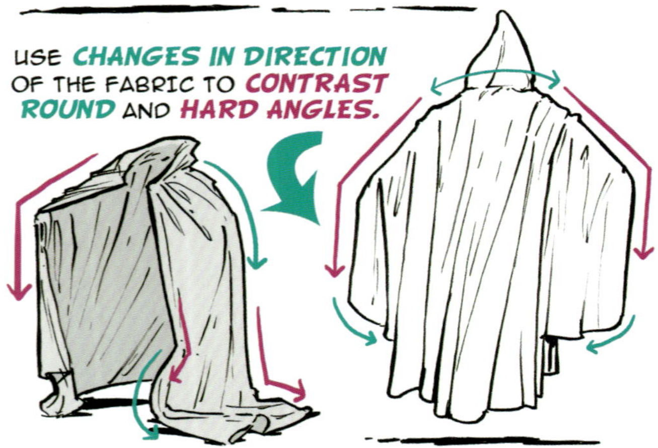

WITH CLOAKS SWEPT OR FASTENED **ACROSS THE NECK**, WE GET A **DIPPING SWATHE** WHEN WE RAISE THE ARM **OPPOSITE** TO THE FASTENING.

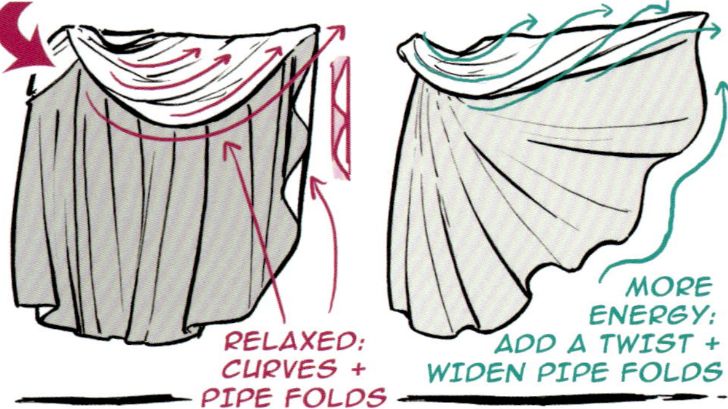

CAPES IN THE WIND WORK BEST WHEN THE **BOTTOM EDGE** FEATURES A **RANGE** OF HOOPS.

FROM BEHIND, DRAW THE BOTTOM PROFILE, AND RUN **CREASES** TOWARDS A **SINGLE POINT.**

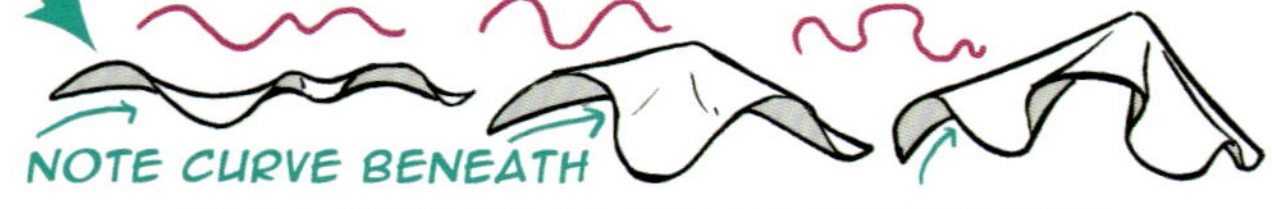

FOR A **DEEPER** SENSE OF **SWEEPING PERSPECTIVE**, HAVE THE PIPE FOLDS **CURVING UP** TOWARDS THE **NECKLINE.**

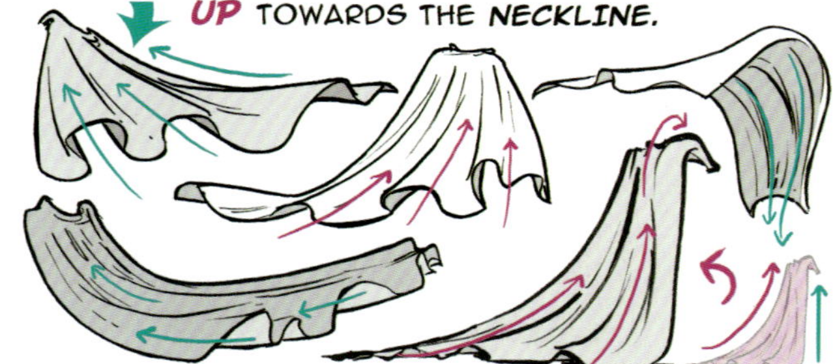